D0871739

# The Ruby-Oswald Affair

ROMAR
BOOKS

# THE RUBY OSWALD AFFAIR

**ROMAR BOOKS, LTD.**
Seattle, Washington

Published by Romar Books, Ltd.
18002 15th Ave. NE, Suite B
Seattle, Washington 98155-3838

First Edition.

Printed and bound in the United States of America.

ISBN 0-945265-03-4

Library of Congress Catalog Card Number 88-062694

Cover design by Lee Wallat

# Contents

# Publisher's Preface

When Alan Adelson first met Earl Ruby, brother of Jack Ruby, he was a young attorney just starting out in Detroit. Little did he know when he agreed to be Earl's attorney that he would someday be asked to probate the will of Jack Ruby. And little did he know that in that entangled legal process of trying to have Jack Ruby's last wishes honored, that the pain and distress that he would witness the Ruby family go through would compel him to initiate his own search to sort out the truths and fairy tales about the man who shot and killed Lee Harvey Oswald.

For twenty years Adelson studied the two men and the event in history that brought them together. The more Adelson discovered about Jack Ruby, the less tolerant he became of the accusations made about this man—that Jack Ruby helped assassinate the president, that he was a Mafia hit man or a CIA pawn, that he shot Oswald to keep him from telling what he knew about the conspiracy to shoot the president. Adelson used every opportunity to speak the truth about Jack Ruby, his Chicago roots, his life in Dallas, his preoccupation with being a Jew, and (in his own peculiar way) his constantly trying to make things right.

In 1984 Alan Adelson completed his rough draft of *The Ruby-Oswald Affair*, and in late 1987 completed negotiations to have his book published by Romar Books, Ltd. Knowing that his reflections on Jack Ruby and Lee Harvey Oswald would be in print for the public to read, Adelson and his wife went to Hawaii to celebrate. In Hawaii he came down with pneumonia and died on February 3, 1988. He was 54.

In the final preparation of Alan Adelson's book, the executive editors of Romar Books, Ltd. worked closely with Alan's widow Charlene Adelson and with Jack Ruby's brother Earl. The editors soon discovered the reason for Alan's burning desire to tell the story about Ruby and Oswald. The brothers and sisters of Jack Ruby have been betrayed by a number of people—some authors, some reporters, some lawyers. They have granted interviews, only to see their statements quoted out of context, twisted to make a sensational but false point. They wanted to see in print the truth about their brother—even that which is painful and unflattering but nonetheless the truth—and they believed that Alan Adelson's reflections on their brother would accomplish that.

The brothers and sisters of Jack Ruby were prepared to release to Alan for use in this book pictures and documentation kept private by the family. They did not fear Alan's exploiting them for his own personal gain. Romar Books has been able to continue this relationship of trust, and the family has consented to release the documentation and photographs even in Alan's absence. *The Ruby-Oswald Affair* contains never-before-published pictures and letters of Jack Ruby. For the first time Jack Ruby's story appears in his own handwriting.

In 1967, Alan Adelson told the Texas press, "My chief job is to continue vindicating Jack Ruby's name." Even though Alan did not live to see his book in print, *The Ruby-Oswald Affair* is a lasting tribute to this mission.

# The Ruby-Oswald Affair

# 1

Detroit, Sunday, November 24, 1963. I was at home, like most everyone, watching TV. I saw a man the media identified as *Luby* gun down Lee Harvey Oswald. Even after the reporters began to say the correct name, I still did not make the connection between Jack Ruby and my client, Earl.

My earliest connection with Jack Ruby's family was through his brother Earl. Earl had come to Detroit to purchase Cobo Cleaners in the early sixties. At the time, Cobo's was owned and operated by the brother of Detroit's late mayor, Albert E. Cobo.

Earl was new in town, and needed an attorney for the transaction. Since my law practice was new and I needed clients, my sister's mother-in-law, who was related to Earl's wife, gave him my business card.

After examining the documents Earl brought me, I agreed that they were in order; consequently, I became Earl's attorney. I took over several business transactions and a few minor lawsuits for him, but for the most part, until November 24, 1963, it was Mr. Ruby and Mr. Adelson—a strictly formal relationship.

It was not until the week following the shooting that I realized Jack Ruby was Earl's older brother. Earl called my office: he had just returned from California by way of Dallas, and had some papers regarding his securing power of attorney for his brother Jack that he wanted me to look over. Until he mentioned his brother's name, I had never connected the two Rubys. I invited him to bring the papers over to my office.

Earl arrived at the appointed time. "What a shock," I said.

"You think you were shocked," he replied slowly. "I was at the plant working last Sunday. I had been talking on the phone to an old friend in Chicago. He told me something was happening on TV, so we hung up. That day about noon, I left the plant to go home. When I heard the news on the radio, I had to pull over to the side of the road. I could hardly believe my brother had shot Oswald. I was stunned.

"Anyway," he continued, "that night I went to Dallas, and the next day on to California to meet Bill Woodfield. Bill's a free-lance writer who's been engaged to write the 'original byline story' by Jack. The story will be syndicated throughout the world with Jack and Bill splitting the royalties. We're sure going to need them to defend Jack."

Earl handed me some legal documents. I looked at the papers and saw that one was a contract for Woodfield to write the story, as if Jack were telling it. Actually, Earl's sister, Eva Grant, would give the required information to Bill Woodfield. Earl needed a power of attorney to sign Jack's name to the contract. I dictated it while we sat there.

The topic turned to attorneys who might represent Jack. Since I had no experience in criminal law, I was not too familiar with the procedure, particularly since the trial would be in Texas.

"Tom Howard is the assigned attorney," Earl said, "but we want someone with more prominence." He named several nationally known legal giants.

I handed Earl the completed power of attorney and wished him luck.

As a result of our conversation, I called a prominent member of the Detroit Criminal Bar, Joe Louisell. I had referred a client to him for representation in a criminal matter some years earlier. He immediately understood my problem and suggested that Earl and I meet at his office the next day.

At two o'clock the following afternoon, I walked into Louisell's office. Earl was just behind me. We were quickly ushered into a large office where Louisell, sitting behind a desk with his feet propped up, was talking on the phone.

He smiled as we entered, and indicated seats across from him. As he hung up the phone, I stood, shook his hand, and introduced Earl.

After we explained that we needed an attorney for Jack, Louisell expressed the opinion that someone from Dallas should try the case.

"Preferably a WASP," he said. "Dallas is Baptist country. If you retain a Jew or a Catholic, you may find yourself in trouble."

The meeting was short. We thanked him and found our way out.

I was about to learn my first lesson about the news-making potential of "big lawyers," for even as we left the building, newspaper headlines announced: "Louisell Invited to Join Ruby Defense Team."

The following week, Earl called to say the original byline story contract with Woodfield had been signed, and he asked if I had ever heard of Melvin Belli.

"Of course," I said. "He's the King of Torts. He has gained more damage awards for his clients than any other litigator in America."

"Well," Earl said, "I think we will retain him to defend Jack."

I felt instantly this decision was wrong. Melvin Belli certainly was one of the most prominent attorneys in the country, but I had never heard that he was a criminal lawyer.

"How did you meet him?" I asked.

"You remember the agreement with Woodfield for the original byline story?" he inquired. "Well, Woodfield's wife is a good friend of Belli's. He wants this case so badly he can taste it. He'll do everything that's necessary, and we'll pay only the expenses. He'll get his big money from the book he'll write."

"That's fair enough," I responded, but in the back of my mind, I knew Melvin Belli was not the proper attorney for this case. He was Italian Catholic, and Dallas has the highest percentage of Protestants of any city in Texas. Dallas is also well-known as the insurance capital of the Southwest, and Belli was the nemesis of insurance companies.

Earl and I spoke of the case almost every time we talked, but I did not become directly involved until late 1966.

After the trial in March 1964, with Jack sentenced to die, a new string of lawyers emerged, many very well-known. If Jack was going to win his appeal, he certainly had the talent behind him. I was later to meet these men, for whom I have a great deal of respect.

Jack did win his appeal, and was granted a new trial. Almost immediately afterwards, however, it was announced that Jack was dying of cancer. The media reported that he was being removed from the county jail to Parkland Hospital.

After reading this announcement, I asked Earl if Jack had a will. He said he did not know, and at his request, I prepared a Last Will and Testament for Jack Ruby. Earl took the will to Dallas with him, but it was never signed. Jack was under heavy security, with few people allowed to enter the room. The family spent several days trying to arrange witnesses for the signing of the will. I was unaware that under Texas law at that time, Jack could have signed it anyway.

Jack Ruby died on January 3, 1967, at 10:30 A.M., a patient in Parkland Hospital, not the convicted murderer of Lee Harvey Oswald, but facing trial for that crime.

Sunday, January 8, 1967. It was bitterly cold, but clear. The drive from Detroit to Chicago was uneventful. The funeral service was scheduled for ten o'clock the next morning. Earl had made reservations for me at a motel near his sister's home just north of the city limits. His sister's house was to be the place the family would sit *shivah* for the following week. The *shivah* period in Jewish culture is the week of mourning following a funeral.

I drove up to the motel office. Headlines of newspapers inside the coin-operated racks told the story: "Jack Ruby Returns Home. Burial Tomorrow." I went through the usual formalities of motel registration, making sure I had enough change to buy all the papers.

With the papers under my arm, I went to my room and called Earl, to let him know I had arrived. He told me that Phil Burleson, an attorney on the Ruby case, would meet me in the morning, and suggested that I bring him to the funeral chapel.

I sat on the bed and read the articles about Jack. Most of them repeated the story of the assassination, his trial, and the recent reversal of the verdict. Had he lived, Jack would have been preparing for a new trial.

As arranged, I met Phil Burleson at nine. With him from Texas was Hugh Aynesworth, who had covered Jack's trial for *Newsweek*.

I drove the short distance to the funeral home, where I let Phil and Hugh off at the door and circled through the parking lot. The attendant asked if I were going to the cemetery. I nodded, and was directed to park behind the black Cadillac in the street.

I was filled with self-importance as I walked toward the front door of the chapel. Here I was, attending the funeral of a man whose name had become a household word. I was going to be the director of all legal affairs for his family from then on. My self-importance disintegrated, however, when I reached the front door. A security guard had just admitted several people, apparently recognizing who they were. He stopped me with an abrupt, "Who are you?"

"Earl's attorney." I responded.

"It's someone called Earl," he said to the man next to him.

In the few moments it took for Earl to reach the door, I was mortified. I felt as if I were trying to crash the funeral.

Earl vouched for me, and I was admitted. He took me around the room and introduced me to everyone, including his family, whom I would get to know in the days to come. As the rabbi was already approaching the podium, I took a seat near the rear of the room.

Rabbi David Graubart, who had known Jack, asked us to pray for the repose of his soul.

"The eyes of the world are upon us now," he said, without looking up from his papers. "Jack Ruby linked himself with one of the most tragic moments in American history. He acted as a patriot, but as a misguided patriot-avenger. He would be called in scriptural idiom 'an avenger of blood' who, while his heart is hot, pursues a manslayer and overtakes him.

"Jack Ruby thought he could acquire his spiritual world in one grand moment, to use the idiom of ancient rabbis. Unfortunately, he destroyed his world in that one moment.

"Shall we condemn him? No. I speak as a religionist who believes that a man is loved by God because he is created in His image."

Jewish funeral services are generally short and to the point. I had never seen one last more than thirty minutes. This service lasted only ten. As I filed up the aisle with the others, Earl called me over to the door.

"They want to open the casket," he said.

"Who are 'they?'" I asked.

"The news media."

The funeral had been a closed-casket affair. I realized immediately that the closed casket would raise questions. Who was to know if Jack was really in the casket? I had heard rumors that Kennedy was not really dead, but was hidden away in South America.

"Earl," I said, "let them see. I know it sounds grisly, but let's put it to rest."

The lid of the casket was opened, and for the first time I

saw Jack, the man I would learn to know almost as well as I knew myself.

I walked outside; the air was still crisp. It must have been ten degrees that morning, although the sun was shining brightly.

Phil Burleson was at the car when I arrived. As we drove to the cemetery, there was something I had to ask. He was the only lawyer who had been in on the case from almost the beginning until now.

"Phil, may I ask you a stupid question?" I began.

"Sure," he said. "I ask them all the time."

"How could Jack have been convicted of first-degree murder if he didn't conceive of the crime until the moment it happened?" I had read bits and pieces of the Warren Commission report as they were published in the newspapers, and I had just finished Mark Lane's *Rush to Judgment*. I was about to embark on the most serious study of my life.

"That's not a stupid question," Phil said. "Under Texas law, first-degree murder is called murder with malice; that's what Jack was convicted of."

"Well," I asked, "doesn't the malice require premeditation, just as it would in Michigan?"

"Yes," he said, "that's when they lied."

Hugh Aynesworth was in the car by this time, and joined in the conversation. He explained, "On that Sunday morning, Jack was at home at ten o'clock. The night before, Chief Curry told the reporters waiting at the station that Oswald would not be moved until ten the next morning, so there was no need for them to stay around. If Jack had premeditated killing Oswald, he would have been there before ten.

"But shortly after ten that Sunday," he continued, "Jack received a call from an employee in Fort Worth. She wanted Jack to wire her money because her rent was due, and she had not been paid yet. He promised to go to Western Union that morning and send her the money. So Jack drove downtown and pulled into a lot across the street from Western Union. The office was just east of the police headquarters where Oswald was being held. Elaborate preparations were under way to move the prisoner. There was an armored car to be used as a decoy vehicle, while Oswald was to be moved in a police car.

"Jack went into the Western Union office, where he was time-stamped twice, once at ten-seventeen, and then again at ten-eighteen. When he finished his business, he walked out of the office and noticed a small crowd at the entrance ramp to the police station. He walked over just as a car driven by Lt. Pierce came up. As the policeman guarding the ramp stepped aside to let the car pass, Jack started down the ramp.

"At ten-twenty, he shot Oswald, three minutes after being time-stamped at Western Union."

"Anyhow," said Phil, picking up the story, "Jack was wrestled to the ground and immediately taken to the jail section of police headquarters. A policeman, Sergeant Patrick Dean, was in charge of security that day. At the trial, he testified that Jack told him that he had made up his mind to shoot Oswald right after he had found out that Oswald was being held in the Dallas police station."

The black Cadillac in front of us began to creep forward into the street. As we pulled out behind it, several school-age youngsters threw snowballs, but that was the only disturbance the entire twelve miles to Westlawn Cemetery.

Phil continued, "With that testimony, the jury was given the impression that he had planned the shooting at a prior time."

"Wait a minute," I said, "How could that testimony get in?" Although I'm not a criminal lawyer, I did do trial work, and such testimony seemed to be hearsay to me.

"*Res gestae,*" Phil answered.

*Res gestae* is the Latin term for words said at the time of, or as part of, an occurrence. *Res gestae* testimony is allowed into evidence as an exception to the hearsay rule, which usually excludes such secondhand evidence.

"I know Jack was supposed to have made comments like 'dirty s.o.b.' and 'Jews got guts,' but I didn't know he also had a conversation with the police while they were wrestling him to the ground!" I exclaimed.

"He didn't," Phil explained. "The statements were allegedly made after Jack was taken upstairs and stripped to his underwear."

"Jack was actually interrogated by the chief of security for the Secret Service before he said that to Dean," Hugh interjected.

"Boy," I commented, "you have some crazy laws in Texas. How about the judge?"

Both Phil and Hugh laughed.

"Judge Joe B. Brown," Phil explained, "was never considered a great student of the law. He even allowed radio and television reporters in his courtroom to broadcast the verdict."

"I know," I added, "I heard it that Saturday morning."

"Believe it or not," Phil continued, "Judge Brown was writing a book about the trial."

"He was what?" I said in amazement.

"We got hold of some of his correspondence with Holt, Rinehart & Winston, his publisher, stating that he was making progress but wasn't quite ready to submit anything."

"Holy Toledo!" I said, as I followed the black Cadillac into the cemetery grounds on Montrose Avenue. "The publisher of Mark Lane's *Rush to Judgment.*"

I parked the car. Since they were pallbearers, Hugh and Phil walked to the hearse. I stayed behind.

To pass the time, I counted the cars behind the hearse and the black Cadillac. There were fifteen. As we all moved toward the grave site, the rabbi chanted Hebrew prayers. It was over in moments.

The flag that draped the coffin was folded and given to Eva, Jack's sister. I heard her remark that she would give it to Earl.

We followed the black Cadillac back to the home of Eileen Kaminsky, Jack's younger sister, but agreed we would not stay long. Phil had never seen Chicago, and I offered to show him around.

He asked to be shown the downtown area. As we had a few hours to kill before his plane took off, we went to the Playboy Club. The Chicago Playboy Club at that time was housed in a building with four stories of unusually decorated rooms. After examining all the rooms, we returned to the main level for lunch. I wanted to learn all I could, and who knew more than Phil?

"Tell me about Jack," I said.

"Well," Phil began, "he certainly had friends. No less than five of them had attorneys down at the police station to represent him soon after the shooting. Only Tom Howard, called in by Jack's partner, Ralph Paul, remained on the case for awhile.

"Howard operated out of a storefront office across from the police station. You know the type."

I nodded in assent, for I knew such lawyers exist and are very successful in every city. "Numbers runners and prostitutes are their usual clients," I said.

"That's the type," Phil continued. "However, Earl somehow hired Melvin Belli, and the day before the trial, Tom Howard quit. Belli brought in Sam Brody, his associate from California, who hired Joe Halbert Tonahill of Jasper, Texas, and me. I had been a staff attorney in the Texas Court of Criminal Appeals and had worked for the prosecutor's office on the appeals staff. I was to do research for the defense.

"Tom Howard would probably have pled Jack to a lesser crime and he would have gotten a few years. Remember, Dallas was very sensitive at the time. Howard would have kept the whole thing low-key. Belli had other ideas. I believe he thought he was going to walk Jack out a free man.

"Well," he continued, "the first move we made was a motion to release Jack on bail. If we could have shown that Jack's action was not premeditated, he might have gotten out. The only way to show that, of course, was to show why Jack was in the area. The lady I mentioned earlier, the one who called Jack that morning."

"Yes," I responded, eager to hear more.

"Well, she was really the only witness who could establish that she called and requested Jack to send her some money. Since the only Western Union office open on Sunday was downtown, we would establish Jack's motive for being there.

"However, because of previous loose security, the sheriff searched everyone going into the courtroom. That little lady had a small gun in her purse."

"So," I added, "her testimony was not credible."

"That's right. Judge Brown ruled against us, but it wasn't a definite no. The judge set January 10, 1964, as the date for the second bail hearing, which was adjourned to January 20. Belli planned to show that Jack needed psychiatric testing, which could not be conducted in jail. Jack went on the stand and began to cry when asked about President Kennedy's death.

"It was agreed by both sides that the judge would appoint a panel of eminent psychiatrists who would examine Jack. Belli, according to the agreement, withdrew the motion for bail. We felt we had a victory.

"Through all this, Jack behaved as if he were an actor on stage. He felt he was a hero in the limelight. Each time he was brought into court, he actually posed for photographs."

"Didn't he realize he was on trial for murder?" I asked.

"Not really," Phil replied. "Belli gave him such a feeling of confidence that he would never be convicted, that he strutted before his audience. Everyone involved was acting a part. The judge and the prosecutor spoke through their press releases.

"Belli's next move was for a change of venue."

"But where could Jack have gotten a fair trial in Texas?" I interrupted.

"Texas," Phil replied, "is a big state with different philosophies. I would have chosen San Antonio with its high population of Mexicans and Catholics. A town with a lot of minorities wouldn't have hurt Jack's case at all.

"The change of venue was a hearing conducted by the defense. We called the only witnesses. The prosecution introduced affidavits to the effect that Jack would get a fair trial in Dallas. The witnesses, leading citizens, all stated that Jack would not get a fair trial in Dallas, but Judge Brown deferred his ruling until we made an attempt to impanel a jury."

"What a predicament," I blurted out. "That put Belli in an impossible position. He had to try to select a jury that would be fair to Jack, but if he did so, he was conceding the argument for a change of venue."

"Exactly," Phil replied. "After a hundred sixty-two prospective jurors were examined and a hundred twenty-one dismissed because of bias, Judge Brown should have realized that a change of venue was in order. Anyway, the trial began, and between prosecution and defense there were almost sixty witnesses.

"Belli attempted to show that Jack suffered from a variant of psychomotor epilepsy, a condition in which a person may commit an act without knowing it. Therefore, a lot of the testimony was medically technical. Personally, I felt we should have attacked Sergeant Dean for stating in his testimony that Jack had told him he planned the thing from the beginning, while omitting this significant piece of evidence from his earlier reports. Then Dean could have been discredited. Anyway, the jury began deliberation after one in the morning. The verdict is history."

Suddenly realizing the hour, Phil quickly departed to catch his plane with the observation that we would be speaking again soon.

# 2

I planned to spend the next few days in Chicago with the Ruby family. If I were to represent these people, it would be wise, I reasoned, to learn as much about them as I could. Each member had recollections of Jack that would help me evaluate the man.

It soon became clear that the family was extremely close-knit, a fact one does not get from reading newspaper accounts. Up to this time I had the impression that because they lived so far apart, their emotional closeness had dissipated over the years. I was also struck with the family's strong bond with the traditions of Judaism. Although they did not attend services at the syna-gogue or observe strict dietary laws, their deep feeling for tradi-tion was evident.

From my conversations with members of the family, I was able to obtain a biographical sketch of Jack. This background was important: my conclusions about Jack's behavior on that fateful Sunday morning in 1963 took root during my discussions with his family during those few days in Chicago.

Hyman Rubenstein, the oldest brother who had retained the old family name, provided the family history.

Their father, born in Russia, was drafted into the imperial army in 1893. There he learned carpentry. He also learned, as all soldiers did then, how to consume great amounts of alcohol. While stationed in Zembroba, Poland, he deserted, together with two comrades. A farmer's wife discovered the ex-soldiers hiding in a barn near town and detained them long enough for each to marry one of her daughters.

A few years later, Rubenstein decided to bring up his family in America. He worked his way from Europe through England into Canada, and finally arrived in the United States. He settled in Chicago in 1902; his wife and family followed the next year.

Although English was spoken in the home, the primary language was Yiddish. Like New York City, Chicago was a melting pot. Italians, Irish, and Jews from the "old country" lived in tenements on or near Maxwell Street on the city's near west side.

Jack was born the fifth of eight children, but because the family used the Jewish calendar, his exact date of birth is unknown. Jack selected March 25, 1911, when he found it necessary to have a birth date for official records; this is the date that shows on his discharge papers.

The family occupied several different residences in the vicinity of Maxwell Street during Jack's early years. Although they were poor, they always had food on the table. They never thought of buying toys in those days. The children attached old roller skates to orange crates to make carts; rubber bands found in the trash behind the bank became balls to use in games.

In this setting the children of Maxwell Street had to make a choice that children with more privileges never faced: they had to choose between joining the mob or going straight. No matter which choice they made, the children still went to school together and knew each other. Later, in Jack's trial, this fact of neighborhood life would be distorted.

Jack loved the street. He also loved money, a commodity he was destined always to be short of. He learned practical economics early. At the age of nine he walked fifteen miles to Maywood, Illinois to purchase firecrackers. Returning to Maxwell Street, he sold them at a nice profit.

He was nine years old when his mother and father began

squabbling. Although they never actually struck each other, the verbal battles grew louder and more constant. The elder Rubenstein's drinking increased until finally, in 1921, Joseph moved out of the family home. The conflict in the family and his father's departure evidently had a profound emotional effect on young Jack. He became an incorrigible truant. At age ten, he was well known as a quick-tempered and disobedient child.

Because of the breakup of the family, the younger Rubenstein children were sent to live in foster homes. This move was a great blow to Jack, because he was sent to a farm far from his street. He could not sell; he could not buy; he could not do business.

Two years later the family was reunited, and Jack was back on his street. He became the protector of his sisters, keeping the Italian and Irish bullies at bay while he walked them down his street.

At sixteen, while in the eighth grade, Jack quit school. Now he could go into business full time. With the aid of his brothers and sisters, he bought novelty items which he sold door-to-door. In the evening he parked cars at the Chicago stadium. He hustled and scalped tickets to sporting events.

In 1933, the World's Fair was held in Chicago. Jack did a land-office business in novelties. During this time, Hitler's Nazi party was on the rise in Germany. His sympathizers in the United States formed what was called the German-American Bund. They held meetings and wore German brownshirt uniforms. Jack, with the aid of other Jewish young men, enjoyed breaking up the meetings. These incidents may have been a prophecy of what was to come: one of the main tenets of the Bund was anti-Semitism.

Earl told me that when the Holocaust became public knowledge near the end of World War II, Jack decided that he was going to go to Germany, on his own, to kill Hitler. He really thought he could pull it off, until Earl explained to him the difficulties involved. This story was never made public for fear that, at the trial, the jury would take this to mean that Jack could kill.

After the World's Fair ended, Jack decided to move to the West Coast. He had been there about one year when his sister Eva divorced her first husband, Hyman Magid. With her young son, she joined Jack in San Francisco. They engaged in the door-to-door sale of newspaper subscriptions. Although the country was deep in the Great Depression, Jack did quite well. He used the gimmick of giving a novelty to anyone who bought a subscription from him. It worked.

In San Francisco Jack met and fell in love with Virginia Belasco, of the very wealthy and influential Belasco family. Because of the divergence in their social and religious backgrounds, however, they soon parted company. Jack returned to Chicago in 1935.

At this time workers all over the United States and Canada were organizing into trade unions. One afternoon while Jack and his old friend Leon Cooke were having lunch, the two decided to form a union. The idea was not farfetched, for Cooke's family had been in the iron and scrap business for years. Leon was an attorney with no clients; Jack was unemployed.

Cooke applied for and received a federal charter for Local 20467, Scrap Iron and Junk Handler's Union. Jack became the organizer and negotiator, Cooke became the financial secretary, and another acquaintance, John Martin, became president.

Those who knew Jack back then came forward and testified for the Warren Commission that Jack was a good negotiator, and that the union had absolutely no connection with the criminal element in Chicago at that time.

Unfortunately in December 1939, John Martin and Leon Cooke had an altercation; Martin shot and killed Cooke. He was later acquitted on the grounds of self-defense. Jack was extremely distraught over the death of his friend, and left the organization at the request of the new union leadership. Afterward he took

Cooke's name as his middle name. Jack's union dealings are stressed by those who insist he was involved in a conspiracy to silence Oswald after Kennedy's assassination.

Sometime after Jack left, Paul Dorfman succeeded Cooke as secretary-treasurer of the local. Dorfman became extremely rich during his tenure from 1940 to 1956, when the AFL-CIO suspended him and placed the union under federal trusteeship. There is no question that Dorfman was connected to Chicago underworld figures. He was investigated in the same probe as James R. Hoffa, with whom he was a partner. Later Jack would be linked to Paul Dorfman and Jimmy Hoffa because of his earlier association with the union.

When the war began in Europe, Jack was back on the streets hustling. He was drafted in May 1943, and served in the U.S. Army Air Force until 1946, when he was honorably discharged.

Earl was the first of the family to be discharged from the service. He returned to Chicago to establish a business, Earl Products Company. The company manufactured small novelty items such as key chains, small cedar chests, and salt and pepper shakers. As Jack and Sam came out of the service, Earl gave each brother an equal share in the business. It was at that time three of the Rubenstein brothers had their names legally changed to Ruby.

During this time Jack's sister Eva married and soon after divorced Frank Grant in San Francisco. In 1945, she moved to Dallas where she opened the Singapore Supper Club.

Dallas of that era was a wide-open city with several gambling establishments flourishing. In the spring of 1946, Steve Guthrie became the sheriff-elect of Dallas County, after a campaign in which he promised to clean up the gambling in the county. Previously, illegal activities had been carried on with alleged payoffs to the lame-duck sheriff and members of the Dallas police department.

In late October 1946, Paul Roland Jones of the Chicago

mob called Dallas Police Detective George Butler, requesting that he arrange a meeting with sheriff-elect Guthrie. Butler and Guthrie made sure that the meeting would be recorded. During the conversation that ensued, Jones indicated that several people from Chicago had moved into the area and named them. Jones proposed that they keep a local man in charge of the only gambling house in the county and promised that he would install only one of his men from Chicago to oversee the operation. He specifically stated that the man from Chicago would look like a preacher and would not be a "Dago" or a Jew.

Several meetings were held, all of which were recorded. The sheriff-elect and Butler carefully guarded against a situation that Jones could later label an entrapment. Finally, on December 18, 1946, Jones was arrested for attempted bribery.

Back in Chicago, Jack was not happy at Earl Products Company. In 1947, Earl and Sam Ruby bought Jack out.

Looking for work, Jack contacted Eva. It was not long before Jack was in Dallas assisting Eva at the Singapore Supper Club. At the same time, Eva was dating a physician of questionable reputation. This physician was a close friend of Jones. Thus, Jack met Paul Roland Jones. While out on bond for the bribery case and also a federal narcotics charge, Jones became friendly with Jack and began to frequent the Singapore.

Since Eva wanted to return to California, she arranged to give Jack the power of attorney to run the club. This was Jack's first venture into the nightclub business. He quickly changed the image of the club by naming it the Silver Spur and introducing a country-and-western theme. In 1952, Jack opened his second club, the Bob Wills Ranch House, another western-type nightclub.

Soon the pressure of running the two nightclubs got to Jack. He sold both of them and retreated to a hotel where he remained a recluse for four months. Finally his depression was so great that he returned to Chicago, presumably for good. Being back "home" in Chicago was good for Jack. He started to relax and come out of his depression. The stay was short-lived, however. The party who had purchased the Silver Spur was having financial problems with the club and stopped making payments to Jack and his sister. Jack returned to Dallas once more to resume ownership of the club.

The rest had given Jack a new spurt of energy, and he turned the Silver Spur back into a profitable business. The next year he acquired an interest in the Vegas Club, one that he was to own until his arrest. At the end of 1953, he disposed of the Silver Spur to concentrate his efforts on the Vegas Club.

In 1959, Eva returned from California to manage the Vegas Club, allowing Jack to move "downtown." He became a partner in the Sovereign Club, located on Commerce Street directly across from the prestigious Adolphus Hotel. The Sovereign Club was a private club, for members only. The next year Jack's partner decided to sell his interest in the Sovereign Club because of disagreements with Jack. Ralph Paul, Jack's best friend, arranged to acquire the partner's interest. Paul insisted that the club be changed from a private club to a striptease establishment. Thus was born the Carousel Club.

# 3

It was Thursday night following Jack Ruby's funeral when I returned to Detroit. I wanted to speak with the dean of the Wayne County Probate Court bench, Thomas C. Murphy. Judge Murphy had taken a liking to me when I first started practicing law. In those days, a probate judge could appoint lawyers to listen to claims against estates and make recommendations to him. These cases were lucrative as well as prestigious. I handled at least one a month in those lean years when I began practice.

Friday morning I called the judge's secretary to arrange an appointment. I was told he would be off the bench about eleven o'clock.

Arriving in his chambers a little early, I sat and discussed the weather with Mrs. Mooney, his secretary. Not long after, the judge opened the door from his courtroom into Mrs. Mooney's area. He removed his robe as he entered his chamber and signaled me to follow him.

I sat on the couch watching the judge hang up his robe. If anyone looked the picture of a judge, it was Tom Murphy. With his white flowing hair and blue eyes, he seemed the embodiment of justice.

He sat at his desk. I was bursting to tell him where I had been, but I retained my composure.

"Judge," I began, "I know you have presided over the estates of some of the most prominent people in the country." He nodded but made no comment.

"What would you say was the most important legal case in the country in the last twenty years, if not in the whole history of the United States?" I asked him.

I paused for effect. The judge looked puzzled, but did not answer. I continued, "I have been retained to probate the estate of Jack Ruby." I told him about my connections with Earl and that I had just returned from the funeral. What I did not tell him was that there was nothing to probate. Interestingly enough, that was the first question he asked.

"He had the gun, the watch he was wearing, his suit, and maybe the rights to a movie," I responded.

"No asset estate?" the judge inquired.

"Well," I continued, "it is the family's wish that the things that do belong to Jack Ruby be donated to the National Archives in Washington, where the Warren Commission has placed all the other artifacts of the assassination. They definitely do not want them to wind up in a wax museum somewhere. Moreover, if Ruby left anything, it was his $40,000 debt to the United States government for back taxes."

The judge looked at me pensively for a moment.

"Alan," he asked, "what would Jack Ruby have done, if he had not died, after he was released from prison?"

"Earl Ruby told me Jack would have come here to Detroit."

"I see," the judge mused. "Is there any property belonging to Jack Ruby in Detroit?"

"Yes, his sisters packed all his clothing and belongings and shipped them to Earl for storage."

The judge stood up, reached for a book on the shelf behind his desk, opened it, and read silently for a moment. "Yes, here it is," he said, handing it to me. I made a mental note of the citation and read the scope notes in the beginning. The case, decided by the Michigan Supreme Court, involved a man who left another state to reside in Michigan. His belongings were sent ahead, but he died en route. The court decided that the proper place to probate the estate was Michigan.

"Alan," the judge asked, "have you ever noticed on the petition you file to probate an estate of a deceased person, exactly how it asks where he lived?"

"Yes," I answered.

"What I'm getting at is that it doesn't say *residence* or *domicile;* it says *inhabitant of,* and then leaves a blank space."

"But aren't they saying the same thing?" I inquired.

"Not really. *Residence* or *domicile* is a fact; *inhabitant* is a state of mind. In the former, you must physically be present; in the latter, you only have to want to be there."

I understood what the judge meant. I had the requisite authority to probate Jack's estate in Detroit.

*What a break*, I thought. When I got back to the office, I called Phil Burleson. I could hardly wait to tell him.

His comment was, "At last I can send instructions, rather than do the work."

I prepared the petition for probate and sent the necessary papers to the family members for their signatures. Within a week I had the papers back and took them to the filing counter at the Wayne County Probate Court.

I placed the papers on the counter, face down, waiting for my turn. The clerk took them from me and began his routine check for a prior filing of a recorded will. The papers clearly said: In the matter of Jack Ruby, deceased inhabitant of the City of Detroit, lately of Dallas, Texas.

About halfway through this procedure, he looked up at me with his mouth open. "Is this the . . .?"

"Who else is lately of Dallas, Texas?" I answered. He fumbled through the rest of the stamping and filing and gave me the papers.

I took them down the hall to Judge Murphy's chambers, where Mrs. Mooney set a hearing date, one week from that day.

One of the very first matters I ever handled as an attorney involved a lawsuit against the government for a tax refund. It was a complicated situation with a ring of governmental unfairness about it. By the time I returned from the courthouse after filing that suit, the newspapers had me on the phone to find out the "real story." Ironically I had just filed for probate of the estate of a household name, and received not one phone call.

The following week, I picked Earl up at his plant and we drove down to the courthouse. After parking the car, we walked into the lobby and entered the elevator.

On the thirteenth floor, we were confronted by cameras, lights, and reporters from every radio and television station in town. In view of the Joe Louisell episode, however, I instructed Earl not to answer questions.

We entered the courtroom followed by the reporters. I recognized most of them from local news broadcasts.

We did not have to wait long. The court clerk stood and proclaimed, "Everyone please rise; the Probate Court for the County of Wayne is now in session, The Honorable Thomas C. Murphy, presiding."

The judge entered and took the bench.

"You may be seated," the clerk said. The audience mumbled and shuffled into place.

"In the matter of the Estate of Jack Ruby," the clerk bellowed, as I approached the bench.

"Alan Adelson, on behalf of the Estate," I said. "Your Honor, today is the time and date set for the petition for appointment of administrator."

I called Earl to the witness stand. He testified that Jack had wanted to come to Detroit, and that all of his personal belongings were in Detroit. He also testified as to the heirs and the assets of the estate. Then I requested the court to appoint Earl with a nominal bond, which the judge did.

Judge Murphy, at that point, went into a dissertation on

why he, in Michigan, had jurisdiction, citing the law and expounding on the facts. The media people wrote as quickly as they could, because recording devices were not allowed in the courtroom.

The entire hearing lasted almost fifteen minutes; under normal circumstances, it would have taken only a minute or two. "This was history in the making. It deserved more time," Judge Murphy later told me.

In the hallway, the bright lights came on again. Reporters shoved microphones in our faces from every direction. One of the reporters for an ABC affiliate asked me to interpret Judge Murphy's pronouncements from the bench, obviously because he hadn't been able take it down as fast as the judge had explained it in the courtroom. I did, and soon all of the reporters began asking questions.

It was here I began to realize that anyone associated with the assassination was bound to generate a certain excitement. Yes, this *was* history. I was later to learn that the local media people were as thrilled as I was with this story, because the reports they filed would gain national exposure.

Out of respect for judicial ethics, the judge could not come into the hallway right after the hearing. I called him later. "Judge," I said, "is this as exciting to you as it is to me?"

A long pause.

"You darn well better believe it is," he said.

# 4

After Ruby's trial ended with a guilty verdict, Belli was removed as chief counsel. New attorneys were selected to begin the appeal process. Several attorneys became involved, but two became the driving force in preparing the appeal: Elmer Gertz of Chicago and Sol Dann of Detroit.

I had met Gertz briefly at the funeral. That same night he had publicly debated Mark Lane on television. By then, Lane was considered an authority on the assassination. I felt sorry for Gertz at the time; Lane seemed to have all the answers, whereas Gertz was not as versed in the Warren Commission findings and conclusions. I decided as I watched the debate that I would read all there was on the subject, not only the trial transcript and the Warren documents, but also the essays and commentaries on those documents.

The day after the hearing for Earl's appointment as the administrator of Ruby's estate, Gertz called me. At first he seemed hostile. I got the impression that he felt I was encroaching on his territory and trying to upstage his position in the public limelight. After about five minutes, however, his tone became more congenial. Possibly he admired my being able to get a non-Texas court to take jurisdiction of the estate. I felt he also liked the plan of action that I outlined to him on the phone. It became clear to him in our conversation that my chief objective was to turn Jack's property over to the Archives, and to do that we had to obtain the property first.

I explained that I was preparing orders directed at four officials in Dallas to show cause in the Michigan court why they shouldn't turn over Jack Ruby's assets to Earl. These orders were directed at Police Chief Curry (who I discovered later, much to my embarrassment, was no longer police chief); Sheriff William Decker; Henry Wade, prosecuting attorney for Dallas County; and, for good measure, William Alexander, Wade's assistant.

We both knew the orders would not mean anything—that in Texas they were not worth the paper they were printed on—but serving the orders was a first and necessary step in a long process. I explained that I would take the papers to Dallas to serve them myself. Knowing that all flights from Detroit to Dallas changed planes in Chicago, Gertz invited me to meet with him at the airport on my return.

When I arrived at Dallas' Love Field, Eva met me at the gate. Since she did not drive, I arranged for a rental car. When it was brought up, I threw my briefcase in the back seat, and Eva began directing me toward downtown Dallas.

To the first-time visitor, Dallas is impressive. Unlike Detroit and Chicago, Dallas' skyline is almost totally limited to post-World War II construction. There is a clean and stark crispness about this twentieth-century city. Instead of taking the freeway, we drove down Lemmon Avenue. Eva confessed that the freeway system confused her. She guided me through one-way streets to the Statler Hilton, where I would be staying.

As we pulled into the valet parking area, I felt an elbow jab into my right arm—something I would experience several times during my stay in Dallas. Eva pointed at the police station across the street.

"That was where it happened," she whispered.

After I registered at the hotel, we walked across Commerce Street to the police station. The graying marble building stands on the corner of Commerce and Harwood and extends north to Main Street. Eva led me west on Commerce to Harwood, and we proceeded down Harwood.  We passed a narrow marble stairway going down and another marble stairway going up to a set of large doors.  Eva hurriedly continued past the stairways and directed me down a dark ramp that appeared to go to the basement.

"We are going down the up-ramp," she explained, holding onto my arm as we descended.  On the right at the bottom of the ramp was a garage, and to the left were several doors.  The walls were painted dull orange.  Again I felt Eva's elbow.

"This is the spot.  Jack came down that ramp over there."

"Eva," I asked, "Jack was friendly with officers in the Dallas Police Department, wasn't he?"

"Jack knew most of the policemen," she responded.  "It began back in 1954, when Jack ran the Silver Spur *for me*."  She wanted me to know it was her club.  "One night at another club that Jack was visiting, two police officers got into a conflict with a number of the customers.  They were badly outnumbered and the crowd started hurling beer bottles at them.  Jack jumped in and helped the officers come out of it safely.

"When Officer Mullinax was killed on duty a few years ago," she continued, "Jack grieved for quite a while.  He had some of his employees go to the funeral with him and he gave some cash to the widow.  You know," she sighed, "he gave that woman the money he needed to pay his light bill at the club with."

"Eva," I asked, "did Jack pay off the police?"

"No," she quickly responded.  "He had a great deal of genuine respect for the police.  He did give them bottles of whisky at Christmas time, but that's legitimate."

"Where is the back door that some of the critics of the Warren report claim Jack came through?" I asked.

She had me follow her into the garage area.  There was a door leading out to a stairway.  I wanted to examine the door from the outside.

We started to walk up the other ramp.  I asked Eva to stay to the right, and I went to the left.  We stood on the ramp about three quarters of the way up, waiting for a car to drive down. When one did, I noted that there was at least a two-and-one-half foot clearance on either side of the passing car.

"Eva," I asked, as we reached the street level, "if we just came up the *down*-ramp, how did Jack see Lt. Pierce's car coming *up* this ramp?"

"Oh," Eva replied, "that day they turned it around. The armored car they were going to use for a decoy got stuck on the other ramp we first came down, so they had to use the only ramp available. Lt. Pierce drove out to make room for the other cars in the basement to move around."

I looked back down the ramp and saw a sign that read: Clearance 7 ft. 5 in.

We walked east on Main Street to the corner of Pearl, where Eva pointed to the Western Union office.

"Jack came down here that morning. He parked his car across the street," she said, pointing to a parking lot, "and went into the Western Union office."

"I want to pace this off," I said as I set my stopwatch.

We walked from the door of the telegraph office, down the ramp, to the spot where Oswald was shot; then we went back and repeated the process. No matter how we did it, it took about three minutes, which was exactly the period of time between Jack's last time stamp and the shot that killed Oswald.

"Jack," she said, "came out of Western Union, saw a crowd at the ramp, walked toward it, and as he reached it, the policeman guarding the ramp moved the crowd to one side to let Lt. Pierce's car pass by. Jack just walked down the other side."

"But why, Eva?" I asked the $64,000 question.

"He didn't want Mrs. Kennedy to have to come back to Dallas for a trial."

"That's no reason to kill a man," I exclaimed, knowing she had given me the stock response to my question. Eva looked hurt.

My comment had disrupted the dramatic effect of her reenact-
ment. Her brother had killed a man. She couldn't deny it; nor
could she give any satisfactory answers as to why Ruby had
murdered Oswald.

"Eva," I asked, "will you arrange for me to talk to as many
people as possible about Jack?"

She agreed.

That afternoon Eva and I went to Phil Burleson's office in
the LTV Tower. Phil came right out to greet us and seemed
genuinely glad to see us. He showed me the four-foot-tall package
that contained the trial transcript.

Phil addressed me, "You all feel free to take it and read it."
I noticed that the title of the transcript was:

The State of Texas
-vs-
Jack Rubenstein

I wondered if Jack's Jewish name had been used to
prejudice the jury.

"Alan," he continued in his Texas drawl, "Tim Timmins
is the new U.S. attorney for the northern district of Texas. He
would like to meet with you."

"When?"

"Right now, if you can."

"Sure. I'm not on a schedule today."

Eva said that she would be content to wait in Phil's office
for our return. Phil and I left the building and got into his car.

"How far do we have to go?" I asked.

"Oh, just down the street," Phil responded. In less than a
block he pulled up to the curb, and a rather slender young man
opened the back door.

"Alan, this is Tim Timmins, " Phil said, as Tim got in.
There were no amenities. Tim got right to the point.

"You want Ruby's gun, watch, ring, and suit," he said,

"and we want to help. Ruby owed the U.S. government about $40,000 in back taxes. We would consider it an even trade if you delivered that property to us for storage in the National Archives in Washington."

"Tim, that is exactly what I was going to propose to you." I knew Phil had laid the groundwork for this short exchange.

"Alan, can you stay in Dallas through Saturday morning?" Tim asked.

My plans were flexible, so I agreed.

"Good. There's a meeting you ought to attend. I'll meet you at ten o'clock in your hotel lobby."

Tim got out of the car and left. I looked at Phil and asked, "Why all the cloak and dagger?"

"Let's go serve the papers," was his response.

# 5

"Dallas County has just completed its new county building," Phil explained as he pulled his car into a parking lot on Elm Street.

We left the car and headed south. He pointed out Bryant's cabin, the oldest structure in Dallas, the county jail behind it, and the building where Jack's trial took place. Directly in front of us stood a new, impressive building with a marble exterior.

"This is the new county courthouse," Phil said, and ushered me toward the door. "Sheriff Decker is in the basement; Henry Wade is upstairs. Where do you want to go first?"

"The prosecutor," was my instant response.

As we waited for an elevator, Phil spoke to some attorneys waiting with us about the recent United States Supreme Court's Miranda and Escobedo decisions that required law enforcement officials to warn prisoners of their right to remain silent.

The elevator stopped at several floors before it came to ours. At the right floor, Phil nudged me out of the elevator toward the sign: DALLAS COUNTY PROSECUTOR'S OFFICE.

"Is Henry in?" Phil asked the receptionist.

"Yes," she replied, as she called Mr. Wade on the intercom. "Mr. Burleson and a gentleman to see you, Mr. Wade."

"What have you brought me, Phil? Another Melvin Belli?" Wade roared as we entered his office. He was a robust man with the personality that matched his physical dimensions.

"Not quite," Phil laughed, as he introduced us. "Alan has

some papers for you."

I reached into my briefcase, making sure the papers I took out were addressed to Henry Wade, and handed the proper set to him. He sat back and pondered them.

The papers were titled:

STATE OF MICHIGAN

IN THE PROBATE COURT FOR THE COUNTY OF WAYNE

"Michigan," Wade drawled, "I was there once. It was a convention of prosecutors on a small island in northern Michigan. No cars. Yeah, Mackanack was its name."

I didn't bother to tell him the name of the island—Mackinac—was correctly pronounced "Mackinaw."

He continued to read the papers, which ordered him to appear in the Wayne County Probate Court to show cause why he should not turn the pistol over to Earl Ruby, administrator of Jack Ruby's estate.

Henry Wade knew as well as I that the Michigan court had no jurisdiction over him, and that this was simply my official way of beginning negotiations with him. I was fully aware that I was not dealing with just any district attorney. This man was graduated from the University of Texas Law School on a football scholarship, and had been the president of his class. He had also been the roommate of John B. Connally, the Texas governor who had been shot along with Kennedy that fateful Friday morning.

"I haven't decided what to do with the pistol yet," he said, looking up from the papers.

We were all aware that he would soon have to sign an order terminating the Ruby prosecution case. The state could not try a dead man. When Wade signed that termination order, the pistol would no longer be evidence and would have to be released. It was just a matter of time, I thought.

Wade gave the impression that the gun was in his safe and that's where it would stay.

"Henry," I finally spoke, "please just make sure the gun doesn't go anywhere until you decide to whom you're going to release it. When and if I get the gun, I want to be able to verify its authenticity." I did not want the gun exchanged for a similar one, thus losing evidence that I thought would eventually assist in proving that Jack was not part of a conspiracy.

Eva had told me that Jack's gun was broken. It no longer was double action, but had to be cocked before each shot. When Jack shot Oswald, he had only one shot to kill him. Would a man involved in a conspiracy attempt an assassination with a gun he could fire only once without recocking?

"Henry," I said, to change the subject, "now that Ruby's dead and there will be no need for a trial, would you subject Sergeant Patrick Dean to a polygraph examination? Not that I believe he lied," I continued before he could answer, "but to set the record straight."

"I'll have to give that some thought," Wade responded, obviously taken aback by my question. I later found out that the Dallas police did, in fact, give Sergeant Dean a polygraph test. The test indicated that Dean had lied in his statement about Ruby's planning to kill Oswald.

"Well," I continued, "have you read any of the testimony before the Warren Commission?" I was going to ask about Forrest Sorrels' testimony. Sorrels was the first person to speak to Jack after the shooting. He and Sergeant Dean were both with Jack after he had been taken to the confinement area in the police headquarters. Sorrels' testimony contradicted Dean's assertion that Jack had planned the murder ahead of time.

"I've read some of it," Wade responded curtly. I could see he was getting irritated.

Turning to Phil, he asked, "Are you going down to Houston for the seminar next week?" The seminar was on recent

Supreme Court decisions. My conversation with Mr. Wade was over.

We left the office with little formality, and Phil directed me down the hall to the office of William Alexander, Assistant Dallas County Prosecutor. We did not enter the office but just stood at the door. A man with a dark complexion and pocked-marked face stood behind his desk. He glanced at the papers I handed him, and put them on the upper-left corner of his desk.

"I would have seen him fry, but he died first," Alexander commented. One would find little respect for the deceased Jack Ruby in this office. We left quickly.

As we headed back toward the elevators, Phil explained that Jack had always considered Alexander his friend, even when he sought to "fry" him.

"During the trial," Phil continued, "Belli accused Alexander of referring to Jack as 'that Jew boy,' but when the transcript was read back, it was clear that Belli was wrong. Alexander just gives the impression that he's said something bad."

I knew what he meant.

Phil inquired whether I wanted to meet the third member of the prosecution team, A. D. "Jim" Bowie, now a judge.

"Sure," I answered. Bowie was, I had learned, the real brains on the team. I might learn something from him. We went to his courtroom but he was on the bench, precluding any conversation.

"Let's get Decker," I said.

The west side of the basement of the Dallas County Courthouse is the domain of Sheriff J. E. "Bill" Decker. Inside the office, the walls were all glass. I could see the colorful sheriff in his inner office as we spoke to the receptionist. We were invited in immediately even though there were several other people waiting in the reception area.

We were introduced, and Sheriff Decker gave me a toothy grin as he regarded me from behind his oversized eyeglasses. Phil began to converse with the other men in the office.

"I would like to speak to you," Decker addressed me with a deep Western accent. Taking with him his large Stetson, he led me down the hall to one of the glass interrogation rooms. Inside the room he placed his Stetson on the table and turned to me.

"I see you travel in the East," he said, noticing my Shrine lapel pin. This expression is used by one person to inform another that he is a fellow Mason.

Then, without warning, Decker faced me directly and asked, "Is the family planning to sue the county?"

I had absolutely no idea what he was talking about. *Possibly,* I thought, *Decker thinks the family is trying to recover the funds people sent to Jack in jail. Surely Decker knows that Jack never received any significant amount of money in the numerous letters he got from people around the world.* Many did contain small checks, only to assure the sender of receiving Jack's autograph on the back.

"Sheriff," I answered, "the family does not intend to create any more publicity. I think they have had enough." It was a safe, political answer.

It was not long before I found out the reason for Decker's question. When we returned to Phil's office, Eva was sitting patiently in the waiting room reading a magazine.

"I'm glad you're back. Did you serve them all?" she inquired in the same breath.

"Yes," Phil told her. I had forgotten to give the papers to the sheriff, but it really was not necessary.

"I have a 4:30 appointment at Parkland Hospital," Eva said. "Would you take me there?"

"Sure. What's wrong?"

"It's not for me," she responded. "They're releasing Jack's autopsy report to me."

# 6

Parkland Hospital, where President Kennedy had been taken within minutes of the shooting, was not far from downtown by freeway. Once again, however, Eva directed me away from the freeway, down Lemmon Avenue.

"You know," she began, "Jack won his appeal last October. Not only did they set aside his death penalty, but they also gave him a new trial in Wichita Falls."

"Yes," I replied. "That's called change of venue. The appellate court decided that Jack could not get a fair trial in Dallas."

"Well, anyway," she continued, "in December, when the sheriff from Wichita Falls came to get Jack, he took one look at him and refused to move him because he was so sick. The jail doctor thought Jack was having stomach trouble, so he gave him Pepto Bismol."

"Pepto Bismol for cancer?"

"No, they didn't know he had cancer. They took him to the hospital and at first diagnosed his problem as pneumonia." She started to cry.

"He was there a day before they realized it was cancer," she said, taking a handkerchief out of her purse. "The worst part was that the news media was told immediately and Jack heard on television that same day that he was going to die. Alan, is it possible that they injected him with the cancer in the jail?"

"Perhaps you should ask the pathologist." I felt the

situation called for another political answer.

Parkland was a much bigger complex than I had imagined. From reading the Warren Commission testimony about Kennedy's being worked on in the emergency area, I had pictured it as a small hospital.

We found our way to the pathology department in the basement and looked for Dr. Earl F. Rose, the county medical examiner.

Dr. Rose was a direct person who pulled no punches. His small, dull, gray-painted office had just enough room for him to sit behind his desk, with Eva and me on the other side. When he got up to get something from his black filing cabinet, I had to stand to let him get by.

He handed me the original and a copy of the document titled:

## OFFICE OF THE
## COUNTY MEDICAL EXAMINER

On both sides of the title were fingerprints labeled left thumb and right index.

"The number, you will notice," he began, "is sixty-seven, dash, double 0 seven, which means it's the seventh autopsy report done this year." I found the similarity to James Bond's 007 ironic.

"Did they inject my brother with cancer?" Eva blurted out.

Dr. Rose looked at her and answered gently. "Mrs. Grant, there is no way known to me or medical science that one can be injected with cancer. Cancer is developed within the individual, based on his environment and his makeup. External causes can, however, contribute to the development of cancer.

"Lung cancer can develop in nonsmokers as well as smokers. But your brother didn't die of cancer; he died of a blood clot that traveled from his leg and lodged in his lungs. His cancer was a secondary cause."

Eva admitted she had seen the clot in Jack's leg, but was

confused about the cause of death.

"I thought he died of cancer," she said.

"That's a common assumption. Until an autopsy is performed, there may be no way of knowing the actual cause of death. I would say, however, that I don't believe your brother could have been cured, even though he was responding to the treatment. When did you first notice the symptoms?" Dr. Rose looked at Eva.

"When Eileen, our youngest sister, was here in Dallas last July. Jack had developed a dry, nagging cough. For several weeks Dr. Callahan, the jail doctor, gave him cough syrup and Pepto Bismol. Jack got steadily worse. Finally it got to the point that he couldn't keep food down. Jail officials finally ordered that Jack be admitted to the hospital on December ninth."

"Let's see," Dr. Rose said, as he reached for a piece of paper from his desk. He took an old-fashioned fountain pen from inside his white coat and began to write.

"According to my findings," Dr. Rose continued, "he was just beginning to respond to drugs. The nodules in his left lung were decreasing in size. The cancer had spread through his cavities and ducts. He had extensive cancer involvement in his liver and some nodes in his brain."

"Is it possible that he may have had the disease in November, nineteen sixty-three?" I asked, thinking that maybe Belli could have been right when he proposed his psychomotor epilepsy theory.

"No, he would have succumbed much sooner," Dr. Rose replied.

"Dr. Rose," I asked, "how long would it have taken Jack Ruby to contract cancer and die from it?"

"Precisely what I was about to show you. Look at this paper," he said, handing me the notes he had just made. "I would say that Mr. Ruby's disease should have been detected approximately September of nineteen sixty-five, fifteen months before he died. The earliest record of detection we have is four months before his death."

"Who should have detected it?" I asked.

"Doctor John W. Callahan," he said, making sure I had the full name of the jail physician.

"Do you mean, Doctor, that there may have been malpractice involved?" I asked, hoping the legal implications of the word would not bring the conversation to an awkward halt.

"Yes," he answered. "If the cancer had been detected earlier, there would have been an excellent chance Mr. Ruby would still be alive today. They definitely neglected him while he was in jail."

Now I understood why Sheriff Decker had asked me about litigation.

I thanked Dr. Rose. As we rose to leave, I asked if I could have the notes he had jotted down. He handed them to me, a clear indication that he would be willing to repeat this information in court.

As we were leaving, a thought occurred to me, and I asked if I could speak to him privately for a moment.

Eva waited in the outer office while I returned to Dr. Rose's little office

"Dr. Rose," I asked, "didn't you do the autopsy on Lee Harvey Oswald?"

"Yes," he answered.

"Could I get a copy of that report also?"

"I could have one made for you if you like, but it is in the exhibits of the Warren Commission." His tone implied I should have known that.

At that time, I was just reading the testimony in the first fifteen volumes that related to Jack and the president. The exhibits were a hodgepodge of documents contained in the last ten volumes, assembled with no rhyme or reason.

"You might find it very interesting," he said. I thanked the doctor again and departed.

Eva and I left the hospital through the emergency exit so that I could become familiar with the area. We had to walk all the way around the hospital to find the car.

Returning downtown on Lemmon Avenue, Eva asked, "Do you think we have a malpractice case?"

"We probably do," I responded, "but do you want to go through a malpractice suit?"

"Do I want to?" she replied. "Do you have any idea what this city has done to me? Since this terrible thing happened, I haven't been able to get a job or do anything. I hate this city and its people."

"But Eva," I tried to reason, "suppose we did start a malpractice lawsuit, and suppose we won. What would we win? From a legal standpoint, Jack's life was not worth much. A jury in Dallas would feel that Jack was on his way to the electric chair, anyway. It would be absolutely useless and probably do us more harm than good. Right now we want Jack's property, and by starting a malpractice action against the county, we will get an awful lot of people angry with us, the same people who could help us get the property."

I dropped Eva off at her apartment and continued downtown to my hotel. Then I went next door to the public library to look through the exhibits and volumes of the Warren Commission.

I entered the main branch of the Dallas Public Library and asked where the Warren volumes were kept. I was directed to the balcony at the rear. Rather than take the elevator, I walked up the stairs. The Warren testimony and exhibits were in a locked case, together with just about every other book and paper on the subject of the assassination. I was allowed one book at a time. Finally, an hour and several volumes later, I found it.

I began to read the autopsy report, careful not to miss a word. The document traced the wound inflicted on Oswald. It entered at the seventh rib and exited at the eleventh.

As I had earlier realized, if Jack had been involved in some conspiracy to silence Oswald, he would not have waited until after eleven o'clock in the morning that day to come down to the police station. He would have been there before ten o'clock, because the chief of police had announced the previous evening that Oswald would not be moved before then.

Furthermore, if there were a conspiracy to silence Oswald, Jack would have been a poor choice to be the executioner. His actions marked him clearly as an amateur. When a professional shoots to kill, he doesn't shoot the victim in the stomach. Even if the victim did die, he might live long enough to tell all. A professional at point-blank range would have shot Oswald in the heart or head.

I was convinced Jack was not involved in a conspiracy, but I still did not know what had motivated him to shoot Oswald.

# 7

I went to Dallas to serve the show-cause papers in 1967. By this time several books on the assassination of President Kennedy had been published. The most popular one was Mark Lane's *Rush to Judgment*. Fewer than one thousand copies of the testimony and exhibits to the Warren Commission were published, whereas more than one million copies of *Rush to Judgment* were sold.

Mark Lane had been the fifth person to testify before the Warren Commission. In an unprecedented move, Lane asked that his testimony session be open to the public, a request which was granted by Chairman Earl Warren.

Lane had apparently been retained by Marguerite Oswald, Lee Harvey Oswald's mother, to represent her son before the Warren Commission. But since the Commission was conducting an inquiry, not a trial, his services would be unnecessary; in fact, useless.

At the end of the questioning, Lane was asked if there were anything else he would like to present to the Commission. Lane responded, "Yes."

He told the commission of a meeting in Jack's Carousel Club between Officer J. D. Tippit, the police officer shot by Oswald after the assassination, and Bernard Weissman, a former noncommissioned officer who had been stationed in Germany. Weissman had strong right-wing tendencies and had authored a full-page advertisement in the *Dallas Morning News* the day of the assassination. The advertisement was black-bordered and directed at President Kennedy, asking why he had been so soft on communism.

Later, in executive session, Lane identified a third person at the meeting of Tippit and Weissman—Jack Ruby. Lane could not reveal any information about the conversation at the meeting, only that it took place.

Lane maintained that Oswald was innocent, that he was a patsy framed by the Dallas police. Any conspiracy did not include him. The alleged meeting in Jack's club would give the impression that there was a conspiracy among the three men in attendance. The presence of Weissman added a right-wing aura to Lane's conspiracy theory. Oswald, of course, was Marxist.

Lane refused to identify his source for this information, standing behind what he considered a moral commitment. He agreed, however, to inform the commission as soon as he received permission from his source.

Shortly before the Warren Commission disbanded, Lane was asked to appear again. He testified that he had spoken to his source twice since his first appearance before the commission, but that he had not secured permission to reveal the source's name. Lane was told, in no uncertain terms, that his failure to divulge the source of his information did nothing but handicap the Commission.

Lane's book, *Rush to Judgment* (New York: Holt, Rinehart & Winston, 1966), was published almost two years after the Warren report was made public. On page 249 of his book, Lane recounts his meeting with the Warren Commission:

> On March 4, 1964, I gave information to the Commission suggesting that on the evening of November 14, 1963, a two-hour meeting had taken place among Weissman, Jack Ruby, and J. D. Tippit at the Carousel.
>
> This information came to me from a witness to the

alleged meeting. The Commission was right in asserting that I declined to give the witness's name because of my promise not to do so without his permission. I was unable to obtain his permission. But had the Commission wanted his name, it need only have asked one of its witnesses, Thayer Waldo, a reputable journalist on the staff of the *Fort Worth Star Telegram*, who was questioned by counsel (of the Warren Commission) in Dallas on June 27, 1964. Waldo, from whom I had originally heard of the meeting, was well acquainted with the witness and was probably the first person to be told of the circumstances under which it occurred. Counsel, however, did not ask Waldo about the meeting.

Lane implies that the Warren Commission supported his refusal to reveal his source. Yet the Warren Report states:

Lane declined to state the name of his informant but said he would attempt to obtain his informant's permission to reveal his name. On July 2, 1964, after repeated requests by the Commission that he disclose the name of his informant, Lane testified a second time concerning this matter, but declined to reveal the information, stating as his reason that he had promised the individual that his name would not be revealed without his permission. (Vol. II, page 60)

Lane's book contains hundreds of footnotes, giving it an aura of authenticity and authority. But in many of his footnotes Lane is merely citing his own testimony before the Warren Commission. Some footnotes are innocuous. One footnote is merely a reference to the list of people who testified before the Warren Commission.

Thayer Waldo did testify before the Warren Commission,

but there is no mention of the Weissman-Tippit-Ruby meeting in his testimony.  In fact, Waldo testified that he first met Ruby the weekend of Oswald's murder.

I wanted to talk to Thayer Waldo.

# 8

The day after we received the report on Jack's autopsy, I called Eva at 8:00 A.M. I wanted to be in Fort Worth to see Thayer Waldo by 9:00. To avoid arousing suspicion, I had not called for an appointment.

It was approximately 9:30 A.M. when we walked into the lobby of the Fort Worth Star Telegram Building. I walked up to the reception desk and asked to see Thayer Waldo.

"Just a moment," the receptionist replied, as she made a call within the building. After a few minutes a tall, dark man approached us from one of the doors on the side.

"I'm John Tackett," he said, extending his hand in greeting. I shook his hand and introduced myself and Eva. He indicated that he recognized Eva as Jack's sister.

"Why do you want to see Thayer Waldo?" he inquired.

I explained that I wanted to question Waldo about his association with Mark Lane.

"Well," Tackett replied, "Waldo is no longer with the paper. As a matter of fact, he was here only a short time and he had to be dismissed."

"Why?" I asked.

"Sensational journalism," he replied.

"Do you know where he is now?"

"I heard he was in Mexico, but I'm not sure." His answer ended my hopes of speaking to Waldo.

"What was the sensational journalism?" I asked, hoping to

get a clue to the Lane-Waldo connection.

"Let's go to my office," Tackett suggested. He led us through the door to the rear of the building. The office was fairly large, suggesting a position of some importance.

As we sat there, it struck me that as I was attempting to get a story from this man, he was also trying to get a story from Eva and me.

"On February 9, 1964," Tackett began, "Waldo received a call from Mark Lane, who was on the West Coast at the time. Lane asked him to accompany Mrs. Marguerite Oswald to Love Field in Dallas. She was scheduled to testify before the Warren Commission the next day."

"In Washington?" I asked.

"Yes, that's why she had to go to Love Field. Waldo complied with Lane's request and went to Mrs. Oswald's home so she would have someone she could trust to go with her to Dallas.

"That Sunday when Waldo arrived at Mrs. Oswald's home, there were two police officers there to drive Mrs. Oswald to Dallas. The four of them drove to the airport together. On the return trip the two officers, not realizing that Waldo was a newspaper reporter, talked about an employee at the School Book Depository Building who had witnessed Oswald shooting Kennedy.

"The next morning's paper proclaimed under banner headlines—and Waldo's byline—that an eyewitness saw Oswald shoot the President and that Oswald ran right past him on his way out."

"Banner headlines?" I inquired. "How large would that be?"

"Eight columns," he replied. "Apparently Waldo told Lane the story. Although Waldo's account did not give names, two weeks later Lane published the story in the National Guardian with all the pertinent names. He cited Waldo as his source of information."

Tackett's information about Waldo had been helpful. Lane had refused to give Waldo's name to the Warren Commission, but he did include Waldo's name in the article he wrote on that subject.

On the trip back to Dallas I told Eva that when a lawyer writes a brief, a paper submitted to a court citing legal precedent, the worst thing he could do is footnote erroneous material. Lane's book had become known as a brief for the defense of Oswald.

# 9

In order to answer the question of why Jack shot Oswald, it is necessary to learn more about Jack's adult life. Who had he become? What made him tick?

I had asked Eva to introduce me to as many people as possible who might help me to get to know Jack better. For two days we had appointments all over Dallas. I spoke to friends, business associates, attorneys, former employees, and news media people. I also obtained several handwritten pages of notes Jack had made while he was in jail.

From these interviews, Jack's notes, and testimony before the Warren Commission and the House Select Committee on Assassination, I was able to piece together a picture of Jack that helps explain his frame of mind the day he shot Oswald.

Prior to the assassination, Jack was completely apolitical. If he had been asked to name a political affiliation, he probably would have said Democratic because he admired both President Roosevelt and President Kennedy. He read the newspapers every day, but he skipped the front section and turned directly to the entertainment or sports sections.

He was always involved in one promotion or another. Just prior to the assassination, he became involved in the sale of the then- hard-to-acquire Wilkinson razor blades, for which he claimed to have a distributorship. He gave away several as door prizes at his clubs. He also promoted and sold the "twist board," an exercise device that consisted of a small platform mounted on ball bearings. It was operated by standing on the platform and swiveling the hips, imitating the movements of the popular dance the Twist.

At the 1963 Texas State Fair, Jack opened a booth to sell novelties; the enterprise died the first night for lack of interest. Since he had already paid the rental fee, he had some of his employees from the Carousel come to the booth to promote the twist board. One evening, while visiting the other booths at the fair, Jack came upon H. L. Hunt's Lifeline booth and picked up some literature.

The extreme right-wing literature of the Lifeline was a shock to Jack. He could not believe that such literature could be printed. However, he did not know the difference between right-wing and left-wing, having referred to all radicals as Commies and Birchers, as if they were both the same.

The particular leaflet Jack picked up at the fair was *Heroism*, a radio script which espoused a neo-Nazi philosophy, complete with its message of anti-Semitism and a call for the impeachment of Earl Warren. One radio disk jockey told me that on the morning of November 23—the day before Jack shot Oswald—Jack asked him who Earl Warren was. Ironically Warren, Chief Justice of the Supreme Court, would later come to Dallas to interview Jack.

On the morning of November 22, 1963, Jack went to the *Dallas Morning News* to proofread his ads for the coming week-end. Once there, he discovered the black-bordered, full-page "Welcome Mr. Kennedy" ad. He became very upset, not so much with the content of the text in the ad, but by the fact that it was signed by the American Fact-Finding Committee, Bernard Weissman, Chairman. The name *Weissman* seemed clearly Jewish to Jack, and he wondered if the name had been used to stir up feelings of anti-Semitism. Others who had seen the ad were also upset with it. It was the main topic of conversation in the News building that morning.

About 12:30 that afternoon, the announcement came that President Kennedy had been shot. Immediately after the announcement, most people found a radio or television set and stayed by it so they could follow the events. Jack, still at the newspaper, also found a television in the News building and watched it until the announcement that the President had died. Jack then left the News and drove either to Parkland Hospital or directly to the Carousel Club. Two people claimed that they saw Jack outside the Parkland Hospital that afternoon; such a visit could be interpreted as proof of Jack's deep concern about the tragedy. A point of interest is that the Warren Report chose to discount the possibility that Jack might have gone to Parkland— a point that has been noted by many critics of the Warren Report.

Whether he went to the hospital or not, he ended up at the Carousel Club. There he began making telephone calls all over the country. In all these calls, Jack expressed his grief and remorse over Kennedy's death. Jack instructed Andy Armstrong, his bartender and general man Friday, to close the club out of respect for the president.

Eva was at home recovering from surgery. Each day since her release from the hospital, Jack had stopped at her apartment to bring food and generally cheer her up. He arrived there about 5:30 P.M. and immediately called the *Morning News* to advise them to run his ad with a "Closed" sign across the face and to have it run like that all weekend. He also inquired whether his competition, Abe Weinstein's Colony Club and the Weinstein's Theater Lounge would be closed. No one at the paper knew.

Jack left his sister to attend memorial services at the synagogue. There he cried like a baby. After services he drove around the streets of Dallas to observe which establishments were open that evening. He was particularly concerned if the owners were Jewish. He made mental notes of the places that were open.

He then thought of the police, who would be working overtime. Because he occasionally brought food to them, he stopped at a delicatessen, ordered several sandwiches, and while they were being made, called the police station. Lieutenant Simms informed him that they had already eaten. Rather than waste the sandwiches, he decided to take them to Radio Station KLIF; he might even get one of the disk jockeys to plug his club.

His problem, he soon discovered, was that he did not have the night phone number for the station. Since most of the media people were at the police station covering the case, he thought that would be the logical spot to get the phone number. On the radio, Jack had heard a report from the police station by a Joe DeLang, one of the disk jockeys at KLIF, so he went to the police station to find Joe DeLang.

Following are Jack's own words from his notes:

Really, all I wanted was to find this fellow and get out of there, but somehow I got caught in the swirl of things. As I was standing in the long hallway when a door opened and they brought this fellow out. I was very close to him. All of the reporters kept shouting and asking questions. Then someone said "Do you have a larger room?" One of the officials mentioned a room down in the basement. Now I wasn't too anxious to leave, because this was making history, and I was part of it.

I walked down the steps or rode an elevator, I don't remember, and before I knew it I was in the large room, and they brought this fellow out, and made an attempt to ask him questions, but it was useless, and they had taken him back. Then they all left. I was in the hallway and two fellows walked by. I recognized one because he used to work in a service station across from the Vegas Club. I asked the other fellow if he was Joe DeLang. He said no, what do you want him for? I told him I had some sandwiches for KLIF and I wanted to get in there. They said they were from [radio station] KBOX. "What about us, don't we get any?" I said, "Next time." He gave me the direct number to call. I was talking to the tall fellow, I think his name was Sam, for about half a minute.

After getting the number, I walked around to use the phone and was to contact a fellow by the name of Ken and told him about the sandwiches. Then suddenly I asked him if I should try to get [Dallas County Prosecutor] Wade over to the phone. He [Wade] was on the phone talking to someone. I motioned and said someone would like to talk to you. He didn't answer, he went over and conversed with him on the phone. After he finished I got on the phone and the disk jockey didn't know how to thank me enough. He asked me how long I would be, and offered to leave the door open for me. I answered, five minutes.

In Jack's own words, he "got caught up in the swirl of things," not only at that time, but from then until he pulled the trigger some thirty-six hours later. He felt the black-bordered ad signed with a Jewish name was somehow linked to Kennedy's death. He would investigate and find out.

Jack left the police station for KLIF, where he distributed the sandwiches. He was proud to have arranged the interview between Wade and the KLIF reporter, and he was basking in the glory of it.

The conversation at the radio station focused on the assassination and the black-bordered ad. Jack was thinking about the Lifeline papers he had picked up at the Texas State Fair the week before. He felt that all of these things were somehow connected.

Leaving KLIF, Jack drove to the *Times Herald*. On his way he met one of his employees, Kathy Kay. She was sitting with a police officer. Jack joined them for awhile, and the three discussed the events of the day. Miss Kay, of English descent, told Jack that had the assassination happened in England, the assassin would have been dragged through the streets and cut into ribbons.

Jack left the couple to continue on to the *Times Herald*. There he checked his ad for the weekend. More discussion ensued concerning the black-bordered ad in yesterday's *Morning News*.

At 4:30 A.M. Jack was still awake and brooding over the assassination of Kennedy. He returned to his apartment, awakened his roommate, and then called a handyman at the Carousel to bring him his Polaroid camera. The three went to where one of the "Impeach Earl Warren" signs stood. Jack made sure they took several pictures of the sign. They then drove to the post office downtown. He looked into the post office box assigned to the American Fact-Finding Committee to see if it contained any mail. He aroused the night watchman to question him about why the United States Postal authorities would rent a box to such a committee. The night watchman didn't know and didn't care.

After the post office, Jack stopped for coffee and then finally went home. Having slept for less than three hours, he was awakened by a call from his handyman at the Carousel. He followed the news reports on television until early afternoon. He then drove downtown to check out the Carousel. From the Carousel Jack walked to the Dealey Plaza, the site of the assassination. He looked at all the wreaths that had been placed there. Walking back toward the Carousel, he stopped in a bar where he talked with Frank Bellochio, a jewelry designer whom Jack had known for years.

Bellochio had cut out the black-bordered Weissman ad, and he showed it to Jack. In Bellochio's opinion, Jack felt the ad was placed in the newspaper to stir up feelings of anti-Semitism—that the ad was part of a complex conspiracy that included blaming the Jews for the assassination. Jack showed Bellochio his photographs of the "Impeach Earl Warren" sign. The signs, too, were part of the conspiracy.

Shortly after his conversation with Bellochio, Jack called Stanley Kaufman, a close friend and attorney, and described the Weissman ad. He told Kaufman that the black border on the ad indicated that the person who placed it had known President Kennedy would be assassinated.

Jack then visited his sister Eva and spent several hours with her. He seemed restless. He made several calls and left Eva's apartment, only to return again. Jack did not return to his own apartment to stay until after midnight. He finally went to bed about 1:30 A.M.

The next morning he received the phone call from Fort Worth. After promising he would wire twenty-five dollars to the lady who called, he dressed and got into his car for the last time. Accompanying him was his dog, Sheba. He entered the Western Union office and sent the money order.

Outside, he saw a commotion near the entrance ramp to the police station and walked over at the moment Lieutenant Pierce's car was leaving. He walked down the ramp, reaching the bottom just as Oswald was brought out. While millions of people watched on TV, Jack pulled out his .38-caliber Colt automatic and, at point-blank range, shot Oswald in the stomach. As he was wrestled to the ground, he proclaimed, "The world should know that Jews got guts."

It was his revenge for the ad that he felt linked Jews to the Kennedy assassination. Little did he know that other Jews named Lane, Popkins, Weissberg, and Epstein would capitalize on his act, becoming wealthy from the books they wrote about the event.

Joe Tonahill reported that Tom Howard, Jack's first attorney, told Jack to say that he shot Oswald so that Mrs. Kennedy would not be forced to return to Dallas for a trial and relive the tragic loss of her husband. With both Jack and Tom Howard dead, only Joe Tonahill knows the truth about this.

A more logical reason for Jack's action is that he became strongly preoccupied with the idea that the events surrounding

Kennedy's assassination would generate a wave of anti-Semitism, and he felt compelled to change the course of events. When the opportunity arose, Jack did exactly that.

# 10

Many of those who insist there was a conspiracy, including the House Committee on Assassinations, claim that someone helped Jack gain entry into police headquarters. None of the police personnel questioned saw Jack go down the ramp. If any of them did, they obviously did nothing about it. Certainly an officer would hesitate to admit that he saw Ruby; he could have been charged with dereliction of duty.

On the other hand, Jack was able to identify Lieutenant Pierce in the outgoing automobile and also to describe the commotion on the street. This tends to confirm Jack's presence on the ramp, whether or not he was seen there. Had he gained entrance through the alley door, as some theorists suggest, he would not have known who was in the exiting car, nor would he have known that the entrance ramp was temporarily serving as the exit ramp. In addition, that door had an automatic lock when I examined it.

Critics of the Warren Commission's findings also point to Jack's increased telephone activity in the months prior to the assassination. His calls increased by as much as seventy percent, according to Bell Telephone Company records. The critics and the House Committee claim Jack was then conspiring over the telephone. In truth, the calls were business related.

When Jack and his partner Ralph Paul changed the name of the Sovereign Club to the Carousel and gave the club a new image, they ran into direct competition with two clubs owned by the Weinstein brothers, Abe and Barney. While the Sovereign

Club had catered to residents, the Carousel catered to the itinerant businessman, in town for a day or so, looking for a night's entertainment.

The competition between Jack and the Weinsteins became fierce. Jack built an extension on his stage so his girls could walk out into the audience; he hired employees away from the Weinsteins' clubs; he tried anything that might woo patrons from the Weinsteins' clubs into the Carousel.

Then the Weinsteins inaugurated amateur night—a night on which nonunion strippers performed. Theoretically, amateur night featured women who had no experience, but came out of the audience on a whim. Actually, amateur night cut the costs involved in employing union strippers.

Jack attempted to copy the Weinsteins' amateur night, but the Weinsteins countered by holding their amateur nights the same evenings that Jack did. This effectively cut into the Carousel's business.

Jack then tried another tactic. He reasoned that since the amateurs were nonunion, there had been a violation of the union contract with the American Guild of Variety Artists (AGVA), and he began phoning officials of the union all over the country in an attempt to stop the amateur nights altogether.

During one of my trips to Dallas, I spoke with Pappy Dolsen, the leading booking agent for AGVA talent in Dallas. He told me that the same women went from Abe's club to Barney's club, and that the more unprofessional they were, the more the audience loved them. The Weinsteins even used applause meters.

"At that time," Pappy explained, "the union was having its own difficulties. The local representative of the union, Thomas Palmer, got contradictory directives from the New York headquarters. Sometimes amateur nights would be allowed, and then at other times they were outlawed altogether. At one point it seemed that the Weinsteins could sponsor amateur nights and Jack could not."

In August 1963, Jack personally went to New York to see Bobby Faye, AGVA's national administrative secretary, but Faye refused to meet with him. Jack began calling other people in an attempt to find someone who could get through to the union officials. He called Irwin Weiner in Chicago, a bail bondsman well-known to the organized crime syndicate. Weiner had also gone to school with Earl. Weiner's description of the telephone call was that Jack had spoken to an attorney who told him that he would need a bond to get an injunction against the Weinsteins.

Jack also called Barney Baker and Murray "Dusty" Miller, both individuals who have been linked to organized crime. Since neither knew Jack at all, they refused to be bothered by his problems with the AGVA. While all of these telephone calls have led critics to link Jack mistakenly to organized crime, they do explain the increased telephone activity by Jack prior to Kennedy's assassination.

The only conspiracy that Jack was involved in was his unsuccessful attempt to solicit influential people to stop what he felt was a conspiracy against him and his club. Tony Zoppi, a good friend of Jack Ruby's and the entertainment editor of the *Dallas Morning News*, believes that the Weinsteins probably got preferential treatment by paying off union officials. A former president of AGVA, who held office several years after Jack's "battle" with the Weinsteins, has conceded that in the early 1960s there was serious corruption in the union.

# 11

I still hoped to make progress toward securing Jack Ruby's possessions before I left Dallas. Tim Timmins, the U.S. district attorney I had met earlier, had set up a meeting that he'd suggested might help me toward that goal. At ten o'clock Saturday morning, I found Timmins sitting in the lobby of my hotel reading the morning paper. He looked up as I approached.

"Have you had breakfast yet?" he asked.

I nodded and sat in a chair across from him. He had told me very little about the meeting we were to attend that morning, and I was curious about it.

"Who exactly are we going to see?" I asked.

"There are several people here in Dallas," he began, "who might be able to assist you in getting Ruby's property to Washington." Although he did not directly answer my question, this information was reassuring.

I tried again. "Will any of these people be at the meeting?"

"I guess you could say so." Tim smiled. "The meeting is at the office of Mark Martin, president of the Dallas Bar Association. You will meet some of Dallas's leading businessmen. It's just a short walk."

We left the hotel and began walking west.

"A little background might help you to understand our meeting this morning. About three years before the assassination, Lyndon Johnson, then vice president, and his wife visited Dallas. In the lobby we just left, both Johnson and his wife were cursed and spat on by a very nasty crowd.

"A month or two before the assassination, Ambassador Adlai E. Stevenson, after trying to give a speech here, was struck with a placard when he tried to leave. Just months prior to that, someone painted swastikas on the downtown stores owned by Jewish people."

"Except for the swastikas, all these incidents seem political," I interrupted.

"No, that's not what I'm getting at," Tim replied. "To many people around the country, the assassination was just a culmination of all these events. Naturally, Dallas and its new convention center began to lose business. Conventions were canceled. People just did not want to come here, and it has hurt Dallas financially. Have you been over to Fort Worth?"

I answered, "Yes."

"Then you must have noticed the difference." It was more of a statement than a question.

I did not answer, because I did not really understand what he was driving at.

"Dallas," he continued, "has been a national trading center from its founding, and still is today. *Business* is the business of Dallas. It's one of the leading cities in the Southwest, but as you can see, it's neither Southern nor Western in character. Fort Worth is Western."

I started to understand what he was trying to say. In Fort Worth the men did wear Western attire, as opposed to the business suits worn in Dallas, just forty miles away.

"Without business from all over the country, Dallas would dry up," he continued. "The meeting we're going to will be on getting back the business we have lost and keeping it here," he concluded.

As we entered the lobby of the Fidelity Union Tower, I wondered why anyone would want to talk to me about this.

We did not have to wait for an elevator that morning. The

building seemed deserted. When we entered the outer office, we were immediately ushered into a large office near the rear of the suite.

Behind the desk sat Mr. Martin. I was introduced to him and took a seat in front of his desk. Around the room were seated several other gentlemen. None of them were introduced, and none of them spoke at first.

"So," he began, "you're here to get Jack Ruby's property?"

"Yes," I replied. I couldn't see the other men in the room. They were all, including Tim, sitting behind me.

"Well," he continued, "you've made arrangements with the United States attorney here to deliver it directly to Washington?"

"That's what I am trying to do," I responded.

"Why can't it be sent from here to Washington without any fanfare?" he questioned.

"I think," I began, "that the family, more particularly Eva, has been through quite an ordeal these past few years, and I really believe she would feel a bit vindicated if she were to make the delivery herself. It's a small thing to ask."

"But that's what we don't want." I heard a voice from the rear. "It's not good for the image of Dallas. We don't need any more press about the assassination."

I was glad Tim had filled me in about these men's concerns on the way over.

"What about you?" another voice came from the rear. "What kind of headlines are you here to make?"

At this question, I turned around to look at my interrogator, but I could not tell who had spoken. I looked at one suntanned man, as if he were the one, and asked, "What do you mean?"

A balding man with glasses spoke up. "I mean what I say."

"Well, I don't understand," I countered.

"We have had a steady parade of foreigners here who call

themselves lawyers." He enunciated his words carefully. "First, Melvin Belly," he said, intentionally mispronouncing his name, "who came here from the West Coast and did nothing but belittle us and our judicial system."

"And what about your Sol Dann from your Deetroit," the suntanned gentlemen entered into the conversation, giving his own version of my city's name.

These were angry men, and I was not prepared for their questions.

Sol Dann was a senior partner in a Detroit law firm that specialized in personal injury matters. Sol himself loved a good legal battle. He had taken on Chrysler Corporation a few years back in a minority stockholder's suit and had won big.

"Gentlemen," I began slowly, "I am not Melvin Belli and I'm not Sol Dann. You have never seen my name in the newspapers nor my face on television. I have learned to subdue my passions," I said. The last phrase would let any Masons in the room know that I was also a Member of the Craft. I found revealing that I am a Mason to be very valuable in Texas, where there is a high percentage of members.

I spotted a slight smile on the suntanned man's lips, so I knew I had at least one listener.

"My job is much the same as yours," I pointed out. "I want to quietly probate this estate, turn the property over to the federal government, and close it up with as little fanfare as possible."

"Lawyers who like to see their names in print," I continued, "are not helping their careers. First of all, prospective clients are afraid to go to them because of the high fees they might charge. Secondly, with a well-known defense counsel, a jury might presume the client is guilty, or why would he retain such a noted lawyer? And thirdly, and probably most importantly, a jury will expect such a lawyer to perform magic before them, and you can't change the facts of a case."

I must have said the right thing, because the mood of the

meeting changed. I was informed that the men in the room were on a committee empowered to spend thousands of dollars on advertising or on anything else that would "take the taint off Dallas." We discussed the procedure for transmitting Jack's property to Washington. The first step, we decided, would be to offer the articles to the government.

At the conclusion of the meeting, as I was about to leave, I was informed that if I ever repeated any of our conversation, or even reported that the meeting took place, it would be denied.

# 12

About 9:00 P.M. on the same day as my meeting with the Dallas businessmen, my American Airlines jet touched down at O'Hare field and taxied to the gate. I saw Elmer Gertz in the waiting area, watching the faces of the deplaning passengers. I doubted he would recognize me; I had seen him only briefly at the funeral. To my surprise, he gave a clear sign of recognition when our eyes met. This was the man responsible for the release of Nathan Leopold.

I walked toward him and he stood up saying, "Welcome to Chicago, colleague."

*I'm in the big leagues now*, I mused.

He was anxious to know what was happening, so I suggested that we find the closest coffee shop or bar where we could compare notes.

Before we sat down at the table, I removed from my briefcase the copious notes I had taken over the past few days in Dallas. I had written everything down as it was happening, a habit I learned when I was with the Treasury Department. In precise detail I told Elmer of all the meetings and interviews, including the encounter that morning.

I wanted to know more about Sol Dann and why he had incurred the wrath of the Dallas business community. Earl had often mentioned Sol's name in connection with the case, but I did not remember anything that would explain the hostile attitude I had encountered.

Earl had focused more on the state of shock the family was in after the trial. They were shaken by the guilty verdict and angered at Belli's exploitation of Jack. Belli had taken several photos of Jack in his cell to sell to *Life*. Percy Foreman, a Houston attorney, offered his services to the family as their exclusive agent. He would assume the burden of handling all contracts concerning books, movies, television productions, music productions, plays, magazine articles, and photographs—all for the fee of $300,000. They did not retain his services.

I realized that I knew very little of the legal proceedings from the period after the trial to the day Jack died.

"Elmer," I asked, "what was it Sol did that caused those men to come down on me?"

"March 14, 1964," he began, "the day the guilty verdict was returned, Belli was removed from the case. The family realized that a new team of lawyers was needed to perfect an appeal. Somehow Sol Dann and Earl got together."

"I know Sol Dann," I interjected. "We had offices in the same building in downtown Detroit. He is one of the most tenacious advocates I have ever met."

"Yes." Elmer smiled. "Sol certainly can be pugnacious. It was he who brought William Kunstler and me into the case. Kunstler then brought in Sam Houston Clinton, Jr. The team was Dann, Kunstler, Clinton, Burleson, and I. We stayed together until Jack died.

"Now, you've been to Dallas and have spoken to people who knew Jack. From that, what can you tell me about Jack Ruby before he shot Oswald?"

I paused for a moment. The question seemed loaded.

"Jack Ruby was a middle-aged man, concerned about going bald and gaining too much weight. He was streetwise and tough. He liked his women. In spite of rumors, he was definitely not a homosexual. He liked dogs, sometimes introducing his own dog as a member of the family. He had a quick temper. Jack would strike first and then ask questions. He was always very kind to those down on their luck." I quit speaking, expecting to be challenged for an answer that was more definitive.

Elmer sat pensively for a few moments and then said, "Interesting observations. I had the feeling that few people would like Jack. There was nothing lovable or interesting about him. It was hard to defend his mad act. We, his defense team, only had the redemption of American justice as our cause. Of course, we wanted to win Jack's case, but we had an even greater desire to challenge the mockery of justice that had occurred."

Now it was my turn to be pensive. I had not heard this side of the story before.

"After the verdict, Jack went into a state of shock. As his condition deteriorated, we as defense counsel faced a dilemma. We were concerned that a sanity hearing would determine that Jack belonged in an institution. A new jury would definitely consider Jack insane. Although we couldn't ignore his mental condition and that he needed help, we were very reluctant to proceed with a sanity hearing.

"In the meantime, Joe Tonahill remained probably a bigger nemesis than our adversaries, the prosecution. Tonahill, who had been part of the Belli team, had not been formally dismissed as counsel after the trial. When the Warren Commission came to Dallas to take Jack's testimony in June 1964, Tonahill appeared with Jack as counsel. Since Jack was under oath, what he said at the deposition could certainly be used against him at a new trial. He was thus taking the witness stand when he had a right to remain silent. But if he were insane, could he waive that right?"

"An interesting legal question," I commented.

"It certainly is," Elmer answered. "During his testimony he was telling the truth. Tonahill, on the record, agreed to allow Jack to take a polygraph test and arrangements were made.

"Sol became furious when he heard about the polygraph.

When the test was given, he became absolutely livid. Sol accused Tonahill of calling him a Jew-bastard, white nigger, and other anti-Semitic epithets. Sol's accusations made the newspapers. He was going to get Joe Tonahill off the case at any cost."

Sol Dann was a foreigner in Dallas but Joe Tonahill was a down-home Texas boy. Dann had become another Belli in the eyes of the Dallasites.

Looking at my watch, I noticed that my connecting flight into Detroit had just left, but I was not going to leave at this point.

"Meanwhile, to get Tonahill out," Elmer continued, "it was necessary that we get in. Yes, we were the attorneys of the client's choice, but it was necessary, according to the court of criminal appeals, to have Jack sign a request for substitution of attorneys. Normally this wouldn't be a difficult process, but the court of criminal appeals wanted Judge Brown to hear the sanity issue first since the results of that hearing, according to Texas law, could affect a substitution of attorneys and also the imposition of the death sentence."

"Then it would seem," I added, "that Jack had to be proved sane before he would be allowed to select his own attorneys."

"Yes, but remember," Elmer continued, "we really felt by this time that Jack was over the brink. We needed to delay the hearing. Finally, we convinced Phil Burleson, who was quite reluctant, to file papers to remove both Tonahill and Judge Brown from the case."

"I can understand why Phil was reluctant," I offered. "He was the only one of the team who practiced in Dallas."

"Precisely," Elmer agreed. "The motion to disqualify Judge Brown stated that we had information that the judge was writing a book about the trial, that he had already received an advance on the book, and that any future decisions the judge would make would be additional chapters. We also cited his posing for photographs for the media and his securing the services of a public relations agency. Yes, that was difficult for Phil.

"The motion to substitute for Tonahill also contained castigating remarks. In order that the blow to Phil not be so strong, we did agree, at his insistence, to allow him to do all the talking in the courtroom, and to merely sit at counsel table with Jack. At the hearing, Judge Brown, without allowing Phil any argument, ruled against all of the motions. Because this was an obvious violation of Jack's civil liberties . . . "

"The federal court granted the request," I interrupted, for I knew that, once the case went to the federal system, it was possible to remove Judge Brown with no appeal in the state court. I looked at my watch again. I wanted to continue, but I knew I would miss the last plane to Detroit. I thanked Elmer for his time and excused myself.

On board the plane, I wondered if my luggage and the transcripts would arrive in Detroit. And then it suddenly hit me. On that first trip to Dallas, I had never gone to Dealey Plaza.

# 13

I was relieved to find my baggage waiting for me at Detroit Metro Airport. I retrieved it and headed home.

Sunday I began to pore over the transcripts, and to my delight I had not only the transcript of Jack's trial, but also all the transcripts of every court hearing, including the ones in federal court.

There is some danger to understanding in reading a transcript in that you do not get the full flavor of the proceeding. Take the simple sentence, "I didn't say Tom stole the money." Emphasizing the *I* implies that someone else might have accused Tom of taking the money. Put the emphasis on *didn't say,* and you imply that the statement is just not true. Putting the emphasis on *Tom* provides a third interpretation of this simple sentence: perhaps someone besides Tom took the money. It is for this reason that appellate courts will not overturn a trial court's decision by just reviewing the transcript.

Even given that element of uncertainty in interpreting the transcript records, the facts of the proceedings seemed clear.

On March 18, 1965, Sam Houston Clinton, Jr. appeared before United States District Court Judge T. Whitfield Davidson. Also appearing were Bill Alexander and Jim Bowie for the state prosecution, with Tim Timmins on behalf of the United States government. Before the court was a petition for *habeas corpus,* which literally translated means "you may have the body." It is a procedure in which the state must justify the imprisonment of an individual to the court.

Clinton explained to the court that he believed Judge Brown planned to have Jack in his courtroom the next day to ask some questions. Clinton felt this appearance was improper, and that the United States marshal should have jurisdiction over the prisoner, not the county sheriff.

Bill Alexander opposed the petition on the ground that there was no federal question involved; that is, the federal court did not have the right even to entertain the petition. Jim Bowie, of course, agreed with Alexander, explaining that the hearing before Judge Brown was for the removal of Joe Tonahill.

Clinton argued that Alexander and Bowie were wrong, and that his cocounsel, William Kunstler, could explain the law to the court. Upon being asked if Kunstler was available, Clinton asked for a one-week postponement in order to bring Kunstler to court. He also informed the court that he was to begin a trial in Austin, Texas, the next day.

The court wanted to get on with the matter, and adjourned it to the next afternoon, based on a phone conversation the judge had with Tonahill.

The next day, Jack was in the courtroom as required by the petition for *habeas corpus*. Also present were Alexander, Tonahill, and Burleson. Except for Burleson, none of the current attorneys were present; the judge, however, allowed the proceedings to continue.

After Alexander advised the court that Clinton was not present, Jack asked the court if he could speak. The court saw no objection, but before Jack could begin, Tonahill informed the court that he had been on the case longer than anyone else, and it was necessary for him to stay to assist in the appeal. I noted that nothing was said about Burleson, who came into the case at the same time as Tonahill.

Tonahill said, "There are a lot of things I could be doing that would be better for my family and my income, but I couldn't quit Jack Ruby; I couldn't respect myself and continue to practice law."

Whether Tonahill was speaking sincerely or not, only he can say. Certainly the words imply a high moral standard. Ironically, the same week that I read his statement in the transcript, I received a letter from Mr. Tonahill asking how he could file a claim against the Jack Ruby estate.

Tonahill accused the present group of lawyers of commercializing Jack's case, emphasizing that they were from New York City, Chicago, and Detroit. He questioned Sol Dann's stand against the polygraph test when that was what Jack wanted.

Tonahill explained that Jack no longer wanted him as his attorney because Jack was mentally ill and did not know what he was doing. After reading Jack's statement, my first inclination was that Jack really was ill. (I had not as yet read his testimony before the Warren Commission.) Nevertheless, the judge was eager to hear Jack. He allowed Jack to speak from where he stood, without requiring that he be sworn in.

Jack began, "This is the most tragic thing in the history of the world. One of the most tragic conspiracies in the world." The "conspiracy" Jack referred to was the conspiracy among Tonahill, Burleson, and the district attorney to convince the public that he was insane. From these opening statements, Jack rambled on about his killing Oswald and the various attorneys with whom he had come in contact.

The transcript reads as follows:

MR. RUBY: Now, for a person to recall of this, I think I'm doing pretty well for an insane man.

This is the most tragic thing that ever will happen. I am going to die and I don't care.

During the time of my incarceration, Phil Burleson knew all my witnesses, and knew what upset me. He knew of certain things that happened in the jail. I have never been easy in that jail, certain things that scare me in jail, and he knew the breaking point at a certain time for Jack Ruby. In the meantime, unbeknownst to me, I didn't know there were tricks to get verbal statements from persons that will be used against them at an opportune time. Maybe I didn't know.

Yes.

I never had any defense. I never had any defense. Anything that was said in court went back to the District Attorney from Phil Burleson. Right now there is a good policeman and a bad policeman between Phil Burleson and Joe Tonahill, and here is Henry Wade; when he states that Henry Wade wants to get a *habeas corpus,* he uses the names of his dear friends to talk against him.

Getting back to the incarceration. This particular guard of mine works on the Bible with me. As a matter-of-fact, he has taught me various phases of the Bible in which I am not well-learned. He said, "Jack," and I became enthused.

THE COURT INTERRUPTED: I might say to you, you have no right to feel ashamed of Abraham or Moses or any of those men, so just move along.

MR. RUBY: This was an ulterior motive, the question of my confidence, and I became very close to this particular person because he told me he studied for the ministry, and during that time, there were so many things in my past; one little item that will come out later on, about me being involved in sending four guns to a friend of mine in 1959, during peacetime, and my association with Cuba, and this particular man, Mr. McWillie—incidentally, I notice in reading the Warren Report, that because of Jack Ruby not knowing the difference between reality and rights, we will not release the results of the polygraph. There is a reason for that, because I know what happened and what took place in jail. Certain evidence that is going to be submitted, that I did know Oswald. So when this was over, Mr. McWillie called me on the phone and said, "You know Ron Hart who has a hardware store?" This is in early 1959, and not realizing what would happen later, I called Ray Brantley and said, "Ray, wants you to send him something." Mac was a prominent gambler around this country. That is all I had to do with it, and all I had to do anything in the future, from that date on. When the FBI picked me up, I forgot to mention the fact that I called Ray Brantley and sent four guns to McWillie. I asked someone to check Ray Brantley about the call, and that particular night Phil Burleson knew I was unnerved, and he has part of the itinerary of what happened from the time I reached the News Building, and everything until I went down to the station.

And I called Mr. Gordon McClendon's number to find a party to get to KLIF, and I recall the radio broadcast disc jockey was at the station house, so my purpose in going to the station, I came down and tried to get the phone number, but prior to that I called Gordon McClendon; I had to get that number.

All these things were coincidental with what happened. It couldn't have happened in a million times how I criminally indicted myself in a conspiracy that will be proven later.

At 10:15. I left my apartment, and the story was out that this particular person [Oswald] was supposed to leave the jail at ten A.M. I received a call from a young girl who wanted some money. I went to the Western Union, which was coincidental, and prior to that, I will admit a letter was to Caroline which broke my heart. I was emotional, and I closed the club for three days. This letter was written to Caroline, telling her how awfully sorry I was for her. And another situation; there was said something about a trial. Don't ask me what took place, and that triggered me off that Sunday morning.

I accepted the call at 10:15, and went down to the Western Union and parked my car across the street, and took off to transact my business. At 11:17, I walked; I don't say it was made up my mind what to do.

From 11:17 until later, I was guilty of a homicide. Which must be the most perfect conspiracy in the history of the world that a man was going to accept a call and came from his apartment down to the Western Union. If it had been three seconds later, I would have missed this particular person. I guess God was against me. I left the Western Union and it took about three and a half minutes to go to the bottom ramp. I didn't conspire or sneak in to do these things, I am telling you. If they had said, "Jack, are you going down now?" that would make some conspiracy on me. I left the Western Union and it was a fraction of a second until that tragic act happened.

Now, it seems that all these circumstances were against me. I had a great emotional feeling for our beloved President and Mrs. Kennedy, or I never would have been involved in this tragic crime. That was completely reverse from what my emotional feeling was.

From the moment that Tom Howard came in, Phil Burleson didn't care whether he got any money or not to work on the case. So I said to my sister, "Eve, I didn't pay them anything, and that is not good, and I didn't think he was willing to do anything that was not good."

And Joe Tonahill was a very charitable person. Well. I am sorry to say this, it is strange that a person like Harvey Oswald, who never worked a day in his life, and

I have reason to think of these things because I know all the things that are going on, a man has never worked in his life is able to secure a job in a bookstore weeks prior to the anticipated arrival of our beloved President. Who else could know that our President was coming to Dallas? I couldn't know. And I am speaking of what I anticipated to happen.

Now, I am standing in front of a court of law, and I am as competent as Joe Tonahill when he looked at you in the eye, and he knew how to tell a lie, and Mr. Tonahill is trained for these things. He can look at you and tell you certain things from his construction of various types.

May my soul never rest, this man sitting here has lied to you, everything he stated right here at this moment when he made that speech.

THE COURT: I will ask you not deal too much in personalities, when you use the word "lie."

MR. RUBY: All right, your Honor. Mr. Wade, some time back, I requested a polygraph test because I could sense certain things; I can't prove them, but I can sense certain things, so Mr. Bill Decker said, "Jack, if you want a polygraph, why don't you send a letter to Henry Wade stating what you want?"

I first wrote a letter in longhand and somebody said, "Why don't you let somebody do it on the typewriter?" And they typed this letter of my desire to want a polygraph. And there was no conspiracy in my mind. Nothing in my heart, from the moment I left that Sunday morning, and any questions put before me, I won't hesitate to answer.

And after I signed this letter, then it dawned on me that there was a half-inch margin between each paragraph.

Now, unfortunately, the time I was arrested, the

Federal Bureau of Investigation came to interrogate me and the Chief suggested I had better not have any breakfast; I was going to have the lie detector test or truth serum.

I went into the reception room and asked what about the polygraph, and they said evidently the FBI didn't want it.

Now, getting back to Mr. Tonahill—whether Mr. Tonahill is in the case or Mr. Burleson is in the case or not, that is not the main issue.

The important issue is this: I didn't believe there was a God on account of the things that happened. Now, I believe there is because of having a chance to be heard before you. And I want to say you are hearing the most fantastic story, greater than Emile Zola who defended his client, because from the moment I was indicted I didn't have any incrimination against Tom Howard. From the time I was indicted, from the time Bill Alexander received a courtesy pass from me, he said, "Jack, I have been your friend thirteen years." On that particular evening he came up to visit me, the prosecuting attorney, and minutes later he met a newspaper man and said he was going to ask for the death penalty for Jack Ruby. From that moment I didn't have an attorney.

Mr. Belli was sincere, but only judging from the time the wire was sent, because the wire was sent at 11:17, and I said I wanted to get on the stand and tell the truth, and I will tell you why I haven't got on the stand; this particular incident of sending four guns to Cuba, and Phil Burleson unnerved me and made me blurt out. I came out openly and stated, "Oh, my God, we killed the President." And the criminally-minded man don't make that mistake. That evening I was shook up and I cried and the guard came to me and said, "Jack, what is the matter, aren't you going to talk to me tonight?" And I came out as if he were my savior and I said, "Steve, I sent guns to Cuba." I magnified something in my mind which incriminated myself innocently. This letter came out later, and I went on to tell the story of how I left the apartment. I was so emotional because of the loss of our beloved President, and not wanting Mrs. Kennedy to come back to this trial.

Then when I left the Western Union I walked down the ramp and I said to this guard, I said, "I saw it." He knew what to ask, and he said, "Jack, your lawyer said you blacked out." He was able to divulge a weak spot in my testimony. So like a little boy that tells a lie to his teacher, I said, "You promised you wouldn't tell, because we are biblical buddies now." Not knowing it, but he had this little microphone in his pocket. He made the greatest scapegoat in the history of this world, which will be proven later, that I was party to a conspiracy in the assassination of our beloved President.

The only way I can be vindicated is for unbiased people to give me a lie detector test, and not some doctor, because Dr. Beavers said I had an unsound mind. I wish I could think of all the other things regarding my status, but as far as Joe Tonahill is concerned, he doesn't care what happens to me, nor does Phil Burleson, and I am not saying this just to make the headlines; I am not remembering this from rehearsal, I am speaking word-for-word that I know what took place. And I am, like the stupid idiot that loved this country so much, and loved the President so much, and felt so sorry for Mrs. Kennedy when she was standing on that plane with blood on her dress, and they were bringing the casket back with our beloved President, and now I am going down in history as the most despised person that ever lived.

Judge Davidson interrogated Jack regarding his various attorneys. Then, looking at Phil, the judge inquired whether he was employed in this hearing. Phil said no, but upon further questioning, he agreed there was no reason why he could not have been so employed.

Turning to Alexander, the judge finally asked why they should not adjourn and continue the hearing so that the questions raised could be explored more fully. Alexander brushed off the question, saying that the case was ready to be heard now, and then produced an affidavit signed by Judge Brown which he read into the record as follows:

Accordingly hearing was set on March 1, 1965, to determine in a pretrial hearing whether the defendant Ruby desired to go forward with his previous trial motion for a sanity trial or withdraw it. This hearing was postponed at the request of William A. Kunstler until March 8, 1965.

On March 8th, 1965, on preliminary hearing, Mr. Sol A. Dann and Mr. Elmer Gertz were present at counsel table, along with Mr. Joe H. Tonahill and Mr. Phil Burleson. Mr. Dann and Mr. Gertz were not presented to me nor request made for them to be admitted to practice. At this hearing a number of motions were untimely and prematurely presented for my consideration and immediate ruling demanded. These untimely and premature motions were by me overruled, but would have been considered by me as they became timely and full hearing with evidence allowed at proper time and in proper order. As regards the motion for my disqualification, I was and am prepared to give full hearing to said motion at a proper time after due notice to all parties, allowing time for the preparation and production of evidence on all issues.

In an effort to adequately protect the rights of this indigent person, I appointed both Mr. Burleson and Mr. Tonahill to prosecute the appeal, basing this upon the fact that both are duly licensed, competent attorneys of the State of Texas, and the Federal courts, and both appeared throughout the trial on the merits for defendant, and should one be removed by death or disability, that the other could proceed, having full personal knowledge of all the proceedings theretofore.

On March 8, 1965, it was brought to my attention that members of the Ruby family and the foreign lawyers objected to Mr. Tonahill being in the case. Therefore, I personally visited Jack Ruby in jail to determine his preference. He informed me he wished Mr. Tonahill released, whereupon I contacted Mr. Tonahill and informed him I set this matter for hearing on Friday, March 19, at 9 A.M., this being prior to the filing of petition for removal to Federal Court of the Ruby matter by the Texas Civil Liberties Union attorney, Mr. Sam Houston Clinton.

As a matter of courtesy, if not of law, to the most Honorable T. Whitfield Davidson, Judge of the United States District Court of this Northern District of Texas, I have continued the hearing on all matters until Judge Davidson may review the records of this case.

The federal judge pondered a bit and then pronounced his decision from the bench:

The petition for writ of *habeas corpus* is now before the Court, also the motion for a continuance.

Counsel stated that if I would continue the case or postpone the hearing until two o'clock today, he would either be present or have his co-counsel here. His co-counsel was from New York, and was temporarily hearing a case in Montgomery, Alabama.

In his motion for a continuance, he says he is unable to contact his co-counsel in Alabama because he is busy. In his motion this morning he says he is unable to be present because he is in the trial of a case in Austin.

This case is just as important as the Austin case, and at the time he filed his petition here he should have associated some counsel in Dallas and not depended on someone in New York to get here at that time. There are some 1200 able lawyers in Dallas. You heard one say a minute ago that he was open to employment on this very issue if he had been approached. Any of the lawyers that have served him in the past would have done so.

I don't think it was fair to the Court or fair to counsel to file that case, under the circumstances, and walk away. I see no reason why the motion for postponement should be granted, particularly so, that the decision we intend to render will not likely be contingent on the facts, but on the law.

In the first place, when the petition for *habeas corpus* was presented, the question came to my mind, "Why should not this State prisoner have had the benefit of the great *habeas corpus* in the State Court of Dallas?" Dallas has capable judges. It has a Court of Appeals that, in my mind, is the peer to any court anywhere. Why should it not be heard at Dallas instead of being brought here? Maybe I flatter myself that somebody wanted to try this case before me, and I would not mind hearing the case. I would not shrink from the trial of any case, but when the law of the land, of the State of Texas and the United States of America, places the jurisdiction of this question in the State Court, it doesn't lie within me to say that the State doesn't have jurisdiction.

Now, what is the law that pertains to the writ_of *habeas corpus*?

The United States Statute, Title 28, Section 2254, an application for a writ of *habeas corpus* on behalf of any person in custody pursuant to a judgment of a State Court shall not be granted unless it appears that the applicant has exhausted all remedies available in the State Courts. And the State has authority over it.

I would have to hold that the facilities of the State Court of Dallas, and the Court of Appeals were not capable of protecting the right this man has in order to grant the writ.

. . . they tell us that the Civil Rights Law alters that. The Civil Rights Law does not repeal this law; it gives certain rights and privileges, but this law still remains in effect.

. . . Judge Brown has been attacked, and I shall not either condemn or exonerate Judge Brown, because that is not within my power. Neither will I pass upon the question of the attorneys in the case, or the right of any man to appear as attorney.

This case remains on the docket of the Dallas Criminal Court.

I shall remand this case to the Dallas Court, and in order that no thought may be left that Judge Brown is unfair, or that he has let this long litigation make him partial, or cause him to form an opinion that would be unfair to this man, there is a way that some of these other judges can hear it, and I will remand this case back to the State Court, subject to the orders of the Administrative Judge of that district; I believe that is Judge Blankenship.

So this case will not be continued and the writ of *habeas corpus* will not be granted, but the petition will be returned to the Dallas Court without prejudice, and the Dallas judge who is selected to hear it will hear it without prejudice to any ruling of this Court.

Thus, although the relief requested was not granted, the remand was to the administrative judge and not to Judge Brown. This, in effect, was a victory, for it was the beginning of the process for the removal of Judge Brown.

# 14

With the matter back in the state court, the administrative judge immediately assigned it to a visiting judge for the matter of selection of counsel.

I found an interesting comment about Jack's own view of his legal counsel in his personal notes. On January 25, 1964, he wrote:

> Tom Howard evidently feels that he has a chance to gain his recognition back by taking a strong lead in my case which I feel he is not worthy of. I've lost all confidence in him. [I] caught him in a few lies. He is not entitled to the cut of the money.
>
> At the start he pushed his way into the case when I kept asking for other attorneys—Charles Tessmer.
>
> One incident happened when I suggested another attorney, he remarked "there would be more cuts to the pie."
>
> Later, on another visit, I asked him about it and what he meant, and he denied he ever said it.
>
> When there was a situation with Jim Martin [another attorney in Dallas] that he said he would take care of him. The other day when I saw Tom I mentioned Jim Martin. He said it was his own fault and just shrugged it off.
>
> At the start of my troubles, Tom had illusions of grandeur and said to himself that this is the case of a lifetime. For me not to worry that I can count on him.

That he knows just what to do, and that he has handled these cases before.

From that time on I've had nothing but untruths from him and his knocking the other attorneys—jealousy.

Now the situation has arisen that after taken back in [Tom had been fired by Belli], he has gotten out of control again. Something must be done to harness him.

First, he has always known that I wanted Charles Tessmer, and I have a plan regarding him; to get him in the case to sort of dilute and push Tom back to the sidelines.

Either I or him will have to take the initiative and make a statement that he will only come in if he is considered one of the two in the lead to handle the strategy along with Belli, who he thinks will be a big help to get a change of venue. The reason I want Charles is that he has been in quite a few cases lately and won them. I prefer his appearance to Tom Howard. I am sure he is highly respected here, and I'm certain he is too big to show any jealousy and willing to work as a team; not like Tom, who is tearing my morale down.

I'm sure Joe Tonahill will understand why I am doing this only because of Tom Howard.

Also, the other attorneys will understand.

I feel that I want someone of great prominence that is very familiar with the Dallas Courts to have charge in this area, while Belli is on the West Coast. Of course, it will be the three that will be working together: Tonahill, Tessmer, and Burleson. If Tessmer isn't in it, we'll give Howard the chance to make himself the kingpin, and I certainly don't want that, because I won't have the confidence I should have. I'm sure he feels that way about himself. He has expressed himself on different occasions to that effect. That no matter who we would get to represent me, he would consider himself the Texas Attorney.

After listening to him speak to me last night, and his criticism of the way things are going, that from now on he and Belli were going to handle the masterminding, he must really think I'm so naive. However, he is in for a surprise, because all I did was listen.

He referred to Belli as an egotist and glamorous, etc.

He said he didn't recommend this latest piece of strategy [change of venue]. In other words, if it didn't pan out, he would be sitting on both sides of the fence.

He said that Belli and he were going to be the wheels in the case, and that Tonahill and the others are just so and so. That he knows what to do and I don't have a thing to worry about.

The visiting judge, Louis Holland of Montague, Texas, set May 24 as the date for the hearing on choice of counsel.

Earl was the first witness. Of all the members of the family, Earl was the businessman. He spoke with firmness and gained the respect of his peers. He stated under oath that Tonahill came with Belli, and that when Belli went, so did Tonahill. Earl further charged that Belli and Tonahill were making a movie about Jack, and that they secretly took photographs of Jack to sell to *Life*.

A letter sent to Belli and Tonahill was introduced as evidence. This letter corroborated Earl's testimony regarding the movie-making incident, and it was over for Tonahill.

Judge Holland announced he would remove Tonahill as attorney of record and would proceed to a hearing for the disqualification of Judge Brown.

The disqualification of the trial judge could nullify the entire trial and thus Jack would be granted a new trial immediately. At the very least the appellate court would have the records of the disqualification when they reviewed the entire case. Even if Judge Brown had removed himself, it still would have been wise to have the hearing. Consequently, on June 1, 1965, an amended petition to disqualify Judge Brown was filed. The petition concerned the book the judge was writing, the circus atmosphere of the original trial, and the hiring of a public relations expert.

Evidence was presented to show that Judge Brown had received a $5,000 advance from his publisher, Holt, Rinehart & Winston, to write a book entitled *Dallas, Ruby, and the Law.* Copies of extensive correspondence between Brown and the publisher were also presented.

The most incriminating piece of evidence uncovered was a letter from the judge to the managing editor of Holt, Rinehart & Winston, dated March 12, 1965. The judge addressed the progress of his book, stating he had approximately 190 pages completed. He wrote:

> As you probably read in the papers, the Court of Criminal Appeals tossed the case back to me to determine Jack Ruby's sanity and I have set the Sanity Hearing for March 19, and don't know the outcome, but it is my opinion that they will never prove Ruby insane, but the case is far from being over. Therefore, I ask your indulgence and patience, as actually we may have a much, much better book than we had anticipated; but I do not want to put myself in the position of being disqualified.

When this information was filed with the court, it was immediately picked up by the newspapers. Judge Brown removed himself from the case.

This did not satisfy the Ruby defense team. They wanted a full-blown hearing with a judicial determination disqualifying the judge. The prosecution argued that since the judge was disqualified by his own act, the question was moot. Moreover, since the matter was in the court of appeals, the trial court no longer had jurisdiction.

To overcome these objections, the defense team decided to file another writ of *habeas corpus* with Judge Holland, claiming that Jack was being detained unlawfully, because the judge who presided over his trial had a pecuniary interest in the outcome. If Judge Holland issued the writ, it was possible to set aside the death sentence without the appeal.

The effect of the filing of a petition for writ of *habeas corpus* would be to place Judge Brown on the witness stand and ask him questions under oath.

Judge Holland issued the writ. The problem facing the defense team on September 9, 1965, the date for the hearing on the *habeas corpus*, was to prove that Judge Brown did, in fact, have a pecuniary interest in the outcome of the trial.

Phil did a masterful job cross-examining the judge. The judge explained that his reason for such a book was to defend Dallas from the outside news media characterization of the "Big D" as Murder City, and to show that Jack Ruby was not a scapegoat; he had received a fair trial. When Phil finished with him, it was clear to everyone involved that Judge Brown had used Jack for his own end, even to the death penalty, to increase sales of his book.

Judge Holland did not rule on the granting of the writ, for had he ruled on what he heard that day, Jack would have been freed. By certifying the record to the court of criminal appeals, he made available to the appellate court the benefit of the evidence taken that day, clearly affecting the overall appeal.

May 18, 1966, was the designated day for the hearing on the appeal from Judge Holland's denial of the writ of *habeas corpus*.

The ruling was an insult to the defense team. Although no one really thought Jack would be released, it was hoped that something less than the death penalty would be arrived at. The appellate court stated that it had been waiting to decide the main case, including the claim of denial of due process and the validity of the judgment and conviction of Jack:

> . . . controversy continues as to whether Hon. Joe Tonahill, one of the Appellant's trial counsel, should be permitted to represent him on appeal from his conviction for murder.
>
> Judge Holland has indicated his readiness to impanel a jury and determine the question of Appellant's present sanity or insanity. He is directed to do so without further delay and to certify to this court the result of such hearing.
>
> At such hearing, Appellant's trial attorney, the Hon. Joe Tonahill, as well as counsel representing Appellant in this *habeas corpus* proceeding, should be given the opportunity to present any competent evidence relevant to Appellant's present sanity . . .

The defense team was now faced with the dilemma of a sanity hearing complicated by the presence of Joe Tonahill. If they showed that Jack was insane, as they believed, he would thus be placed in an institution where he probably would not get the help he desperately needed. On the other hand, if he were found sane and then lost the appeal, he would die.

They decided that they would rather have Jack be declared sane. Their strategy would be to avoid participating in the hearing. They were confident that the prosecution would succeed in establishing Jack's sanity—but for radically different reasons.

The prosecution put several of the jail guards on the stand who testified to Jack's alertness, his good memory, and his ability to play cards and other games. Without the defense taking a role, the jury returned a verdict of sane.

The defense team reassembled again on June 24, 1966, this time in Austin. They argued Jack Ruby's case before the Texas Court of Criminal Appeals. They did their job well. On October 5, the death sentence was reversed and a change of venue decreed.

# 15

Aside from the circus atmosphere and the fact that Judge Brown was writing a book, should the verdict of guilty and the death sentence have been set aside by the Texas Court of Criminal Appeals?

There were three basic legal issues before that court which were in formation before the United States Supreme Court:

1. The right not to incriminate oneself.
2. The effect of television viewers having witnessed the crime or confession prior to a trial.
3. The use of television in the courtroom. (Judge Brown allowed television coverage of the announcing of the verdict in Jack's trial.)

The right of not incriminating oneself is a key issue in examining the Jack Ruby trial.

A point of Texas law important to understanding Jack Ruby's trial is the nature of the murder charge itself. In Texas during the early sixties there were only two degrees of murder. "Murder with malice" carried the death sentence, but "murder without malice" carried a maximum of five years in prison. The difference was determined by premeditation. If the murder had been planned in any way, it was committed with malice, but a murder committed because of spur-of-the-moment circumstances was committed without malice. The term "in cold blood" as opposed to "hot blood" is often used to describe the distinction.

The defense at Jack Ruby's trial avoided the issue of premeditation and propounded the theory of temporary insanity. The form of "insanity" they proposed was a variant of psychomotor epilepsy. In the novel *The Terminal Man* by Michael Crichton, the main character suffered this disease. During a seizure, he would kill but not remember committing the crime afterwards. If Jack had suffered such a disease, Belli would have been on the right track and Jack might have gone free. The neurologists and psychiatrists that Belli paraded before the court most likely did more to confuse the jury than to convince them of Jack's having epilepsy. Belli failed, and the autopsy performed on Jack after his death confirmed that the jury was right to disbelieve Belli's contention.

On the other hand, the prosecution kept the idea of premeditation firmly in hand. They used the testimony of Sergeant Patrick Dean to establish clearly for the jury that the murder was planned in advance. Dallas law enforcement officers have been extremely reluctant to question the reliability of Sergeant Dean's allegations—even to set the record straight after Jack's death. Henry Wade had certainly proven this to me by his refusal to even discuss Sergeant Dean taking a polygraph test.

Sergeant Dean's testimony was based on a conversation that allegedly took place in the detention area some forty minutes after the shooting. Belli objected to Dean's being allowed to testify, but Judge Brown permitted the jury to hear it in accordance with the *res gestae* (things done) exception to the hearsay rule. This exception allows any deed or statement that is in any way part of the event of the crime to be admissible as evidence. Judge Brown could have justified his decision based on the precedent established by the United States Supreme Court in June, 1958, in the case of *John Russell Crooker vs. The State of California.*

In that case, the defendant was arrested and accused of murder. He immediately asked for an attorney, but the request was denied by the police. Subsequently, the same evening and before he saw his attorney, he confessed. His confession was later used against him at his trial and he was convicted. The case came before the high court and the conviction was affirmed, establishing a precedent for future cases. However, it was a 5-4 decision. Judge Brown obviously would have disagreed with the dissent written by Chief Justice Earl Warren:

> The witness has no effective way to challenge his interrogator's testimony as to what was said and done at the secret inquisition. The officer's version frequently may reflect an inaccurate understanding of an accused's statements or, on occasion, may be deliberately distorted or falsified. While the accused may protest against these misrepresentations, his protestations will normally be in vain. This is particularly true when the officer is accompanied by several of his assistants and they all vouch for his story. But when the public, or even the suspect's counsel is present, the hazards to the suspect from the officer's misunderstanding or twisting his statements or conduct are greatly reduced.
>
> (337 U.S. 433, 447)

If one accepts the validity of Justice Warren's statement, which had the concurrence of Justices Douglas, Black, and Brennan, Sergeant Dean's testimony should never have been allowed. Eventually the Supreme Court did uphold Justice Warren's position on the Crooker decision—one of many reversals that came to be identified with the Warren Court.

The process of the Supreme Court changing the position it took on the *Crooker* case started with its decision on the *Danny Escobedo* case. Escobedo had been convicted of murder in the criminal court of Cook County in Chicago, Illinois. The conviction was based largely on incriminating statements he made to his police interrogators before he was formally indicted. He had requested to see his retained attorney before making such statements, but the police refused his request. Moreover, they never told him of his right to remain silent.

Mr. Justice Goldberg wrote the 6-3 opinion:

> This court has recognized that history amply shows that confessions have often been extorted to save law enforcement officials the trouble and effort of obtaining valid and independent evidence . . . .
>
> We have also learned the companion lesson of history, that no system of criminal justice can, or should, survive if it comes to depend for its continued effectiveness on the citizens' abdication through unawareness of their constitutional rights. No system worth preserving should have to fear that if an accused is permitted to consult with a lawyer, he will become aware of, and exercise, these rights. If the exercise of constitutional rights will thwart the effectiveness of a system of law enforcement, then there is something very wrong with that system.
>
> (378 U.S. 478, 490)

The decision in *Escobedo* established the right of anyone accused of a crime to have an attorney present to give legal advice during any interrogation. The Escobedo case became a stepping-stone to the decision the Supreme Court made on the *Miranda* case—a case that would have had direct bearing on the procedures followed in the Jack Ruby trial.

*Miranda vs. The State of Arizona* is one of four similar cases reviewed by the Supreme Court in 1966. All four cases were consolidated into one hearing because of their similarities. Of five justices left on the Supreme Court who played a role in the *Crooker* decision, only one had voted with the majority. This time he was in the minority.

In each of the four cases before the court in the *Miranda* hearing, the accused was not advised of his right to an attorney as in the *Escobedo* case. The court went one step further, however. Justice Earl Warren wrote the majority opinion:

> To summarize, we hold that when an individual is taken into custody, or otherwise deprived of his freedom by the authorities in any significant way and is subjected to questioning, the privilege against self-incrimination is jeopardized. Procedural safeguards must be employed to protect the privilege, and unless other fully effective means are adopted to notify the person of his right of silence and to assure that the exercise of the right will be scrupulously honored, the following measures are required. He must be warned, prior to any questioning, that he has the right to remain silent, that anything he says can be used against him in a court of law, that he has the right to the presence of an attorney, and that if he cannot afford an attorney one will be appointed for him prior to any questioning, if he so desires. Opportunity to exercise the rights must be afforded to him throughout the interrogation. After such warnings have been given, and such opportunity afforded him, the individual may knowingly and intelligently waive these rights and agree to answer questions or make a statement. But unless and until such warnings and waiver are demonstrated by the prosecution at trial, no evidence obtained as a result of interrogation can be used against him.
>
> (384, U.S. 436, 483)

On June 13, 1966 this position became the law of the land. A person accused of a crime must be "Mirandized" before interrogation, or the answers and statements made by the accused will not be admissible in court.

Had Jack Ruby been retried, the testimony of Sergeant Dean would not have been allowed in evidence, for Jack had not been informed of his rights. The legal climate created by the Warren Court obviously influenced the Texas Court of Appeals when they reversed the guilty verdict and the death sentence of Jack Ruby.

Jack Ruby shot Lee Harvey Oswald on live television. The shooting was rerun hundreds of times. In effect—and this made the broadcasts the second important legal issue—the entire population of Dallas were witnesses to the crime. It became virtually impossible to select a jury of persons who had not seen the original or a rerun of the crime. When Belli attempted to have the case moved from Dallas to a different county, Judge Brown refused, claiming that Jack could get a fair trial there.

Just after the trial was completed, the Warren court handed down its decision in *Rideau vs. Louisiana*. The vote, in favor of Rideau, was 7-2. On February 16, 1961, a man robbed a bank in Louisiana, kidnapping three bank employees and killing one. A few hours later Rideau was arrested. The next morning a motion picture was made of an "interview" in the jail between Rideau and the sheriff. During the interrogation, Rideau admitted the bank robbery, kidnapping, and murder. Later that day the film was broadcast on local television, and it was broadcast the next day as well. Local radio stations played the sound track of the film.

Two weeks later, Rideau was arraigned on the charges and his court-appointed attorneys moved immediately for change of venue based on the televising of the interrogation. It was denied. Rideau was tried, convicted, and sentenced to death.

The Supreme Court granted a new trial. The majority opinion read as follows:

> . . . the kangaroo court proceedings involve a more subtle but no less real deprivation of due process of law.

Under our constitution's guarantee of due process, a person accused of committing a crime is vouchsafed basic minimal rights. Among these are the right to counsel, the right to plead not guilty, and the right to be tried in a courtroom presided over by a judge. In this case the people of Calcasieu Parish saw and heard, not once, but three times, a "trial" of Rideau in a jail, presided over by a sheriff, when there was no lawyer to advise Rideau of his right to stand mute.

The record shows that such a thing as this never took place before in Calcasieu Parish, Louisiana. Whether it occurred elsewhere, we do not know. But we do not hesitate to hold, without pausing to examine a particularized transcript of the *voir dire* [sworn to speak the truth] examination of the members of the jury, that due process of law in this case required a jury drawn from a community of people who had not seen and heard Rideau's televised "interview."

Due process of law, preserved for all by our constitution, commands that no such practice as that disclosed by this record shall send any accused to his death.

(373, U.S 723, 726)

On the basis of this case alone, Jack should have received a change of venue. This case was not yet decided at the time of his trial, but it was decided before his appeal was heard.

The third evolving issue, concerning television coverage of a trial, gained national attention as the result of the trial of the infamous Billie Sol Estes of Dallas. The American Bar Association assisted in taking the *Estes* case to the Supreme Court. Mr. Estes was convicted of swindling, but was deprived of his right to due process by the televising and broadcasting of his trial. The defendant was accused of falsely and fraudulently inducing certain farmers to purchase nonexistent fertilizer tanks and accompanying equipment, and to sign and deliver to him chattel mortgages on fictitious property. The case had already received national notoriety before Billie Sol Estes went to trial. Eleven volumes of press clippings were placed on file with the court clerk.

The defense moved that the court not allow television or radio in the courtroom during the hearings, but the court cited a local judicial canon which leaves to the discretion of the trial judge whether or not television and/or photography should be allowed in the courtroom. The canons of the American Bar Association prohibit such activity.

The Supreme Court did not focus on the legality of the canon that permitted television coverage of a trial but on the question of whether Mr. Estes had received a fair trial. The majority opinion written by Mr. Justice Clark (perhaps because he is from Dallas) recognized that many of the jurors, after being in court, probably went home each night to watch themselves on television. It would seem inevitable that some of the jurors would become more interested in how they might look on television than in rendering a just verdict. The testimony of a witnesses is also impaired by the knowledge they are being viewed by a vast television audience. Finally, one must consider the impact on the defendant. Justice Clark concluded that the presence of television is a form of mental—if not physical—harassment.

Jack Ruby experienced this harassment.

It seems like one of life's ironies that Jack Ruby's life following the Kennedy assassination became so entwined with Justice Earl Warren. The morning after the assassination, Jack took pictures of one of the "Impeach Earl Warren" signs, which he thought were the work of either "Commies" or "Birchers." The same Earl Warren headed the commission on the Kennedy assassination and came to Dallas to interview Jack Ruby. And the same liberal judicial leanings of Earl Warren that brought about the "Impeach Earl Warren" movement influenced the Supreme Court in decisions that would have a direct bearing on the reversal of Jack Ruby's conviction. Their entwinement formed a full circle.

# 16

The Monday morning after my flight back from Dallas, I finally returned to my office. My first task was to follow up on the promises I had made in Dallas. I wrote to Tim Timmins:

Dear Mr. Timmins:

Re: <u>Estate of Jack Ruby, Dec'd</u>

As attorney for the estate above-captioned, please be advised that on behalf of the family of the deceased, the offer is hereby made to the United States Government National Archives, a gift of a certain Colt Cobra .38 caliber revolver, two-inch barrel, shielded hammer, blue steel with brown plastic grips, bearing serial number 2744-LW, physical transfer of which, upon acceptance hereof, to be arranged by the parties. Provided, however, the Wayne County Probate Court gives its approval to this gift.

I also wrote to Henry Wade regarding the possible polygraph examination of Sergeant Dean.

February 15, two days later, Phil Burleson called.

"The details are sketchy," he said, "but an attorney here in Dallas has filed what purports to be Jack's will."

If this were true, I realized all the work I had done to probate the estate of Jack Ruby up to this point would have been done in vain.

"Who was named as executor?" I asked. The executor would control the estate.

"The attorney who had the will is named as executor," Phil replied.

"Who is he?" I asked.

"Jules F. Mayer."

"Do you know him?" I asked, wondering if he would be cooperative.

"No," was Phil's response.

We ended the conversation with Phil promising to get back to me with any new developments.

The law requires the holder of a last will and testament of any person who dies to file it with the probate or similar court upon learning of that person's death. Normally, the holder of the will, if not a relative of the deceased, is an attorney. If the will has not been previously recorded, the attorney should contact the family prior to recording the will, to advise them of the existence of the will and to ask their wishes. Wills and death are delicate matters and should be approached cautiously by lawyers.

Mr. Mayer, however, chose another course. He wrote directly to Judge Murphy, who had granted my petition to make Earl administrator of Jack's estate. A copy of his letter was also sent to me. The letter included a copy of the will and the various probate papers. He issued the following warning:

We admonish you, and through you, Mr. Earl Ruby, not to dispose of, convey, assign, sell, encumber and/or in any other way or manner, directly or indirectly, so do or in anywise contract for disposal of any and all property of any kind, nature, or description belonging to the estate of the late Jack L. Ruby, or to proceed further in any manner in the Wayne County Court administration, but to hold any and all such property, subject to the orders of the Probate Court #2 of Dallas County, Texas, in the pending probate proceedings; we will notify you as to the Court's action therein when taken. Please acknowledge receipt hereof by return mail.

Earl had been alerted to the happenings the day before. I called him immediately. He was in my office within the hour.

I had made a photocopy of this apparent will for Earl. The document itself was handwritten on stationery of the Jack Tar Court Hotel at Galveston, Texas. Earl confirmed that the handwriting was that of his late brother. The document consisted of three pages, and was dated August 24, 1950.

The will disposed of his "estate" to his sisters Eileen and Eva, with a portion to Eva's son, Ronald D. Magid.

The document was handwritten, and was therefore what is called a holographic will. I told Earl that such wills had been outlawed in most states. I would have to check Texas law. I made a mental note to do the research.

With Earl on the extension, I dialed Eva in Dallas. She too, had received a letter from Mr. Mayer. Hers, we learned, was not threatening, but, in fact, was rather pleasant.

"If Mr. Jules Mayer, whom I have never met, had possession of this will for the last thirteen years, where was he when Jack had all his troubles?" Eva inquired.

I had no answer but replied, "He probably started looking for the document when he heard Jack died."

"No, he wasn't," Eva retorted. "He was looking for papers with Jack's signature, so he could sell them. He probably didn't even realize he had such a will. The newspapers said he found the will when he was cleaning his garage to throw out old files. A likely story. Why didn't he call Eileen or me directly? Why did he do it this way?"

Again, I really had no answer. I could only speculate. I suggested the only way to find out was to call Mr. Mayer. I said good-bye to Eva, and with Earl sitting in front of me called Mr.

Mayer.

Mr. Mayer answered my call promptly and seemed quite amicable at first.

"Yes, I found the will while cleaning out some old files," he said.

"Would you consider resigning as the executor in favor of a member of the family?" I inquired.

There was a short pause. "No," he said with authority. "Jack wanted me to act as his independent executor, and I intend to do just that."

"But what do you have to administer?" I asked. I was puzzled by his use of the term *independent executor*.

I answered the question for him. "His gun, his suit, his ring. He didn't leave anything."

Before he could answer, I confronted him with another question. "Did you even follow the proceedings during Jack's incarceration?"

"Somewhat," he responded.

"Then you know he took a pauper's oath so he could get the transcripts of his trial and other hearings. Look, we made a deal with the National Archives in return for a release of the tax lien. There's nothing else to be probated. Let the thing be done with," I pleaded.

There was another pause. "You have absolutely no right whatsoever to make deals with my property," he finally answered.

I noted his use of the word *my*. There was no purpose in continuing the conversation.

My next step was to check Texas law. I needed to know if Jack's holographic will was valid. I was afraid it was, since it had been accepted for probate. But was this particular will valid without witnesses?

I soon discovered in the Texas Code that the will was valid. *Holographic* was a word I had not heard since law school. Holographic wills are often associated with nuncupative wills. A nuncupative will is an oral will, usually said on one's deathbed. I checked quickly and discovered that both holographic and nuncupative wills were valid in Texas. In addition, I found that independent administration by the executor required no court approval.

If Jack's holographic will was valid, I reasoned, why wouldn't the will I prepared be a valid nuncupative will? We would at least give it a try.

# 17

Over the next few days there was a flurry of letters and telephone conversations. Elmer Gertz wrote to me asking how the matter was proceeding. One paragraph, in particular, caught my attention:

I am puzzled by a report that appears in today's *Chicago Tribune*, a copy of which is enclosed. I am sure it has appeared everywhere. Just what is this about?

Sol Dann had also written to Phil Burleson about the same article. Carbon copies had been sent to all the other attorneys on the team. Dann hoped someone could explain the cryptic last paragraph of the article:

It would appear that if Alexander couldn't witness the execution of Jack in Texas, he at least wants to have the sordid pleasure of seeing his estate administered in Dallas.

Elmer Gertz next wrote a letter to Mr. Mayer, apparently responding to a letter similar to the one I received. Elmer had cautioned Mayer about the way he was proceeding:

There are certain facts that you must bear in mind before jumping with both feet into a situation. It is notable that when Jack Ruby faced the death sentence, I did not hear from you nor did other counsel in the case. These attorneys and I have rendered services which, among other things, resulted in setting aside the death sentence, and we have not been paid for these services.

I called Phil and asked that he again try to persuade Mr. Mayer to step aside in favor of Earl. I discussed with him the possibility of petitioning the probate court in Dallas County to admit the nuncupative will.

Phil remembered that both Eva and Eileen were present when Jack read the document. Moreover, their testimony would have greater credence, because it was against their own interest to negate the will that Mayer had. The will I drafted left Jack's property equally to all of his brothers and sisters except Earl.

Phil agreed to speak to Mr. Mayer. The result was a letter from Mr. Mayer that arrived the next day. He made it clear that he would fight any move to replace him as administrator of the will:

> I this date received a telephone call from Mr. Phil Burleson, who stated that he was calling in your behalf. I told him, and I repeat for your benefit, that I shall act herein fully as may be proper and necessary under the law; that if, in fact, the named beneficiaries of the Will filed for Probate do disclaim in proper instruments as required by law, and name others to take under the Will, I will honor same fully. I cannot and do not care to agree to answer any question of yours with a "yes" or "no" without having the same placed in writing to me, and without knowing the circumstances.

I called Judge Murphy to bring him up to date. I also wanted his opinion on the validity of Mayer's will. I had not spoken to him since my return from Dallas. The judge invited me over that afternoon.

Earl and I slipped into Judge Murphy's chambers through the back corridor, in order to avoid being seen by media people. Tom Murphy was sitting at his desk and saw Earl and me enter the outer waiting room of his chambers. He waved us in. He was the first to speak.

"I received this letter the other day," he said, handing me the original of Mr. Mayer's letter to him. "What kind of lawyer is this?" the judge inquired. He thought Earl or I would know.

"Judge," I responded, "I don't know the man."

"It would seem to me," Judge Murphy continued, "that when it comes to estates, any attorney named in the will should step aside if the heirs wish it. Unless there is some specific reason not to."

"Well, that's not the case here," I responded. "The man hadn't seen or spoken to Jack for years."

We discussed the wisdom of pressing our nuncupative will, but the judge advised us not to do that until we knew that Mr. Mayer would not step aside.

"Does Mr. Mayer know about this nuncupative will?" Judge Murphy asked.

"Yes," I replied. "I think Phil Burleson told him about it, because Mayer mentioned it in his last letter to me."

"All right," the judge went on, "I will write Mr. Mayer."

We thanked the judge and left. That was on Friday. On Monday he wrote to Mr. Mayer. Although the letter was very reserved, it stated that we would present our nuncupative will to the Dallas County probate court for acceptance. The tone of the letter made it appear that our will was valid. The judge ended his letter:

Should you desire any further information concerning the small estate of Jack Ruby, deceased, pending in

Detroit, County of Wayne, State of Michigan, please do not hesitate to write us. This court will help in any manner possible to bring this matter to a successful conclusion.

Then I sent the papers to the family for their signatures, waiving a formal hearing on the nuncupative will. Three days later the following letter was circulated by Phil:

February 23, 1967

TO: All Ruby Attorneys

Dear All:

Another Chapter in the Jack Ruby Probate matter has come to light.

Attached is a handwritten Will or purported Will giving certain personal effects to a former Deputy Sheriff who was guarding Jack in Dallas County Jail.

This has been set up as No. 67-404-P2, typed in Re: Estate of Jack Ruby, Deceased, and there is a Petition asking that the Will be admitted to Probate and that Norman H. Hooten be appointed the Executor of the Estate. The return on this case is set for March 6, 1967, at which time anyone who objects to such action of admitting the Will to Probate and appointing Hooten as Executor or Administrator, is to appear and object. The attorney for Hooten is Harold C. Adams, 902 Fidelity Union Life Building, Dallas, Texas.

In regards to the Will filed by Jules Mayer, it is my understanding that that date for contest or objection is set for next Monday, Feb. 27, 1967.

...More later, as it develops.

In the same mail I received a letter from Mr. Mayer. He, too, advised me of the Hooten will and, "as a courtesy," enclosed it, stating:

Please note that besides not naming any executor, and not disposing of any items except listed jewelry, this purported instrument of Hooten's does not revoke any prior Last Will of Jack's.

Thus he was telling us that although we have to work together to set aside the Hooten will, he was still holding his position on his holographic will.

I became so preoccupied with this proliferation of wills that I nearly missed an announcement on the late news that the prosecutor in New Orleans had announced that he was reopening the Kennedy assassination case.

On March 1, 1967, I filed by mail the necessary papers with the Dallas County Probate Court to contest both wills, and for admission of the nuncupative will as Jack's Last Will and Testament. Phil followed up my action by filing his appearance as local counsel.

Mr. Mayer immediately responded with an old trick used by lawyers when the opponent is far away. He filed a motion for costs. It is usually granted, and the distant opponent has to post a bond of $100. No matter how trivial, he would fight me each step of the way. The date of the hearing was Friday, March 17, 1967.

Almost immediately after filing his motion for costs, Mr. Mayer tried another tactic. He notified Earl, Eva, and me that our depositions were to be taken in Dallas. Both the motions for costs and the depositions were perfectly legal, and Mayer was technically within his rights to use them. They were, however, very unnecessary. Such tactics are only employed to harass the opposition. He did schedule the depositions for March 17 or 18, at our convenience. Again, in his letter to us he feigned to be the courteous lawyer:

> The above dates are suggested so that you will not be inconvenienced unduly, as we understand you and Mr. Earl Ruby already plan to be in Dallas on March 17, 1967, for our 10 A.M. court hearing.

I wrote back to Mr. Mayer that only I would be in Dallas on that date, as I did not want to inconvenience Earl. There was no way he could get Earl's deposition without coming to Michigan, and he knew it.

Regardless of the deposition and hearing, I wanted to go back to Dallas. My reading of the Warren Commission testimony and exhibits raised many questions that needed answering. I also wanted to speak to Sheriff Decker again.

On March 9, 1967, I called the sheriff and made an appointment to meet with him on March 16, at 2:00 P.M. Then I wrote to Eva that I would be in Dallas at 9:00 P.M. that day, and that it was not necessary for her to meet me at the airport. I did not want her to know I was going to see Decker alone.

Between March 9 and March 16, I obtained disclaimers from all of the heirs. Eva, Eileen, and Ronald D. Magid signed formal papers to be filed with the court, disclaiming anything they were entitled to under Jack's will, in favor of the entire family. The disclaimers also requested the court to appoint Earl as the administrator.

# 18

My plane landed at Love Field, Dallas, at noon. The arrival was scheduled for 10:30 Dallas time, but because of weather problems in Chicago, the flight arrived late. I had only a couple of hours before my appointment with the sheriff. After renting a car, I headed directly for Dealey Plaza.

The air was warm and the sun was bright. My overcoat and jacket were in the back seat. I felt a bit guilty for not telling Eva I was in town already, but I wanted to see all I could this day on my own.

I parked the car and walked westward half a block to Houston Street. There it was. The Texas School Book Depository Building. An eerie feeling crept over me as I stood on the sidewalk and looked up to the last window on the sixth floor in the southeast corner; it was from this position that the President had been shot.

A place that we have only viewed on television or in photographs always looks different when we see it the first time with our very own eyes and not through a camera lens. This was true of Dealey Plaza.

I had believed that Elm Street was the street in front of the School Book Depository Building, but in fact, it is not. Elm Street, when it reaches Houston Street, curves to the left and then down a steep embankment under a triple underpass, along with Main and Commerce Streets. Commerce Street does the same on the other side of the plaza, except that it curves to the right. The plaza serves as an exit from the downtown area.

Seen from the air, the three roads resemble a three-pronged fork converging at the handle. The triple underpass is a bridge cutting across the fork at the top of the handle. From ground level the whole area was scooped out to allow traffic on the three roads to travel beneath the triple underpass, which is a railroad bridge leading to the yard behind the School Book Depository Building.

As I continued past the building, it was obvious that it was closed and in need of repair. The sign on the door indicated it was owned by the municipal court system in Dallas.

Following Houston Street, I found myself first in the parking area of the building, and then in the railroad yard itself. I continued walking out onto the tracks and across the bridge. Looking back to the left, I could see the School Book Depository Building with its Hertz Rent-a-Car sign looming on top.

The expanse of the plaza is much smaller than pictures indicate. From the base of the bridge, and on both sides, there stands a wood fence which goes up to the street level, and then continues to a pergola on each side about halfway across the length of the plaza. On the other side of the pergola the fence continues in stone. The fence was at no point less than five feet tall. If there was a sniper behind that fence, as many of the critics of the Warren report theorized, he must have been quite tall to aim and fire over the fence. Moreover, looking north one cannot miss the tower of the Union Terminal Building. Any would-be assassin in the area would certainly have been seen by railroad personnel watching the motorcade from the tower.

As I stood on the pergola, I could better see the slope of the descending streets. The grade is very steep. Most astonishing was the short distance from the pergola to the street. The whole plaza was like a bowl scooped out of the earth. At the time of the attack on the President, echoes had to abound. These reverberations would explain why so many people differed on the number of shots they heard that day.

While standing there at the pergola on the School Book Depository Building side, I also noticed that the window on the southeast corner of the building could not be seen. If Oswald did have an accomplice, the two could not have maintained visual contact.

It was almost two o'clock. I ended my tour of Dealey Plaza and headed back to my rental car. I did not want to miss my appointment with the sheriff.

As I walked into the sheriff's headquarters, he came out to greet me. We walked back to an interrogation room and went inside. I lit a cigarette and tried to seem leisurely about it.

"Bill," I finally began, "since I saw you last, I have learned quite a lot. When I was here before, you already knew what the autopsy report said, didn't you?"

"I had an idea," he admitted.

"Is that why you asked if the family wanted to sue the county?"

"Yep," he drawled.

"But even with the autopsy report, wouldn't that be foolish?" I responded. "Who needs the publicity or aggravation?"

He liked my statement. "You never know what you or the family might do. We don't know you. For all we know, you might just want to do it for the publicity."

"Bill, I don't want any publicity," I said, repeating what I told the businessmen's group on my last visit.

There was silence. I looked out the window and said nothing. I wanted the sheriff to think about what I had just said. After a few moments I decided to get down to the real reason I had set up an appointment with Sheriff Bill Decker.

"Bill, what really happened to Jack? He's gone now, and the family really wants to keep him buried. Just how sick was he?"

"I can honestly say," he began, "I did not know Jack was as sick as he was. True, his sisters came to me last summer complaining that he was ill. I went up to see him personally. 'Jack,

boy,' I said, 'what's ailing you?' 'Nothing, Bill,' he told me, 'just
a little stomachache.' 'Well,' I said, 'if you have any problems, let
me know.' He looked the same, he acted the same, but to be on the
cautious side, I assigned a special deputy to be with him at all
times, to observe him.''

I sensed that the sheriff was being absolutely candid with
me. No matter what the truth really was, Bill Decker was telling
what he believed to be the truth.

There wasn't much more Bill could tell, and I wanted to go
back to Dealey Plaza. I started to excuse myself when it suddenly
occurred to me that the sheriff might be able to help me on one
more item.

"Bill, is it possible for me to get into the School Book
Depository Building?"

"You are certainly asking the right person," he replied,
smiling. "Follow me."

We walked to his office He made a quick phone call, took
his Stetson from the hat tree, and headed for the door. We each
drove to the plaza in our own cars.

From our cars we walked on Houston Street in front of the
old courthouse and jail, where we crossed over into the plaza.

"The Presidential limousine traveled through downtown
Dallas to here on Houston Street," he began. "It went to the corner
there, and made a slow left turn onto Elm. It had descended down
Elm," he said, pointing down the street, "to about that point, when
the sound of shots rang out." He pointed up to the sixth-story
window. "From there."

We walked up to the front door of the School Book
Depository on Elm Street and waited a few moments for a man to
arrive with a key. When the door was unlocked, the sheriff
escorted me into the building.

"We'll do this in reverse order," he said. There was a
stairway to my right. "The building was used then by a school-
book operation. This was the warehouse where the books were

shipped out." We walked through a door in front of us into a small vestibule. On the right was an office, then through an opening without a door I could see a large room. Along the right wall were more offices. Directly in front of us was a double elevator and large overhead doors on either side. To the left of the closest overhead door was a normal door that led to the loading dock. There were two more overhead doors on the west side of the building.

"At the moment of the rifle reports, Motorcycle Patrolman Baker was directly in front of the Elm Street entrance. He left his cycle and entered the building. He encountered the superintendent on the first floor and the two of them went up these stairs," the sheriff said, and we began ascending a set of stairs in the northwest corner of the building.

When we reached the second floor, he continued. "Now look over there." He pointed southeast to a door with a glass upper half. You could see into the room. "Patrolman Baker spotted Oswald over there in the lunchroom. He pulled his gun and approached. As he got to Oswald, the superintendent came in and identified him as an employee, so they went on elsewhere.

"Oswald had just purchased a bottle of soda from the vending machine when Baker spotted him. After Baker and the superintendent left to continue their search, Oswald coolly walked out of the lunchroom."

I followed him out into a large office area. "He was seen here, walking in this direction." Decker and I retraced the footsteps of the assassin. "Around this counter, down those stairs, and out the front door."

I looked down the stairs to where we had first entered the building.

"Let's go up to the sixth floor," he said. "We'll have to walk, because the electricity isn't on."

"I don't mind if you don't," I said, deferring to his age.

"We'll take the back stairs," he said. "Those were the

stairs Oswald went down before entering the lunchroom."

The stairs went directly from one floor to the next in an L-shaped manner. There were no landings. At the sixth floor we walked directly to the opposite end of a large, open floor to the window on the southeast corner.

I looked out. This had been the view of the assassin. I trembled inside at the very thought of it.

The sheriff spoke again. "The room was full of boxes of books; Oswald had stacked a few boxes about here," he indicated with his foot a spot about two feet back from the window, "to hide himself from anyone on the sixth floor while waiting with his rifle."

I looked out the window as the sheriff opened it. The view was up Houston Street. I looked down Elm Street. The grade I observed earlier in the day was even more noticeable from this vantage point. Cars moving down the grade seemed to be moving slower than the thirty-five to forty miles an hour they were probably travelling. A car traveling at five to seven miles per hour would appear to be standing still.

"It was not a difficult shot," I observed.

"No, it really wasn't," the sheriff responded. We walked back to the middle of the now empty room.

"At the time there were boxes of books all over this area. Oswald dumped his rifle about here, right in the open. His clipboard was found later, right here." The sheriff indicated an area just a few feet away.

"It sure seemed as if he wanted to be discovered, leaving his clipboard and rifle so close together," I observed.

"Well, maybe we would know what was on his mind if your client hadn't shot him."

As we were about to descend the stairs, I said, "Let me see how fast I can make it to the second floor."

"Sure, go ahead, but don't mind if I take my time."

I walked back to the southeast corner, started my stop

watch, and quickly walked to the place where the sheriff indicated Oswald left his gun, then down the stairs into the lunchroom. The entire trip took sixty-six seconds. I was not at all out of breath.

The sheriff caught up to me and said, "You didn't have to do that. The Warren Commission reenacted the whole thing with Patrolman Baker and an agent."

"How long did it take Baker to get to the lunchroom?" I inquired. "Between a minute and a quarter and a minute and a half," the sheriff drawled.

We walked down the front stairs and out the Elm Street door. I turned to the sheriff. "Bill, thank you so much. If you could give this tour to everyone, there would be no doubt about the accuracy of the Warren report."

Having seen enough of Dealey Plaza for the day, I went to my hotel and checked in. In the room I wrote my notes and began to prepare for tomorrow's ordeal. I soon fell asleep.

At precisely 9:30, the phone woke me up. It was Eva, punctual as ever.

"Alan," she began, "how is your family?" I really didn't want to talk. I had been in a deep sleep.

I tried to put her off, but she said, "You must talk to Dr. West; he was the last psychiatrist to speak to Jack, and he's in town right now." She gave me a number.

"Thanks, Eva. I'll see you in the morning at the court-house," I said.

I dialed the number to find it was another hotel in down-town Dallas. The doctor was out, so I left word for him to return my call.

# 19

Friday morning at 8:30, I met Phil Burleson in the hallway outside Probate Court Number 2. The probate court was in the old courthouse building that faces Dealey Plaza. It had not yet been moved to the new county building, Phil explained.

Our adversaries arrived and I was formally introduced to them. Mr. Mayer was represented by Marvin L. Levin, a partner of Mr. Mayer; Mr. Hooten was represented by two younger attorneys, Harold Adams and Julian Foster. We all entered the chambers of Judge Ted Robertson for the pretrial hearing.

After we were seated at a conference table in the judge's office, the judge began. "Gentlemen, we have before us three applications for probate of a will. Mr. Mayer's holographic will dated 1950, Mr. Hooten's dated 1966, and Mr. Ruby's dated 1966. We shall discuss them in inverse order."

He turned first to Mr. Ruby's nuncupative will. "I am looking at Section 65 of the probate code," the judge said, opening a statute book. "Accordingly," he continued, "such will requires three witnesses. I trust such witnesses exist." He looked at Phil.

"Yes, your honor," Phil responded. He knew that Jack had told Eva, Eileen, and Earl that this was his will.

"Very well," the judge said. "With regard to the Hooten will, as well as the Ruby will, the testamentary capacity must be established."

The judge meant that we and the Hooten attorney would have to show Jack was of sound mind at the time he made the wills.

This stipulation, Phil and I knew, placed us in a dilemma. If Jack had the testamentary capacity when our will was made, he also had it when the Hooten will was signed. We knew we had some decisions to make.

"Next," the judge propounded, "does either the Hooten or Ruby will revoke the Mayer instrument of 1950?"

"Our will," I said, "revokes all prior wills by its terms."

"True," the judge observed. "Thus the issues are joined. If the requisite testamentary capacity exists, the Ruby will shall prevail; otherwise, it would appear that the Hooten document, which does not revoke prior wills, might be a codicil to the Mayer instrument."

A codicil is an addition to an existing last will and testament, which modifies rather than revokes the first.

The judge went on to the next subject. "The question of who will be appointed as executor. The Hooten will makes no mention of an executor; however, the Mayer and Ruby wills specifically name an executor. Under the circumstances, I will not name either at this time, but will appoint a disinterested party until the matter can be resolved. I will set a date for the hearing and consolidate all applications into one cause. Is there anything else, gentlemen?"

"Yes, your honor," Phil said, "the newspaper people are outside the courtroom. May I suggest that we all agree not to discuss the matter with them?"

"That's your prerogative," the judge responded. "You can be assured I won't speak to them."

We all agreed that no one would speak to the reporters.

As we were leaving, Mr. Levin suggested that Phil and I meet with Mr. Mayer later in the day. Phil had to decline because of other appointments, but I accepted. I told him I would be at his office at eleven o'clock.

Outside the courtroom, Eva sat waiting. She had arrived after we went into the judge's chambers. Phil and I took Eva to another floor for two reasons. We wanted to avoid the media people, and we wanted to discuss privately what had occurred.

We explained to Eva that if our will was good, then Hooten's was also. If Jack was sane on his deathbed, he was sane when he made the Hooten will. There was no doubt that the Mayer will was good; we knew of no way to attack it.

"But why," Eva asked, "would Mayer want to do this when the family doesn't want him to?"

We had no answer.

"I will meet him this morning and try to find out," I responded.

It was just past eleven o'clock, when I entered the Texas Bank Building. It was an older building away from the new, larger skyscrapers on Main Street. Although the building was not impressive, the offices of Mayer, Mayer & Levin were. There were a large conference room and a substantial library. Whenever I visit another law office, I always make it my business to see the law library. If it is substantial, I know that the attorneys at least have the tools to be competent.

Mr. Levin greeted me and ushered me in to meet Mr. Mayer. There behind a desk stood a short, balding man in his late sixties. On the walls of his office, along with his diplomas, were hung photographs of Mr. Mayer and various dignitaries. When he observed that I was looking at them, he began to explain who each one was. He was particularly proud of some newspaper articles and pictures that were framed and on the wall. They dealt with his brother, the other Mayer in the firm name.

After the amenities were concluded, I again asked Mr. Mayer why he persisted in his position.

"It was Jack's wish," was his response.

I couldn't help but reply, "Mr. Mayer, that was in 1950. This is now 1967. Many things have happened over the years, particularly to Jack. Where were you all that time?"

He had no answer.

"My wife and I were at the Jack Tar Hotel in Galveston when a knock came at the door," he stated. "My wife opened the door and Jack was standing there. He wanted a will."

"He drove all the way to Galveston to have a will drawn?" I asked.

"That's correct. I dictated the entire will for him."

This explained why the will was on hotel stationery.

"Why does it state County of Dallas?" I asked.

Mr. Mayer did not act upset with my question. He just did not answer. Instead he jumped to a different subject as he would do throughout our conversation when he did not want to talk about something.

We spent the entire day discussing how to resolve the problem. It took that long, because he had a habit of taking every phone call that came in without excusing himself.

Finally, we reached what I thought was an agreement. In effect, Phil and I would withdraw our application to probate our will. We realized that we did not have the testamentary capacity. We would join together with Mayer to contest the Hooten will. Mr. Mayer would be appointed an independent executor, but within ten days he would resign in favor of Earl. Earl would engage Mayer's firm as counsel.

The next morning I returned to Mr. Mayer's office to find him seated at a typewriter. He was personally typing the agreement. As he finished a page, he handed it to me. When he was done, the statement consisted of three single-spaced, typed pages. He had spelled out all of the facts leading up to this date, and then spelled out our agreement. Mr. Levin and I signed the document, and I left thinking we had an agreement that satisfied everyone.

I returned to Detroit that afternoon and immediately called Earl from the airport. We met later in my office and I gave Earl a copy of the agreement. After reading it, he remarked that finally everything would move smoothly.

I neglected, however, to tell Earl that we were going to keep it secret. I did not remember until I returned to my home to read the newspaper account of our "secret meeting" held with Judge Robertson the day before. I tried to reach Earl but I was too late.

The next day the *Detroit Free Press* reported that Jack Ruby's gun was going to the National Archives.

# 20

Phil called Monday to advise me that Mr. Mayer was going to rescind the agreement because of the news leak.

"That's ridiculous. What does one thing have to do with the other?" I said. I guess I knew that eventually he would have found some way to rescind the agreement. He wanted full control of Jack's estate, no matter what.

There was going to be a hearing in Judge Robertson's court on Wednesday. Phil said he would let me know the outcome.

Mr. Mayer had filed a petition with the probate court for his immediate appointment as executor. This, apparently, was his way of informing us that he was not going to abide by the terms of our agreement. I hung up the phone and immediately called Mr. Mayer. He could not come to the phone because he was "attending a press conference."

Phil, as well as the Hooten proponents, filed a detailed motion for continuance (adjournment), but the judge overruled both.

Only Eva and Mr. Mayer testified.

Eva said that it was the intention of the family to get possession of the gun and take it to Washington where it would be presented to the National Archives. She said she would like to accomplish this any way she could, and as soon as possible.

Phil tried to get her to say that she would do it in accordance with the procedures of law and rulings of the court, but Eva could not comprehend what he was trying to get her to say. The result was that the court had to appoint an executor to make sure the property was not removed from the state.

Mr. Mayer took the stand and testified that I had breached the agreement by informing the media that the gun was going to the National Archives. Under Phil's cross-examination, Mr. Mayer admitted that I had told him it was the intention of the family that the gun be so handled. He further admitted that there was no real danger of the gun being moved out of the state of Texas, since it was still in Henry Wade's safe.

The court decided to appoint a temporary administrator, a person disinterested in the proceedings.

During this period, Elmer Gertz wrote asking what was going on. He addressed the letter to Phil and me, with carbon copies to all the other attorneys. Part of the letter indirectly questioned the way in which Phil and I had been handling the case:

> I think you owe it to all the attorneys for Jack that there be a full explanation and full consultation with us. After all, we do have a greater stake in the matter than some who purport to be taking the lead, because there are costs and fees due to us.

At first I was very upset. The speed at which things occurred made it impossible to consult with the other attorneys. I was angry that when Phil and I were faced with having what little estate Jack had taken away from us by Mr. Mayer, Elmer was only concerned with costs and fees.

I wrote Elmer back immediately, stating my feelings. I outlined the problems I was having with Mr. Mayer and assured him that any book or movie rights belong to the family, not to the estate. This must have satisfied him because he never mentioned it again.

Phil also wrote Elmer but did not emphasize the same

issues. He gave Elmer a chronological breakdown of the happenings from the time I filed in Wayne County to the present. He
ended his letter by focusing on Mr. Mayer.

> As many things happened in regard to Jack Ruby,
> both while alive, and now dead, there are problems
> created by persons connected with the case that should
> not be created, and I here now make special reference to
> Jules Mayer. To back this up and explain it a little more
> fully, I feel that Jules Mayer has some type of motiva-
> tion, either publicity or money, that is driving him to do
> the things that he is doing, and which I cannot understand
> and must confess that the deduction of either publicity or
> money is the only reasonable basis motivating him.

While in Dallas I never did have my call returned from Dr.
West, the psychiatrist Eva had asked me to speak to. His secretary
finally called me in Detroit. She told me Dr. West would be in
Detroit on May 5, 1967, for the American Psychiatric Association
Convention. He wanted to meet with Earl and me. She also asked
me to send to Dr. West a copy of Jack's autopsy report.

I called Phil to find out about Dr. West. He explained that
throughout the years, both the prosecution and the defense had
brought various psychiatrists into the case. Dr. Louis Jolyon West
was the last one to visit with Jack. According to Phil, he seemed
genuinely interested in Jack's welfare.

The topic then turned to Mr. Mayer. I felt that when Levin
signed the stipulation agreement on behalf of Mr. Mayer, we had
entered into a contract that was enforceable. We decided to
proceed on that assumption. Earl would withdraw his application
to have the nuncupative will admitted to probate and also withdraw the contest of the Mayer will. We would, however, contest
the admission of the Hooten will. The same day I closed the
probate proceedings in Wayne County.

Each of Jack Ruby's heirs signed a letter to Mr. Mayer

asking him to withdraw in favor of Earl. They assured him that they would discharge him of any liability with regard to the estate.

Mr. Mayer was not pleased by our actions. March 31, 1967, Mr. Mayer wrote me, stating his determination to maintain total control over the estate:

> The writer [referring to himself] disavowed that any agreement existed or any representation was then being made, or could ever hereafter be construed in this court or any other court that any agreement or representation existed or exists for him to resign from acting as independent executor of decedent's estate in favor of Earl Ruby, or anyone else for that matter . . .

Phil told me that Judge Robertson had set June 6, 1967 as the date for the contest of the Hooten will.

Soon after, I learned that Mark Lane, author of *Rush to Judgment*, planned to give a lecture on the campus of Michigan State University on April 12, 1967. In an attempt to arrange a debate with him, I contacted the officials at the university. They informed me that Lane had turned me down.

On April 10, 1967, I wrote Mr. Lane:

Dear Mr. Lane:

As you are aware or unaware, this writer represents the family of the late Jack Ruby, and when the authorities at Michigan State University informed me of your refusal to debate with me on April 12, 1967, I felt regret and also suspicious of your true motives.

The general public, not having had the opportunity or inclination to investigate the Warren Commission report, is vulnerable to accept the sensational exploitation that you and others have used.

My personal and professional knowledge of the

accuracy of the Warren Report makes it my duty to expose every inference, misquote, or subterfuge you incorporate for the obvious purpose of publication sensationalism.

Until such time that you yield to debate, I will assume that you are fearful of having the truth substantiated.

On April 12, Earl and I drove to East Lansing, the campus of Michigan State University. We entered the auditorium just as a student was asking Mr. Lane why he would not debate with me. He answered that he knew nothing about me or my credentials. Besides, only so much time was allotted to his lecture.

With that out of the way, he proceeded to give his lecture. He began as he did in *Rush to Judgment.* The assassins were behind the fence. He had affidavits of witnesses. He attacked the Warren Commission for failure to ask particular witnesses the "right" questions.

He examined the Warren Commission's conclusions about the path of the bullets, emphasizing that they came from the right of the limousine. He discussed the path of the first shot. It entered the President's neck at the Adam's apple and exited at the base of the skull. He was positive that was the case because the entrance wound was clean in the Adam's apple area. He stated that the Warren Commission had concluded that this bullet struck the President in the base of the skull, exited in the throat, then took a right turn and struck Governor Connally, who was riding on the jump seat in front of the President.

It was clear to me that Mr. Lane had not seen the assassination site from the southeast corner of the sixth floor of the School Book Depository Building. The only way one bullet could have struck both the President and the governor was if it had been shot from the rear above. The steep incline of Elm Street would have made such a shot possible.

At this point a young lady approached Earl and me and asked if I were Mr. Adelson. I nodded and she asked me to follow her. She took me out of the auditorium into a small office in the front of the building where a gentleman was waiting.

"Are you Mr. Adelson?" the gentleman asked.

"Yes."

"Mr. Lane would like to meet with you immediately after his lecture. He will be at Kellogg Center, the university's hotel."

I went back to the auditorium and got Earl. He followed me up the aisle where I told him that Lane wanted to speak to us. We walked across the campus to the Kellogg Center and waited about twenty minutes.

Mark Lane entered the hotel, said something to the registration receptionist, and walked directly to where I was sitting.

"How did you know who I was?" I asked.

"You look like a lawyer," he answered. We went to a conference room that Lane had reserved. With the door closed, I introduced him to Earl.

"Do you really believe what you wrote in your book?" I immediately asked.

"Of course," he responded quite seriously. He again explained that he could not debate with me because of my lack of credentials. I told him I did not believe him.

I argued that although my knowledge of the assassination was limited, I was an expert on Jack Ruby.

He admitted he would have trouble linking Jack to a conspiracy under debate. I hesitated to share many of my conclusions about Jack Ruby and the Kennedy assassination, in case I should someday have the opportunity to debate Mr. Lane.

I did tell him that while in Dallas I had met Detective Paul T. Rayburn at police headquarters. Detective Rayburn was cited in *Rush to Judgment;* however, Rayburn had told me that the information he had given Lane had come from his father-in-law, and that it had turned out not to be true. He also said that Lane was not welcome in Dallas.

The conversation turned to whether Jack would have gotten out of jail had he survived. We all agreed that had Jack been . released, someone would have taken a shot at him. Earl remarked that the sheriff knew this. That was why Jack's cell door was not locked, and he was allowed to roam about the floor and use the pay telephone at will.

Lane informed us that he was currently working with Jim Garrison in New Orleans. He said that Garrison really had it all together and we should watch him.

It was getting late and we had to drive back to Detroit. We excused ourselves and left. On the way home, Earl remarked that Lane might be right about Oswald's involvement in some sort of conspiracy, but he was certainly wrong if he thought his brother Jack had anything to do with it.

# 21

I had decided to avoid any contact with Mr. Mayer until the June 6 hearing. I did fulfill, however, each of the stipulations to which we had agreed. Our contest of the Mayer will was officially withdrawn on March 29, 1967. By the date set for the hearing, I had an instruction requesting Mayer's withdrawal from each member of Jack's family.

On April 20, Marvin Levin sent a letter to Hooten's attorneys with carbon copies to Phil, the judge, and me. Levin suggested that the items Hooten claimed be appraised, and that some member of the family pay him for them.

If the above is agreed to by you, and is accomplished, there would be eliminated the contest by the Ruby family as to admitting Hooten's instrument as a codicil, and also the expense to which Hooten may be put in connection with offering the same and defending his contest against same, which expense may very well far exceed the value of these items, which in any event now appears would have to be sold in administration of the decedent's estate, and Hooten would in effect obtain nothing.

Levin's wording indicated that a member of the family should pay Hooten off so that the items Jack left to him could be sold and used for administrative expenses. This would include, of course, attorney fees for Mayer, Mayer & Levin.

On May 5, Earl and I went to meet Dr. West at his hotel. Dr. West had three reasons for wanting to meet with us.

"First," he began, "I want to interpret to Mr. Ruby my findings in his brother's case for his personal understanding, and hopefully, for his personal comfort. Second, to explore certain ideas and gain information that I may need to have if I am to be helpful to the family in the matter of the disputed will, as well as anything else the future may bring. And third, I want to check out certain facts, for both accuracy and interpretation, regarding Jack Ruby's life in relationship to a scholarly essay I am writing about the psychiatric and medico-legal ramifications of his case.

"My interest is with the intention of being helpful and being a friend to the Ruby family. I assure you that anything I gain from our conversation will be used responsibly and with the dignity of Jack and the family in mind.

"In essence," he continued, "I intend to show that Jack Ruby was neither an irresponsible hoodlum nor a criminal conspirator, but an emotionally liable and impulsive man. He was profoundly devoted to the President and Mrs. Kennedy and was violently disturbed by the assassination. Jack shot Oswald in a moment of blind passion during which he was capable neither of premeditation nor judgment of the consequences."

Dr. West was a large man. I guessed he was close to six feet, seven inches tall. As he spoke, he exuded dignity. Since Dr. West was confirming our own convictions, I knew Earl liked what he heard.

"Yes, Doctor," I said, "but that form of temporary insanity is not recognized in Texas. It is a doctrine developed in Michigan. Remember the movie *Anatomy of a Murder* with James Stewart? The murder trial in the movie hinged on the irresistible impulse theory."

The doctor was well aware of this.

"I plan to discuss this at some length in my essay," he

responded. "In my opinion the defense in the Ruby case left much to be desired from the psychiatric viewpoint. This will also be discussed. Jack Ruby's life of confinement in the Dallas County Jail, the illnesses he developed there, both psychiatric and physical, the significance of the death penalty in relationship to his health—all of these matters will be major concerns in my analysis of the case."

"Doctor, you say psychiatric illness. What was Jack suffering from?" I asked.

"The medical term is paranoid state," the doctor informed us. "The delusion manifested itself in his belief that President Johnson, who Jack Ruby thought was behind the assassination, arranged a cover-up by finding a scapegoat. In this case, as with Adolph Hitler, it was the Jews. Jack Ruby was very sensitive about his religion. In his mind, he believed that every person of the Jewish faith was systematically being brought into Dallas and killed. Dallas to him had become Johnson's concentration camp."

"Whenever I saw my brother," Earl said slowly, "he did seem surprised to see me. He seemed to think I was dead."

"That's correct," Dr. West continued. "Such disturbances in Jack Ruby's thought processes had been building up since the end of his trial—a trial that ended in his being condemned to death. His persecutory feelings had sufficient time to become well established."

"Doctor," I asked, "if Jack was as sick as you say, why wasn't this apparent to his guards?"

"A person suffering from this form of illness," Dr. West explained, "was not going to reveal his distrust of those not close to him. Also, he might have wanted to keep on the good side of the guards to make things easier for himself. He was perfectly capable of such choice in that the delusionary pattern touched on only one area of reality. This is true in most paranoid behavior. The rest of his thinking was based on reality. Jack would have been capable of concealing his delusions.

"On April 25, 1964, he tried to electrocute himself with the light fixture. At that time, Jack Ruby had just suffered a second psychotic break and full-blown hallucinatory experience," Dr. West explained.

"Dr. West," I asked, "we are attempting to contest a will dated August 5, 1966. You obviously believe Jack did not have testamentary capacity at that time?"

"There can be no doubt about that," Dr. West said emphatically. "The will in question proves his paranoia. By the will, he was giving his only possessions to a guard, not his family. This would indicate that he expected them to be tortured and killed before he died. In his delusions he was to be the last of the Jewish people to be eliminated in one big ceremony."

We spoke further of the legal matter pending in Dallas, and Dr. West agreed to appear to testify.

As we were about to leave, Dr. West turned to Earl, saying, "I understand you have borne a terrible burden, both psychological and financial, for these three and a half years. I feel that this meeting we are having may provide a small note of meaning to an otherwise catastrophic situation. If some significant reforms can be effected through efforts such as mine, then the terrible sufferings of Jack Ruby and his family shall not have been completely in vain."

At home that evening I reexamined Jack's testimony before the Warren Commission. It was taken on June 7, 1964, at the Dallas County Jail. The interrogation was conducted by the chief justice. Much of the testimony has been used by the critics of the Warren report to indicate that there was, in fact, a conspiracy involving Jack. The knowledge gleaned from Dr. West now made it possible to understand Jack's ramblings.

Jack started out by asking Mr. Warren, "Without a lie detector test on my testimony, my verbal statements to you, how do you know if I am telling the truth?"

Without swearing Jack in, Mr. Warren pursued the conversation into the third page of testimony, discussing a polygraph examination. Finally, he swore Jack in and Jack commenced his story, beginning Thursday night before the assassination. He retold his story in detail up to the point where he was about to go to Radio Station KLIF on Friday night. Then, out of nowhere, he asked, "Is there any way of getting me to Washington?"

The chief justice was taken aback by the question, but explained to Jack that it could not be done. Jack continued his story to the point where he went to the Times Herald Building. Then again, completely out of context, he said, "Gentlemen, unless you get me to Washington, you can't get a fair shake out of me."

After some discussion involving Joe Tonahill, Mr. Warren agreed to have Jack submit himself to a polygraph examination.

Jack then said, "I wish the president were here right now; it's a terrible ordeal, I tell you that."

Mr. Warren tried to coax Jack back to his story, but Jack persisted.

"Chief Warren," he said, "your life is in danger in this city. Do you know that?"

The chief justice shook his head no, and suggested that Jack tell him about it after his testimony was completed.

Jack asked if Mr. Warren had the power to take him to Washington. The chief justice said he did not.

"Gentlemen," Jack said, "my life is in danger here. Not with my guilty plea of execution." He probably meant his being found guilty and sentenced to death. He was clearly telling the commission that he feared for his life from another source.

Mr. Warren knew that he was dealing with a delicate situation and that Jack might be granted a new trial. He wanted to eliminate any superfluous testimony. He encouraged Jack to continue his story.

Jack persisted, "I tell you gentlemen, my whole family is

in jeopardy—my sisters, Eva, Eileen, and Mary. I lost my sisters."

Jack told the commission that he had lost his sisters. He went on to name all of his family and to state that they, too, would be included.

"Consequently," he continued, "right at this moment I am being victimize as a part of a plot in the world's worst tragedy and crime and at this moment Lee Harvey Oswald isn't guilty of committing the crime of assassinating President Kennedy. Jack Ruby is."

Jack explained that the Dallas John Birch Society was "giving the people the opportunity to get in power, because of the act I committed . . . has put a lot of people in jeopardy with their lives. Doesn't register with you, does it?"

Because of the "Impeach Earl Warren" signs, Jack thought that Justice Warren's life was also in jeopardy.

Mr. Warren indicated he did not know what Jack was talking about.

"Would you rather I just delete what I said and just pretend that nothing is going on?" Jack asked in an all-knowing manner. Mr. Warren said he would not delete anything and that he was interested in what he had to tell the commission. Jack continued his narrative.

Near the end of his testimony, Jack again seemed to disconnect from reality. He told the commission that had he been able to speak to the President five or six months earlier, a certain organization would not have been formed and would not have been able to use him to commit the most dastardly crime that had ever been committed.

"Can you understand now in visualizing what happened, what powers, what momentum has been carried on to create this feeling of mass feeling against my people, against certain people that were against them prior to their power? That goes over your head, doesn't it?"

"Well," the Chief Justice replied, "I don't quite get the full significance of it."

Jack continued, saying he wished President Johnson would have delved deeper before he allowed those certain people that power.

The Chief Justice was bewildered.

"The Jewish people," Jack continued, "are being extermi-nated at this moment." He again asked to be taken to Washington. "I am the only one who can bring the truth to our President, who believes in righteousness and justice."

Jack ended his testimony on the assurance he would be given the polygraph, and that the president and all the world would know the results.

On July 19, 1964, at 2:23 P.M., in the same room where Jack had testified to the Warren Commission, he underwent a polygraph examination. In fifty-five answers given, Jack did not show any deception. Because of his mental condition, the Warren Commission did not rely on its results.

How differently I viewed Jack's testimony after the conference with Dr. West.

# 22

By mid-May the district attorney in New Orleans, Jim Garrison, was making the newspapers every day. Up to this time he had made no mention of Jack, so I did not follow his "probe" too closely. A whole new list of names was appearing in the papers: David Ferrie, Jack S. Martin, Clay Bertrand, Clay Shaw, Alvin Beauboeuf, and Perry Raymond Russo. The list grew each day.

Two events had occurred in New Orleans the weekend of the assassination. First, the district attorney's office received a phone call from Jack S. Martin, a self-styled expert on electronic detective devices. He was also a professional soldier, philosopher, and adventurer. Martin informed the assistant district attorney that a David Ferrie knew Oswald, and, in fact, had been the one who taught him how to use a rifle. David Ferrie had been in Dallas the two weeks preceding the assassination. Ferrie, a former pilot for Eastern Airlines, had been discharged after being arrested on a morals charge in 1961. He was a dedicated member of a church he called the "Orthodox Old Catholic Church." David Ferrie had an unusual physical condition. He had absolutely no body hair and consequently wore a red wig and glued-on eyebrows.

At the time of the assassination both Martin and Ferrie were employed by a detective agency, Guy Bannister Associates. The agency was involved in an investigation on behalf of Carlos Marcello, the reputed Mafia boss in New Orleans. Marcello had been charged by the federal government with illegal entry into the United States. His trial ended in acquittal the same day as the assassination. That evening everyone involved with the trial had a victory celebration.

Ferrie, who had recently won a severance pay battle with Eastern, had planned a trip to Texas after the trial to examine an ice-skating rink. He planned to open one himself in Baton Rouge, ninety miles north of New Orleans. Accompanying Ferrie were Alvin Beauboeuf, his roommate, and another friend, Melvin Coffee.

On the advice of Martin, the district attorney dispatched officers to pick up Ferrie at his apartment. The visit was not a well-kept secret, for Ferrie learned that he was wanted for questioning when he called New Orleans to check in with his employer. Consequently, when he returned on November 25, Ferrie sent Beauboeuf up to the apartment to remove certain obscene photographs he did not want found in his possession. Beauboeuf ended up being arrested with the lewd photographs in his possession. Ferrie voluntarily appeared in the district attorney's office the next day. Both Ferrie and Beauboeuf were turned over to the FBI for questioning. Later Martin admitted to the FBI and secret service that he had concocted the entire story about Ferrie's knowing Oswald.

The second series of events that became the focus of Garrison's investigation involved Dean A. Andrews, Jr., an attorney whose reputation among his colleagues was at best questionable. Andrews claimed that the day after the assassination, while recuperating from pneumonia in the hospital, he received a telephone call from Clay Bertrand. Andrews said that Bertrand was "a lawyer without a briefcase"—a person who really wasn't a lawyer but referred clients to lawyers for a commission. Andrews said that Bertrand had called to ask him to defend Oswald in Dallas.

Andrews claimed to know Oswald. In May 1963, Oswald

had come to his office for legal assistance in helping his Russian wife become a U.S. citizen. He also wanted to straighten out his dishonorable discharge from the Marines. In his testimony before the Warren Commission, Andrews said that Oswald came to his office accompanied by some "gay" kids of Latin descent.

When questioned further by Garrison's office, Andrews claimed that he had met Bertrand at a "fag wedding reception" some years earlier, and that since their first meeting Bertrand had referred many clients to him. He described Bertrand to the FBI as over six feet tall with brown hair, and well-dressed. Paradoxically, he described Bertrand to the Warren Commission as five feet, eight inches tall, sandy hair, blue eyes, ruddy complexion, and weighing between 165 and 175 pounds.

When Garrison reopened his probe, David Ferrie became the target. Garrison contended that Ferrie went to Texas that fatal weekend to pick up Oswald after the assassination.

Ferrie had been involved with the Civil Air Patrol and became a senior officer in 1958. Oswald, it was reported, was associated with that organization in 1955 or 1956. Ferrie also tended to associate himself with causes. In 1961, he became involved with a group of Cuban refugees who vowed to invade their homeland to expel Castro. Ferrie volunteered to be the pilot for the group.

Garrison theorized that Ferrie knew Oswald from the Civil Air Patrol. Ferrie's involvement with the anti-Castro movement, and the fact that Oswald had brought some Cuban friends to Andrews's office, confirmed in Garrison's mind the connection between Ferrie and Oswald.

Garrison hounded Ferrie, Beauboeuf, and Coffee, but their story remained the same. Suddenly, on Washington's birthday, 1967, David Ferrie died of a cerebral aneurysm. Garrison claimed it was a suicide.

Garrison vowed to continue the probe. He said, "We know the key individuals, the cities involved, and how it was done. The only way they are going to get away from us is to kill themselves." He also announced that a committee called "Truth or Consequences" had been formed for the purpose of financing the probe. Interestingly enough, and perhaps not coincidentally, this was the same name adopted by the group of Dallas businessmen who had talked to me about settling the Ruby estate quietly and keeping the name of Dallas out of the limelight.

With Ferrie dead, Garrison now needed a new target. According to Dean Andrews, Garrison approached him to learn more about the Latins who appeared in his office with Oswald. He also wanted more information on Clay Bertrand. In a nationwide television interview, Andrews explained that he told Garrison that Manuel Garcia Gonzales was one of the gay kids that came to his office, and that all he knew of Bertrand was that he lived in the French Quarter, spoke Spanish, and was a homosexual.

On March 1, Clay Shaw was subpoenaed to appear in the district attorney's office. Shaw also lived in the French Quarter, spoke Spanish, and was considered by some to be a homosexual. At the age of twenty-nine, he left his job in public relations with Western Union to join the Army. He rose from private to major. Not only did he receive decorations from the Belgian and French governments, but he also was awarded the Bronze Star and Legion of Merit by the United States. Upon his return to New Orleans after the war, he developed the New Orleans Trade Mart, an organization established to promote world trade. In his spare time he dealt in art and fostered the restoration of the French Quarter. He had authored several published plays.

On the same day that Shaw was subpoenaed, another witness appeared in the district attorney's office—Perry Raymond Russo. An insurance salesman from Baton Rouge, Russo had met David Ferrie through his association with the Civil Air Patrol. The two became fast friends. When Russo learned of Ferrie's death, he wrote the district attorney, offering to tell all he knew about the deceased. He mentioned nothing, however, about the assassination, Bertrand, or Oswald. In early interviews with the press, Russo denied knowing Shaw, Bertrand, or Oswald. On February 25, Russo was interviewed by one of Garrison's assistants who prepared a 3,500 word summary. According to his statement, Russo had seen Shaw on only two occasions. He had seen him when President Kennedy had come to New Orleans in May 1962, and he had seen Shaw working at a service station owned by Ferrie. Russo identified a picture of Oswald as Ferrie's roommate, but only after a scratch beard was drawn on the photograph. That same photograph with the beard was later shown to other friends of Ferrie's. Not all of them would confirm the identification.

Garrison added Russo's identification of Oswald as Ferrie's roommate to the theory he was weaving. He also had a witness who could put Ferrie and Shaw together. At 5:30 on the same day he had been subpoenaed, Shaw was arrested and charged with being involved in a conspiracy that resulted in the death of President Kennedy.

When an arrest is made in a felony case, the defendant is entitled to a preliminary hearing during which the prosecution must establish to a court that a crime has been committed, and that the defendant probably is the perpetrator of that crime. On March 14, Shaw was given his preliminary hearing.

Russo, the star witness, had undergone hypnosis on three occasions, ostensibly to make sure he was telling the truth. Under hypnosis, however, a subject can be influenced by the manner in which the hypnotist presents the questions. Russo testified that a meeting was held at Ferrie's apartment during which Shaw, Oswald, and Ferrie planned the assassination. Russo said that he heard the three discuss such things as diversionary tactics, availability of exits, and triangulation of cross fire. When asked if any of the conspirators were in the courtroom, Russo pointed to Shaw.

Although Shaw's attorneys, William Wegmann and Irvin Dymond, did a very creditable job in cross-examination, they could not budge Russo. He could confidently respond to all of their questions. The court had no alternative but to bind Shaw over for trial.

On June 19, Walter Sheridan of NBC News got Russo to admit that his testimony was part truth, part fantasy, and part lies. Russo admitted that he was afraid, and that sometimes he was unable to tell the difference between truth and fantasy. Russo's statement to the media made it clear to the district attorney and his staff that Russo would be of no use to them at the trial. The district attorney had to find another "witness." Garrison shifted his attention to Dean Andrews.

It is quite likely that Andrews concocted his entire story, including the existence of Clay Bertrand. Certainly Andrews, like many others in New Orleans, knew Clay Shaw. No one besides Andrews, however, knew a Mr. Clay Bertrand.

This didn't hamper the district attorney. Garrison subpoenaed Andrews to appear before the grand jury. He hoped Andrews would testify that Shaw and Bertrand were the same person, but he was disappointed. In fact, Andrews told the grand jury that they were not the same man. When Garrison questioned him about the height of both men, Andrews answered that Shaw was as much as six inches taller than Bertrand.

For Andrews's failure to verify Garrison's theory, Garrison obtained a five-count indictment for perjury against him. At his trial for perjury, Andrews acted as his own defense counsel, although he was assisted by a young lawyer who happened to be in the courthouse. Andrews was sentenced to eighteen months. He correctly prophesied to newsmen that he would be the only person sentenced to prison in Garrison's entire Kennedy assassination probe.

Why did Andrews get into the mess? One can only speculate. I believe he wanted a piece of the limelight. He hoped that his claim that he was asked to defend Oswald would bring him fame. The fictional Clay Bertrand was created to collaborate his story.

Garrison also attempted to connect Clay Shaw with David Ferrie through Alvin Beauboeuf, who after Ferrie's death moved to a suburb of New Orleans. He had taken a job at a service station. Garrison's "investigators" stepped up their interrogation of Beauboeuf.

At one point, just before Shaw's trial, the investigators advised Beauboeuf that the district attorney had unlimited financial resources for his investigation and prosecution of those involved in the Kennedy assassination. Perhaps Beauboeuf could be rewarded for his testimony, maybe as much as $15,000. Also there was a good chance that the district attorney could secure for him a job with an airline—a goal that Beauboeuf had had for some time. Beauboeuf requested the investigators meet at his attorney's office, where the matter could be discussed.

The next day Beauboeuf, his attorney, and one of the investigators met in the attorney's office. The attorney recorded their conversation. The investigator repeated his offer to Beauboeuf. The attorney then questioned the investigator about what his client should know and be able to present in testimony in order to meet the demands of the offer. The investigator told the attorney that since Beauboeuf was close to Ferrie, he should know about the meeting in Ferrie's apartment that was attended by Oswald, Shaw, and Ferrie. He should know that the conversation at this meeting grew heated when Shaw insisted that they carry out the conspiracy his way.

The attorney questioned the investigator as to whether Beauboeuf would not then be charged with having withheld information during a criminal investigation. The investigator said Beauboeuf could use the explanation that he was afraid to come forward while Ferrie was alive because he had threatened his family.

The meeting ended with the attorney asking the investigator whether there would still be a "deal" if Beauboeuf could not tell what he "should know" about Ferrie and the meeting with Oswald and Shaw.

"No," the investigator replied, "that's not the deal. The deal is that Beauboeuf fills in the missing links." Whether it was the truth or not seemed irrelevant to him.

When the investigator left, the attorney had a tape containing an offer by the district attorney for false evidence. But Garrison still had the lewd pictures that Beauboeuf had had in his possession when he was arrested leaving Ferrie's apartment, and Beauboeuf was in some of the pictures.

News of the tape recording made by Beauboeuf's attorney spread quickly. Beauboeuf was invited to the district attorney's office. He was asked to sign a statement that he did not consider the offer made by the district attorney's investigators to be a bribe. If he refused, certain pictures would be published.

When Garrison released information that Jack's unpublished phone number was found in Oswald's notebook in code, I knew it was time for me to make a trip to New Orleans.

# 23

The May 15, 1967, issue of *Newsweek Magazine* covered the attempted bribe of Beauboeuf by Garrison's investigator. I called Hugh Aynesworth, the author who wrote the *Newsweek* report.

"How did Garrison react to your piece?" I asked.

"Oh, his only comment was that since *Newsweek* is owned by the *Washington Post*, it's an administration paper," Hugh responded.

I really did not understand his answer until I got to New Orleans. Hugh gave me the name of Ed Wegmann, Clay Shaw's attorney, and suggested I contact him.

Ed Wegmann was happy to hear from me. He explained that all kinds of things were going on at Tulane and Broad, the name used by attorneys for the courthouse, which stood on the corner of Tulane and Broad Streets. I invited myself to visit with Mr. Wegmann.

As I entered the building where Mr. Wegmann's office was housed, I noted the most recent issue of *Esquire Magazine* on display at a newsstand in the lobby. The cover showed the now famous picture of Jack the moment he shot Oswald. The cover article was written by Ovid Demaris and Professor Gary Willis. I had completely forgotten that Professor Willis had visited Detroit to interview Earl and me. I purchased a copy, tucked it into my briefcase, and proceeded to the tenth floor.

As I entered the office and announced myself to the

receptionist, a man sitting in the waiting room stood up and introduced himself. He was Clay Shaw.

Ed came out to the waiting room at that moment, introduced himself, and again introduced me to Mr. Shaw. We proceeded to Ed's private office, leaving Shaw in the waiting room. Once seated, I was introduced to William Wegmann and another young attorney.

"Does Garrison really believe his own theories?" I asked as an opener.

"Garrison believe his own theories?" Ed began. "You first have to understand what makes him tick.

"He was born in Iowa, but grew up in Chicago. He served in World War Two as a pilot, graduated from Tulane Law School in 1949, and was appointed to the district attorney's staff in 1953. He worked under District Attorney Leon Hubert, who later became staff attorney for the Warren Commission. Hubert spent most of his time with the Warren Commission on the subject of Jack Ruby.

"Garrison's first venture into politics came in 1957, when he ran unsuccessfully for the office of assessor. In that year Richard Dowling was elected district attorney in a close election decided by the state Supreme Court. Garrison was out of a job and began practicing law.

"In 1960, Garrison ran against an incumbent criminal court judge and made a good showing, losing by only a few thousand votes. In 1961 he ran for district attorney against Dowling. During the election campaign a curious thing happened. All of the television stations sponsored a debate among the candidates for that office. Dowling, the incumbent, refused to participate in the debate. He felt he could gain nothing by appearing on television with his opponents. During the debate Garrison attacked Dowling for his failure to crack down on corruption and vice, and vowed to be a full-time district attorney. The position of district attorney was considered a part-time job and paid only seventeen thousand a year. When Irvin Dymond, Dowling's chief opponent, was asked if he would be a full-time district attorney, he said, 'Not for seventeen thousand a year.' Garrison was elected.

"Soon after taking office, Garrison and his staff began an attack on his predecessor. He accused Dowling of dismissing charges against friends and political allies and took the matter before the grand jury. No indictments were returned, but Garrison received much newsprint.

"Next, the district attorney turned to the vice he claimed existed in the night clubs on Bourbon Street, the main street in the French Quarter of the city. Bourbon Street clubs were financially stronger than Dowling had been, however, and began to combat the Garrison raids. According to state law, judges of the criminal court have to approve any expenditures for investigation by the district attorney's office. The judges suspended the funds.

"Garrison counterattacked. At a local Jewish temple he gave a speech on brotherhood. With television cameras on him, he charged that the parish prison was overcrowded because the judges weren't doing their job. The judges, he said, were involved in a 'vacation racket.'

"The judges charged in retaliation that any overcrowding in the parish prison was due to the lack of prosecution by the district attorney, and *en masse* they signed a complaint against Garrison for criminal defamation. Garrison's staff quickly dismissed the complaint. The judges then called upon the state's attorney general to refile the charge. The charge was refiled.

"The trial was held in early 1963. The judges each took the witness stand and were subjected to bitter cross-examination. It proved quite embarrassing to them in that their pasts were exposed to the public. The news media ate it up with banner headlines.

"In the American system of justice, any witness called by subpoena to testify, must appear and take the witness stand under penalty of contempt of court. All, that is, except the defendant, in this case, Garrison. If after the state rested its case Garrison took the stand, he would have been subjected to cross-examination like the judges had been. The defense rested with the prosecution, however. Garrison was found guilty. He was sentenced to pay a thousand-dollar fine which was overturned by the United States Supreme Court two years later.

"Garrison had a vendetta against one of the judges, Bernard Cocke, and the judge let the district attorney know the dislike was mutual. During a trial at which Judge Cocke was presiding, he asked one of the witnesses on the stand if the testimony he was then giving was the same testimony he had given to the grand jury. Garrison immediately cited the judge for contempt of the grand jury. This was just prior to Garrison's own conviction. After Garrison's trial, he requested of Cocke a voucher for funds to pay for the undercover work his office was conducting on Bourbon Street. When the judge refused, he was then issued an indictment for malfeasance.

"None of the assistant district attorneys in Garrison's office would try the case. Garrison had to try it himself. Judge Cocke was promptly acquitted. Garrison's attack, however, did lead to Judge Cocke's defeat in the next election."

"What kind of justice system do you have here?" I asked. I was taken back by the short history I had just heard.

"It normally works," Ed answered.

"We all know that the man sitting out in the waiting room is innocent of the charges, and we all know how he got into this mess," I said. "What, if anything, can I do to help?"

"As you know," Ed explained, "if Garrison says Jack Ruby was part of the so-called conspiracy that Clay Shaw, Oswald, and Ferrie were involved in, we could prove his whole theory is wrong by just disproving the part about Jack Ruby."

"That, I think I can do. I can certainly provide the witnesses you might need to rebut what Garrison's witnesses would say," I said. I knew I could, because I knew Jack was not involved in any conspiracy. "Of course," I continued, "I will have to know more of Garrison's case to determine who you will need."

"Why don't you go ask him?" Ed responded. "He talks to everyone and anyone who can shed any light on the case."

"Should I call?" I asked.

"No, just go over. He'll see you. But under no circumstances allow him to take you before the grand jury." Ed laughed.

I made my exit and hailed a taxi. When I entered the cab and said "Tulane and Broad," I expected a short ride. The cab drove out Canal Street for what I thought was three to four miles, certainly well out of the downtown area. We made a left turn on Tulane, and in a few blocks I saw the courthouse.

I looked up at the gray building. Stamped in the stone was the inscription, "This is a government of law, not of men." A long, wide flight of outside stairs led to the second floor. I climbed twenty-two steps and was in the building. To my left I saw the sign "District Attorney." I entered a large reception room and gave my business card to the receptionist. I asked to see Mr. Garrison.

I had no sooner taken a seat when a young man came out to greet me.

"You are *the* Mr. Adelson?" he asked. I was so taken aback by the compliment that I almost did not answer. He must have meant someone else.

"Yes, my name is Adelson," I finally replied.

"Would you come with me?" I followed the young man down a long, dark, narrow hallway. When we were almost to the end, the dull carpet suddenly gave way to bright red. He opened a door and asked me to be seated.

I looked around the large office I was sitting in. On a credenza behind the desk in front of me were some volumes of the Warren Commission Report. It is easy to tell if the volumes of this report have been used to any great degree. Since they were printed by the government printing office, they were not the quality one might expect in a normal book. As the volumes are used, the blue dye on the covers wears off on the user's hands, causing the book to lose its deep blue color, especially at the bindings. I could see that the volumes containing the testimony relative to Jack had hardly been touched, while many of the other volumes had been extensively used.

Behind me, toward the window, were several blown-up photographs of Dealey Plaza and what the critics termed the grassy knoll.

I had not been in the room for more than a minute when a second man appeared. He sat down next to me and addressed me with a serious stutter, "Not that we don't believe you are who you say you are, but it's important we do know to whom we are speaking. Will you please describe to me Jack Ruby's cell in the Dallas jail?"

I remembered Earl's remarks to Mark Lane when we met with him at Michigan State University. Lane was working with Garrison alright.

"He didn't have a cell; he was allowed to wander around the floor," I responded. A smile formed on the man's face. He left, and within a few moments Jim Garrison walked in.

The "Jolly Green Giant," as he was affectionately called, was tall, six feet, six inches, handsome as a movie star, and impeccably dressed. He shook hands with me.

"Yes, Mr. Adelson," he said, as he seated himself behind the desk. "You are the attorney for Jack Ruby's family."

"Yes," I responded. I suspected that our conversation was probably being tape recorded. "I realize you are working with Mark Lane by the question I was asked."

"Mr. Lane has assisted in our investigation," he responded in his deep, modulated voice.

"But Lane's theory and yours are not the same."

"Oh," the giant responded. He sat up in his chair and looked me directly in the eyes. "How so?"

"According to all I have read—please correct me if I am

wrong—you believe that Oswald, Ferrie, and Shaw conspired to assassinate John F. Kennedy."

"Yes, with the aid of others," he said.

"Well," I continued, "according to Lane, Oswald was a patsy, a fall guy who had nothing to do with a conspiracy."

"I will have to discuss that with Lane," he said. Changing the subject, he asked, "How well did you know Mr. Ruby?"

"I never met the man," I replied. Garrison brought his legs up onto the desk. "I saw him only in his casket at the funeral."

"Did you know he was an agent for the CIA?" he asked.

"In all my investigation I found no way Jack could have been an agent for anybody. In his whole life he never worked for anybody other than himself." He could tell I was indignant.

"The CIA has a way," Garrison continued, "of enlisting people without their knowledge. Didn't you read the testimony of Nancy Rich?"

*Nancy Elaine Perrine Rich*, I thought, *the lady who requested to testify.*

Nancy Rich was twenty-seven when her husband died at his own hands. She testified that she went to Dallas in 1961 to find her husband. She claimed she worked at the Carousel while she was there. She didn't get along with Jack because he did not think she cleaned the glasses well enough. She spoke of a meeting that she attended with her husband. They discussed rescuing refugees from Cuba. She could not remember where the meeting took place. She spoke of a second meeting with more people, none of whom she could identify. The plot changed. Not only were refugees to be rescued, but military supplies were to be brought in. The hitch was money. At that point, she testified, Jack Ruby walked in with a large bulge in his breast pocket. He and one of the participants at the meeting went into a back room. When they came out, the bulge was gone and everyone was happy. During cross examination, Nancy Rich admitted she had a police record for prostitution, vagrancy, and narcotics.

"You believe Nancy Rich?" I asked.

"Of course, she was absolutely telling the truth, and Jack Ruby's appearance at the meeting proves he was working for the CIA."

"Mr. Garrison," I responded, "Jack Ruby never had any great sum of money in his life. How could he be trusted to carry that kind of money?"

"The CIA has ways of causing people to do things," he replied.

*And the government controls the* Washington Post *and* Newsweek, I thought. I understood Garrison's response to Hugh Aynesworth's story.

"Didn't you see the report of the friends of Mrs. Rich?" I asked. "They admitted she was a psychopathic liar who delighted in telling wild tales."

"Those are not lies," Garrison stated. He had an unshaken confidence in himself.

"Mr. Garrison," I said, "I personally spoke to her attorney. He said she was an habitual liar who found it very difficult to tell the truth."

"We checked into her background," he responded, "and we found her highly reliable. Were you aware that we discovered Jack Ruby's unlisted phone number among Oswald's notes?"

I didn't even care to answer his question, so I changed the subject.

Garrison did not seem to care either. I suspected that Garrison would not base his case against Shaw on this ridiculous piece of "evidence."

"But Rich's testimony is also contrary to Lane's theory," I said. "Lane believes that Jack Ruby was able to murder Oswald because he had the cooperation of the Dallas Police."

"Well, I never asked Mr. Lane about it," Garrison responded.

Garrison attempted to get me to admit that Jack was part

of a conspiracy. He used the English language eloquently and had the humor of a stand-up comedian. His presence commanded attention. He spoke of his theory as an author would speak of his book, or a painter his best work. He was, without a doubt, one of the most captivating men I have ever met.

"Jack Ruby," he stated, "was sent by the CIA to silence Oswald."

I thought of another of Jack's personal notes:

Had I wanted to get him (Oswald), I could have reached in and shot when either Fritz or Curry brought him out in the hall when they told the press that they would bring him down in the basement, and there certainly would be less risk on my life then. I wasn't but two feet away.

"Mr. Garrison, if what you say is true, why didn't Ruby shoot Oswald on Friday, the day of the assassination? He was only two feet away from him."

There was no answer.

An important engagement that Garrison suddenly had to attend came up, and our meeting ended abruptly

I left the same way I came in, only to discover I had entered from the side of the courthouse. I walked around to the front of the building, where I saw these words etched in stone: "The impartial administration of justice is the foundation of liberty."

# 24

From Garrison's office I went directly to my hotel to compile my notes of the day. When they were complete, I called Ed Wegmann and read them to him.

I was now free to visit New Orleans. I have always felt that cities have personalities, which in turn influence the attitudes of their citizens. These attitudes, I believe, are based on the city's history. My hotel was in the French Quarter on Chartres Street. I walked around, noting the names of the streets. Royal, Bourbon, Conti, Dauphine, Orleans—all names associated with the Bourbon family, the last royal family before the French Revolution. The intersecting streets, St. Peter, St. Anne, and St. Louis, were the names of their patron saints.

In the early eighteenth century, France had a grand vision of a vast empire in the new world. The city was founded by a trading company under a charter from the king. The citizens were originally prisoners or political exiles who, by contract with the king, were supplied with female companions, again prisoners or prostitutes.

As the colony grew, a better class of citizens was attracted. These new citizens brought not only their appreciation for the arts, but also slavery. By 1740, New Orleans was the capital of the "idle life." Gambling was its major pastime.

As the slaves cleared the swamps, agriculture became a major force in New Orleans economy. Sugar cane was the chief product. Even though the Mississippi River provided an easy mode of transportation, the French edict that the colony could trade only with the homeland and other French colonies made trade difficult.

With the end of the Seven Years War with England, France ceded its vast empire of forts from the Great Lakes down the Mississippi to Louisiana to England and Spain. Spain gained possession of New Orleans. With this change, the colony was granted a more liberal trade policy, which in turn brought more settlers.

The first wave of French Canadians, later called Cajuns, came as a result of the American Revolution. Longfellow, in his epic *Evangeline*, has his heroine searching for her love, an exile from Nova Scotia, in the swamps of Louisiana. At the same time, settlers were arriving from the Canary Islands and Haiti. By 1800, the city had approximately eight thousand citizens and over fifteen hundred buildings. New Orleans continued its reputation for a fast life built on pleasure. The city was not know for its high moral standards.

After forty years Spain, alarmed by the rapid westward advancement of the Americans, gave New Orleans back to France. As the Americans settled in the city, the original white residents, now known as Creoles, maintained its French character. French was the language in polite society until the Civil War.

Many privateers called New Orleans their home, flying the French flag as they attacked British, Spanish, and American shipping. Among the most famous were the Laffite brothers, Pierre and Jean. At the same time, the city became the embarkation point for revolutionaries in Mexico and Central America. The immigrant population was eager to fight for liberation of these countries, including Texas.

In 1805 Aaron Burr, former vice president of the Union, sailed down the Mississippi. Having lost favor among his own people after he killed Alexander Hamilton in a duel, Burr hoped to take over the area and create a new nation of which he would be the leader.  He quickly got caught up in the wars of liberation against the Spanish to the south and west.  Burr later would be tried for treason.

Burr's escape to New Orleans after he shot Hamilton was only one of the more highly publicized incidents in the city's history.  The city became a refuge for exiles from all over the world.  Dueling became a common pastime at St. Anthony's Square.  Today this square in the French Quarter features promising young artists selling their wares.

During the War of 1812, Andrew Jackson commanded the city.  But the city would have nothing to do with this boorish "Kaintuck." The city fathers plotted to surrender New Orleans to the British, and Jackson threatened to burn it to the ground.  Before either threat could take effect, however, Jackson won the Battle of New Orleans with a stunning victory over the British.  At last the Mississippi was open to trade.

New Orleans now became the trade center of the South.  Its wharves were piled high with merchandise destined for world ports.  It became a city of wealth.  Seeking their fortune, Germans, Italians, and Irish immigrated to New Orleans.  In 1840, it was the third largest city in the United States.  By midcentury New Orleans also became know as a center of culture.  One could always see French opera in New Orleans, and at least three English theaters were operating outside the French Quarter.  It continued to grow.  By 1860, the population had reached over 168,000.

After the Civil War, a large wave of Italian immigrants settled in the French Quarter.  For a while it appeared that the French Quarter would be renamed the Italian Quarter.  This wave was caused by the abolition of slavery and the ensuing need for cheap labor.  Many believe that with the Italian immigration into New Orleans, the Mafia arrived in America.

Throughout the Reconstruction Era, law and order ceased to exist in the South, especially in New Orleans.  Government officials were mostly blacks and carpetbaggers.  Organizations similar to the Ku Klux Klan made protests and riots against this imposed political structure a daily occurrence. In 1876 the federal troops were withdrawn. Reconstruction ended in New Orleans, but the damage had been done. Distrust of the federal government exists to this day.

This distrust enabled Garrison to establish a base for perpetrating his hoax on the American people. His continual attacks on the CIA and the FBI were readily believed by many of the citizens of New Orleans.

By the turn of the century, the city was again economically sound, with the river traffic at its peak. Corruption ran rampant in government circles, while the citizens continued to play. It was called "the city that care forgot," famous for its gambling, horse racing, and prostitution.

Dallas also began by a river—the three forks of the Trinity. In 1840 a lawyer from Tennessee, John Neely Bryan, made a trip to the Three Forks area. He liked what he saw. Bryan broke his ties at home and returned to found the city of Dallas in 1841. History is not clear as to whether he planned to establish a trading post with the Indians or whether he intended to be a part of the Peters Colony, a government land giveaway program designed to encourage settlement in the young Republic of Texas. The Peters Colony did publicize Bryan's town in its advertisements, and the publicity brought many settlers to Dallas.

It is not completely clear how Dallas got its name. When the Republic of Texas became the twenty-eighth state, James K. Polk was president. Some wanted to call the city Polk, but failed to get the necessary support to do so. There is speculation, but no documentation, that they settled for second-best—Polk's vice president, George Dallas.

Bryan planned his city around a public square in the heart of what is now downtown Dallas. In this square stood the courthouse in which Jack was tried. A search of early courthouse records reveals the first civil suit heard in the county was a divorce case. The jury granted the divorce, and the defendant very shortly thereafter married the foreman of the jury—perhaps foreshadowing Dallas's judicial process almost a century later.

When the question arose of what town would be the county seat, Bryan offered free ferry service across the Trinity for five years. Dallas, population 430, was elected the county seat in 1850.

Two years later, Maxime Guillot arrived to establish a carriage factory, the first manufacturing plant in the town. Soon afterward Alexander Cockrell opened a sawmill. Cockrell envisioned a great future for Dallas. In 1858 he initiated construction on a three-story hotel; he did not see it completed. He died in a shooting spree with the city marshal. Apparently the marshal owed Cockrell money and did not like the method Cockrell was using to collect his debt. Cockrell's widow supervised the completion of the hotel's construction, only to have it burn to the ground the next year.

La Reunion, a group of French and Swiss colonists, came to Texas and settled just to the west of the Trinity River. Although the colony ended in bankruptcy, it did bring to Dallas something that few frontier towns had—culture.

In 1860, a second fire destroyed everything in Dallas's town square. The push for abolition had not created a friendlier attitude toward blacks among most people in Dallas, and blacks became an easy scapegoat for Dallas's second disaster. Three black slaves were arrested, tried, and convicted of setting the fire. They were hung the day they were convicted. The cause of the fire was never proven, but three black men were dead because of the fire.

The next year Texas seceded from the Union and embraced the Confederacy. Because of its location, it did not see war in its streets, but it did send many of its young men to fight. With the end of the Civil War, the town saw its first Union soldiers when a 250-man detachment camped nearby.

Although Dallas, like New Orleans, is on a river, the similarity between both the towns and the rivers ends there. The Trinity was dry most of the time, except when it flooded. The idea of water transportation from Dallas to Galveston and the sea was the dream of a few Dallasites. The first boat on the Trinity was called the *Dallas*. On its maiden voyage it made its destination, but on the return trip it sank. The second ship met the same fate.

Because it was obvious that the Trinity would not provide a navigable link between Dallas and the coast, its economic future depended on its becoming a junction for an east-west and north-south railway system. There were two prospects: the Houston and Texas Central Railroad, running north and south; and the Texas and Pacific, running east and west. According to *Dallas Public and Private* by Warren Leslie, neither railroad had originally planned to route through Dallas.

Some Dallas citizens raised money and gave land to the Houston and Texas Central Railroad. The railroad managed somehow to hit Dallas on its way north. The Texas and Pacific had legislative persuasion to link up with Dallas. Legislators in Austin attached an amendment to the Texas and Pacific's right-of-way, making it conditional on its passing through Dallas. The citizens of Dallas had friends in high places.

By 1873 the two railroads formed a junction in Dallas. A steady flow of people began arriving from the East. The town had become a city. Even the panic of 1873 did not bother Dallas. The elegant Le Grande Hotel opened in 1875, complete with gambling and prostitution. The city fathers, however, quickly put a stop to that part of the operation. Four churches and a synagogue established the moral tone for Dallas at that time.

In 1890, the courthouse was completed. It served as the courthouse until 1960, when it was replaced by one of the many new skyscrapers that have become part of Dallas's skyline. Jack was tried and convicted in the new courthouse which also became the battleground for the contesting of Jack Ruby's will.

At the turn of the century, insurance companies began establishing their headquarters in Dallas. The first arrival was the successful Praetorian, which contributed to Dallas's big-city look by building a fourteen-story skyscraper. Second was Southwestern Life, followed by a myriad of insurance and banking institutions that transformed Dallas into a hub of commerce.

This tale of two cities gives some insight into the possible hoax perpetrated by Jim Garrison. One can contrast the atmosphere of Dallas, the introspective, provincial, and conservative capital of the Southwest, with the fun-loving, live-for-today attitude of New Orleans. Unlike the citizens of Dallas, many citizens of New Orleans did not mind being in the national limelight of sensational, exploitive headlines. It was free publicity—an invitation to come to the city of intrigue and excitement.

Garrison's investigation traversed state lines and was extremely expensive. Talk that he purchased an expensive home in the French Quarter during the time of his "probe" solidly confirmed for many people the suspicion that Garrison was receiving supplemental funding. If "the committee of Dallas" was willing to spend a great deal of money to "take the taint off Dallas," might not Garrison be a worthy recipient? In each of his accusations, the premise was the same. The actual shots might have been fired in Dallas, but the key events that led to Kennedy's assassination and "Oswald's execution" originated in New Orleans.

# 25

The next morning, while I was still in New Orleans, the news broke in the papers. Garrison's office had found, among Clay Shaw's papers, a memo which read: "Lee Odom, P.O. Box 19106, Dallas, Texas." Garrison had also found in Oswald's notebook a similar number preceded by two letters which looked like the letters P and 0. Garrison claimed that the cryptic letters and numbers were the coded, unlisted private telephone number of Jack Ruby in 1963. Garrison had alluded to this the day before, but I did not realize its significance.

If this were true, maybe I was all wrong. Maybe Garrison was onto something. I called Eva; she had not heard the news. I told her I would be on the next plane to Dallas.

By the time I arrived in Dallas, Eva had seen the news. As always, she met me at the airport. She had a big grin on her face.

"He's full of shit," she said, as soon as I was within hearing distance. The morning had given me some anxious moments. Even before I knew why, Eva's announcement made me feel better.

"The telephone number," she said, "wasn't Jack's. It was mine. I couldn't get a phone without a deposit, so Jack ordered it for me. True, it was in his name, but it was my number."

"Don't tell anyone," I cautioned. "Let's save this bit of information to spring on Garrison when he introduces it into evidence at the Shaw trial."

Eva didn't tell anyone, but Garrison's new revelation was

soon discredited. It was a coincidence that the numbers in both notebooks were the same. It was not long before the real Lee Odom turned up, explaining that he had gone to see Shaw in 1966 to promote a bullfight in New Orleans. The two met and exchanged addresses. Garrison ignored Odom's explanation and insisted he had established a connection between Jack Ruby and Clay Shaw.

A few days later, Garrison told reporters that the President was killed by a fatal bullet that was fired from the front. It involved four men, two actually doing the shooting, and the other two picking up the spent cartridges. Garrison also announced that, although there were shots from behind the Presidential motorcade, "…it is becoming increasingly apparent that he was not shot from the sixth floor of the School Book Depository Building."

When asked if Oswald was involved, Garrison proclaimed, "There is no question at all about the fact that Lee Harvey Oswald did not fire a shot there." He went on to explain that the bullets used by the assassins were frangible, bullets that disintegrate upon impact.

A reporter asked how this could be true when a bullet, which was ballistically shown to have come from Oswald's rifle, was found on the stretcher that brought Governor Connally to Parkland Hospital.

"It was dropped on one of the cots at the hospital," Garrison explained.

Garrison's announcement was exactly the theory advanced by Mark Lane. I wondered how important my conversation with the Jolly Green Giant had really been. It was I who had pointed out to him the discrepancies between his theories and Lane's. When we met, he had no doubt whatever that Oswald was the assassin. Now his whole story had changed.

From then on, Garrison's charges became wilder. On June 19, NBC aired an hour-long expose of the Garrison probe. His comment was that the NBC program was sponsored by the federal government. "It is obvious," Garrison told reporters, "that the official Washington attitude is that our inquiry must be stopped at all costs."

A few days later one of Garrison's top investigators resigned, announcing that there was no factual basis or material evidence to support Garrison's belief in an assassination plot. Garrison's reply was that the investigator was not privy to the evidence. He accused the investigator of plotting with the CIA to discredit his investigation. Garrison then announced that Officer Tippit was killed by the conspirators so that the police would shoot Oswald on sight.

Garrison had asked for equal time to respond to the NBC special report of June 19. He was accorded that time on July 15. He began with the statement that, "I'm going to talk to you about truths and about fairy tales, about justice and about injustice." He sounded convincing, but he only talked about the fairy tales.

Not long after his response on NBC, Garrison decided that Oswald was a U.S. government agent that had been sent to Russia to observe if U-2s left vapor trails.

On November 16, it appeared that the ego trip being taken by District Attorney Garrison had reached its logical, bizarre conclusion. Before a convention of radio and television newsmen at the Los Angeles Century Plaza Hotel, he announced, "The man who has profited most from the assassination is your friendly President, Lyndon Johnson." It is ironic that Garrison embraced the same theory that Jack Ruby, in his paranoid state, had proposed to friends, family, and (obliquely) the Warren Commission.

In December Garrison added a new piece of "evidence" to his theory. He came across a photograph in the Warren exhibits of a man bending over in Dealey Plaza, with two uniformed police officers beside him. There were no details in the photograph to indicate why the man was bending down, but Garrison proclaimed that this man had to be picking up a piece of a bullet—a .45-caliber bullet. He concluded that the federal government must have known within ten minutes of Kennedy's assassination that Oswald was not the assassin, for a .45-caliber bullet could not have come from his rifle. Obviously, according to Garrison, someone else shot President Kennedy with a .45-caliber pistol and then fled into a manhole.

For twenty-two months after Clay Shaw was bound over for trial, Garrison continued his attacks on the federal government and its role in the assassination. Finally, in January 1969, the trial began. It took two weeks to pick a jury. Although Garrison did not try the case himself, he made the opening statement and the prosecution's testimony during the next four weeks was orchestrated by him.

The jury, on March 1, at 1:00 A.M., acquitted Clay Shaw.

Garrison was in his office when the verdict came in. When informed, he shouted, "The American people don't want to know the truth about the assassination."

# 26

When I went to Dallas to investigate Garrison's "discovery" of Jack Ruby's unlisted private number, I decided to use this time in Dallas also to see for myself the places where Lee Harvey Oswald had lived. Since Eva had already solved the mystery of Jack's phone number, I decided I could start carrying out this secondary plan right away. When I told Eva, she seemed upset. "Why that creep?" she inquired. There was a note of dejection in her voice.

"Eva," I answered, "there is much more to this than just Jack. It is impossible to tell the world about Jack without telling about Oswald." Eva did not understand.

That afternoon after I checked into my hotel, I rented a car and drove over the area that Oswald had traversed after shooting the President. I drove through the Oak Cliff section on Beckley, past his rooming house, then toward Tenth Street where he shot Police Officer Tippit, then to Jefferson Avenue to the Texas Theater where he was apprehended.

I parked at the curb near the theater and reflected on the basic question left unanswered by the Warren Commission. Why did Oswald shoot Kennedy? No matter how severely psychopathic a person is, some reason usually lies behind his actions. The Warren Commission could only establish background factors that might have influenced Oswald to assassinate the president. These elements included Oswald's hostility to his environment, his failure to establish meaningful relationships, his desire for a place in history, his commitment to Marxism, and his capacity to act decisively without regard to the consequences. I could not believe that Oswald shot Kennedy just so he could have a place in history.

I flew back to Michigan without any satisfactory answer to this question, but vowed to research the question further.

During the height of Garrison's investigation and "revelations" on the Kennedy assassination, the litigation of Jack Ruby's wills began, on Tuesday, June 6, 1967. Earl and I flew into Dallas the afternoon before. I spent the rest of that day preparing Eva's and Earl's testimony.

The next morning we met Phil Burleson at the old courthouse building and entered the courtroom. Although Mr. Jules Mayer was present, we did not acknowledge him.

The litigation began with Mayer's team. The first witness was Charles Mayer, a relative and law partner of the man who championed the 1950 will. He qualified as a clinical psychologist, now retired, and testified that Jack was of sound mind in 1950. We could not object to this testimony nor would we because of our agreement with Mayer—in spite of his rescinding it. We wanted to maintain our position of having abided by an enforceable contract.

The Hooten team followed the Mayer team, attempting to show that their will was valid. Norman Hooten took the stand. Short and thin, he did not look like a typical policeman. Hooten testified that he was familiar with Jack's handwriting and showed examples of it on jail menus. The August 5, 1966, instrument was introduced and admitted into evidence without objection.

Phil cross-examined the witness concerning Jack's state of mind during his incarceration. Hooten testified that during the six-month period he was employed as a jail guard, he observed Jack and spoke to him more than one hundred times. Since Jack's cell was not locked, often at night Jack would come out of his cell and speak to him. Hooten said that Jack seemed of sound mind and perfectly normal. "Jack always came out on top in the trades he made with other inmates," he said. "Jack read the newspapers and spoke intelligently about his own case."

Cross-examination brought out the fact that Hooten was also thinking of writing a book or magazine article, or some other form of profitable publication. He had not entered any negotiations yet, but his lawyers had been authorized to do so. He admitted reluctantly that he had been trying to sell his "instruments" on the New York autograph market. This admission discredited the alleged sentimental value to Hooten of the items Jack had left him, and indicated his intent to take commercial advantage of his connection with Jack Ruby.

"Did Jack Ruby ever speak of being killed?" Phil asked, thinking Hooten might comment on Jack's conviction that a mass murder of the Jews had taken place.

"Yes," Hooten responded, "in fact he once said, 'If I'm ever turned loose, I won't live three days on the street.'"

"Did he ever discuss his family and his fondness for them?" Phil asked, again hoping to establish that Jack believed his own family had been victims in the "mass murder."

"No," Hooten answered, "except very briefly, and not as separate people."

"Did he ever speak of a conspiracy?"

"Jack did predict that after his death, evidence would be brought out linking him with the assassination, but it would be false evidence." Hooten's response created quite a stir in the courtroom. That day Garrison had announced the link between Jack and Oswald.

Finally, in exasperation Phil asked: "Did he ever talk about mass extermination of the Jews?"

"No."

"Did he ever speak about mass slaughter of Jews right here in the Dallas County Jail?"

"No, not that I can recall."

"Did he ever tell you that he took a lie detector test?" Phil asked.

"Yes," Hooten responded, "but he said he was forced to take it."

Again there was a stir in the courtroom. It was well-known that Jack wanted to take the lie detector test.

"Did you ever notice that Jack was ill last summer?" Phil asked, changing the subject.

"No," Hooten quickly responded, "except for a couple of stomachaches."

"Did you see Jack vomit during that period?"

"No, but one or two of the other guards did." Hooten's attorneys objected to this line of questions as being immaterial. The judge sustained the objection.

Phil went back to the original line, asking if Hooten had ever told anybody about the will he was purporting.

"No," he answered.

"What other documents or instruments written by Jack do you have?" Phil asked, hoping to elicit an answer with which he could discredit the witness.

"There was a friendship note I was to send to his former landlady. I couldn't find her."

Hearing that, I went to the phone in the hall and looked up the former landlady. She was listed in the 1966 Dallas telephone directory. Upon my call, she came to the court to get her note. I did this to cast doubt on Hooten's reliability as a witness.

After the noon break, Dr. West was put on the stand, out of order. It took at least ten minutes to place his qualifications on the record.

I questioned Dr. West, bringing out all of the medical history the doctor had given Earl and me back in Detroit.

"Why, Doctor," I asked, "would someone in the mental state you described leave property to a stranger such as Hooten?"

"The reason," Dr. West postulated, "was that Mr. Ruby

expected all of his family to be killed before he died, so they wouldn't be around to receive anything." The direct examination of Dr. West ended about 4:00 P.M.

On cross-examination, Dr. West was asked why Jack's mental illness was not noticed by his guards if it were so apparent to his family, lawyers, and doctors. Dr. West responded that Jack was more likely to reveal his distrust to those close to him, since they were more important to him.

"He also might want to keep on the good side of the guards," Dr. West stated, "to make things easier for himself. He was perfectly capable of such choice. The delusionary pattern hit only in the area of unreality; as in most paranoid states, the rest of his thinking was based on reality. A trained observer would have noticed Jack's ailment. The only way I was able to discern Jack's mental status was to draw it out of him."

Dr. West added that in many mental hospitals the attendants, who are untrained, are surprised that many of the paranoid patients are there at all, as they seem normal most of the time.

Dr. West was excused at 6:45. Not one spectator had left the room during his testimony. It was quite clear that evening that Hooten was going to lose.

The next morning the judge promised that court would not be in session as long as it had been the day before.

We had decided not to bring Hooten back on the stand after the landlady appeared and asked for her note.

Hooten's attorneys then called Phil Burleson to the stand for cross-examination. They attempted to get Phil to testify about the sanity hearing held in 1966, but Phil would not answer their questions.

The Hooten proponents rested their case. I called Eva to the stand. I started by asking her to list Jack's personal attributes.

"He was impulsive, warmhearted, and enjoyed helping people he liked; however, he had no desire to save money," she replied.

"How often did you see your brother in jail?" I asked.

"Almost every day the first year, even though I was recuperating from my operation in November; later, at least three times a week. Someone tried to go every day."

The questioning, which was carefully planned, elicited the proper answers. It was really a script.

Eva told the court that Jack lost his spirit in jail. That he was a broken man. That the trial wore him down. That his personality changed as early as two weeks after the trial began. That he thought the Nazis were going to get him and his family. That he did not know what was real and what was not.

"Did he read any books in jail?"

"Yes, he was reading *Exodus*, by Leon Uris," she said, thereby establishing where Jack got the notion of the mass murder of the Jews. "He heard the screams of the people in the mental wing of the jail at night and thought those were Jews being exterminated. You couldn't reason with him. All the time he was in jail, he would call me to find out if Earl or Eileen were still alive. He passed incoherent notes to members of the family."

"What is your present status?" I asked.

"I am unemployed. I have been unable to find employment in Dallas since Jack shot Oswald. I wonder if this is an American city sometimes, where you can't get a job. I'm bitter about Dallas."

She added that Earl had been "adjusted in his mind" better than the rest of the family, so the family was letting him handle all the affairs.

She said that in 1964 Jack had told her he wanted his gun to be sent to the Archives in Washington.

"When did you first notice your brother's physical illness, as opposed to his mental condition?" I asked. I wanted Eva to fill in the unanswered questions in Hooten's testimony.

"As early as June, and particularly in August," she replied. "By September he was throwing up every day."

"When was the last time Jack indicated to you that the Jews were being systematically slaughtered?"

Eva responded that he had mentioned it the day before he died. He was then at Parkland Hospital near Love Field, where he said he could hear the planes bringing the Jews to be slaughtered in Dallas; he said he heard the trains, too. He claimed they made a special whistle as they passed Dealey Plaza on their way to the Dallas gas chambers.

"He had his nurse call to see if everyone was all right and to say good-bye for him." Eva began to cry. "He put his lips up to the glass in the visitor's room at the jail and said he would never see me again."

The questions ended, and no cross-examination was attempted. Eva stepped down, still crying.

Next, Earl took the stand. With his slow, deliberate answers he testified that I had prepared a will for Jack, with instructions that it have three witnesses sign in Jack's presence. He said he could not get people into Jack's room because of the guards. Yes, Jack read the document and declared it was his will.

Then I led Earl through his family history. He testified that even as a boy, no one got into more fights than Jack, that Jack would fight anyone who insulted Jews or his family. He described the tremendous admiration for Kennedy and Roosevelt that Jack had, and Jack's feeling that those two presidents were great friends of the Jewish people.

All of this information was completely irrelevant to the case, but no one objected; they all wanted to hear it.

Earl continued with how he came in contact with an author to write Jack's story, and how he met Belli through him. He narrated what happened during and after the trial, and how he, too, had noticed the change in his brother.

Again there was no cross-examination, and Earl left the stand. We all knew Judge Robertson was going to reject the Hooten will and accept Mayer's will for probate. He did.

Our next step was to challenge Mayer to relinquish his role as independent executor in the federal courts. We felt we had a contract with him, and counted on his honoring it. Unfortunately that hope was soon proved false. Our withdrawal of Jack's 1967 will was already a matter of record, and Mayer refused to budge.

*(left)* Young Jack Rubenstein in 1936, beside the Russian River in San Francisco.

*(below)* In the early 1940s: Jack with his younger sister Eileen, on the left, and one of their cousins.

Jack Ruby (front row, second from left) with his Army Air Force unit, the 300th AAF BU.

Jack, still in uniform, was always on the lookout for a chance to have a good time and to share the spotlight with someone important. *(above)* Jack, right, and his younger brother Earl, center, with a friend and the Condos Brothers, who had a popular '40s tap-dancing act. *(below)* In 1944, Jack being chummy with Barney Ross, the champion boxer, at Ye Olde Tavern in Chicago. The group also includes actor Sonny Tufts, third from right.

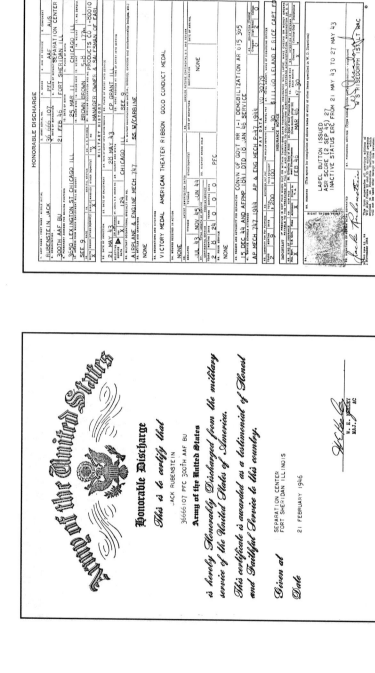

Jack Ruby's separation papers, recording his honorable discharge from the U.S. Army on February 21, 1946, after 2 years, 8 months, and 24 days of service. He returned immediately to Chicago and went into business with his brothers Earl and Sam.

**The State of Texas,** } **Know All Men by These Presents:**

**County of** DALLAS

That I, MRS. EVA M. GRANT, a widow

of the County of Dallas and State aforesaid, for and in consideration of the

sum of ----TEN ($10.00) ------------------------------------ DOLLARS,
cash and other valuable consideration

to me in hand paid by JACK L. RUBY

the receipt for which is hereby acknowledged, have BARGAINED, SOLD and DELIVERED, and by

these presents do BARGAIN, SELL and DELIVER unto the said

JACK L. RUBY

and State of TEXAS

of the County of DALLAS County, Texas, to-wit:

the following described personal property in now known as the
subject to

All equipment, supplies, etc
SILVER SPUR CLUB, located at
the liens of record.

And I do

and assigns, to f

ors

part

and assigns, against every perso...
thereof.

WITNESS my hand at Dallas Texas, this day of Decembe. J. 19 47.

*Mrs Eva M. Grant*

Witnesses:

After leaving his brothers' novelty company in Chicago, Jack moved to Dallas, the city he would love and be linked with in history books. He took over management of his sister's downtown supper club, renamed it the Silver Spur, and bought it from her in 1947 "for the sum of TEN ($10.00)." With its country-and-western theme, the club was a popular Dallas night spot, and attracted big names such as Hank Thompson *(left)* and Tennesee Ernie Ford *(right)*, here with Jack in 1952 *(inset)*.

THE STATE OF TEXAS
COUNTY OF DALLAS

WHEREAS, JACK RUBY, hereinafter styled MANAGER,
and BEN ESTES NELSON, a Minor, by and through his lawfully
appointed Guardian, COLUMBUS L. NELSON, hereinafter referred
to as ENTERTAINER, desires to enter into Business Manager
Contract; and

WHEREAS the said Ben Estes Nelson, a Minor, has
become well known in the Dallas Area under the name of "Little
Daddy", as a singer and performer, and probably can earn large
sums of money if properly managed and promoted; and

WHEREAS the said Jack Ruby is experienced in the
entertainment business and is fully capable of managing and promoting the said Ben Estes Nelson;

NOW, THEREFORE, the parties hereto agree

1.

The said Jack Ruby, hereinafter called Man
in consideration of the services to be performed by th
Estes Nelson, hereinafter called Entertainer, and in c
the mutual covenants hereinafter contained, does agre

(a) To do and perform any and all acts ne
representation of said Entertainer, to promote him i
theater, clubs, on radio and television, and in publi
contests and personal appearance schemes wherever
ment of said Manager such appearance will inure to
financial benefit of Entertainer.

(b) To use the best of his ability to se
the best possible contracts and/or agreements for

It is agreed between the parties that th
Manager shall be final in all matters with referen
said Manager may make such contracts for Enter
fit and as his judgment may dictate.

We, the undersigned, agree to each and every provision
of the above Contract, and to such Agreement we hereby bind ourselves, our heirs, executors and administrators, forever.

EXECUTED in triplicate, this 18th day of March, 1952.

_____
Jack Ruby
MANAGER

BEN ESTES NELSON, A Minor

BY: _____
Columbus L. Nelson, Guardian
ENTERTAINER

Jack thought he had a gold mine in 1952 when he discovered "Little Daddy," a young Dallas singer and dancer. Jack took the boy to Chicago and then New York, trying to get him into the big time. The attempt failed. In the flurry of stories on Jack after the shooting, some reports claimed that he had kidnapped the child. On the contrary, Jack had a contract with the boy's parents, and acted legally as his manager.

Aug 13-53

Dear Bro Jack;

Enclosed is check for $1250.00.

I hope you know what your doing or keep in mind that it will mean plenty of hard work to watch this place and the theatre and the Silver Spur.

If this place doesn't go, any excuse you give me will not go - or if it doesn't go, don't expect anymore money. Its up to you to see that it pays out.

For the time being I think 50% of this deal is enough and also you will have the other fellow to help you. Before I'd even consider sending anymore money, I want to see how it works out. 50% of this deal should be enough, especially since you told me what a terrific money maker it can be.

Good Luck
Earl

over

I had to make check to Chas. Bry as we can't loan you money anymore experience

A letter from Earl Ruby, accompanying a check in loan for purchase of the Vegas Club, which Jack bought into in 1953. Earl warns Jack about the work involved in running another club in addition to the ones he already has; the year before, Jack had retreated from the nightclub business because the pressure was too much for him. Over the years it was Earl Ruby—not the Mafia—that kept Jack supplied with funds to run the clubs. Earl's statement: "All the money he got for the clubs was either mine or Ralph Paul's."

MARTIN Stationery Co., Dallas

D-600  INSTALLMENT NOTE

$ 3,500.00                          Dallas          , Texas,          February 25,    A. D. 19 58

For Value Received   Min-I-Ron Co., Inc.                                                    promise to
pay to    Jack Ruby   Trustee for Earl R. Ruby                                    or order,
the sum of   Three thousand five hundred and no/100 ($3500.00)- - - - - - - - - - - DOLLARS,
with interest from date at the rate of       eight (8)        per cent per annum, both principal and interest payable at
     Dallas, Texas                              XXXXXXXXXXX
This note is payable in    one year from date.

        All past due principal and interest on this note shall bear interest at the rate of    10%    per cent. per annum.
     It is understood and agreed that the failure to pay this note, or any installment as above promised, or any interest hereon,
when due, shall, at the option of the holder of said note, mature the full amount of said note, and it shall at once become due
and payable.
        And it is hereby especially agreed that if this note is placed in the hands of an attorney for collection, or collected by suit,
or in probate or bankruptcy proceedings   Min-I-Ron              agree to pay ten per cent. additional on the principal and
interest then due thereon as attorney's fees.                            MIN- I - RON CO., INC.

Address                                                             By                       President
                                                                                          Secretary
Phone

$ 5,000.00                              March 9,                          19 60
                                                                    after date, for value received
     Upon demand                                          promise to pay to the order of
     The S & R Incorporated
     Earl Ruby                                                              Dollars
        Five thousand and no/100 ($5000.00)- - - - - - - - - - - -
                                              with    6%    per cent interest per annum
at    Dallas, Texas                          until paid. All past due principal and interest shall bear interest at
from    date                                 the rate of ... per cent per annum until paid. And in the event default is made in the payment
the rate of        per cent per annum until paid.  And in the event default is made in the payment of this note at maturity and it is placed
in the hands of an attorney for collection or suit is brought on the same or same is collected through Probate or Bankruptcy proceedings
     agree that an additional amount of ten per cent on the principal and interest of this note shall be added to the same as collection fees.

                                                        S & R INCORPORATED
Due                                                     By                    President
Address

PURCHASER'S RECEIPT                              537176
RETAIN FOR YOUR RECORDS

PURCHASED BY                        APRIL 13 1960
   EARL  RUBY
                                             2800.00
PAYABLE TO    JACK  RUBY ••••••••••••

                                    MEMORANDUM
RECEIPT FOR BANK MONEY ORDER DRAWN ON
                    TO                     FOR
      NATIONAL SECURITY BANK
        CHICAGO AND OGDEN AVENUES
          CHICAGO, ILLINOIS

Earl Ruby first learned the novelty business from his older brother Jack, but
Earl proved to be the better businessman, and provided financial support for
Jack's enterprises. Above are records of three such transactions. The second
is signed by Joe Slatin, Jack's first partner in the Sovereign Club. In addition,
Jack took out an almost continuous series of small bank loans. It is unlikely that
someone with the long-term, important mob connections that conspiracy
theorists claim for Jack would need these mundane sources of financing.

# TWIST WAIST
### EXERCISER

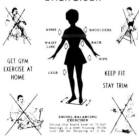

GET GYM
EXERCISE AT
HOME

ARMS ◇ SHOULDERS
WAIST ◇ BACK
LINE
◇ HIPS
LEGS ◇

KEEP FIT

STAY TRIM

SWIVEL BALANCING
EXERCISER
Strong chip board base on 10 ball
bearings in a steel housing. Holds
over 200 lbs. Shipping wt. 3 lbs.

**$3.95**

Compare this unit with the most expensive · For quality, price, results
and compactness

Why pay HUNDREDS $ for home equipment of health and salon when
TWIST gives the results plus fun to the entire family for
only pennies!

### EARL PRODUCTS CO.
P. O. BOX 5475        DALLAS, TEXAS

*(above)* His dogs were a love as well as a sideline business with Jack. He sold puppies to buyers across the country. The animals spent much of the time with Jack at his clubs, and he was usually accompanied by at least one of them when he went out. Sheba, on the left, was a favorite and was with him the morning of November 24, 1963. He left Sheba in the car when he parked and walked to the Western Union office. This is a strong argument against premeditation in Jack's shooting Oswald: he would never have left his beloved pet locked in a car if he expected to be gone more than a few minutes. *(left)* A flyer advertising the Twist board, one of the gadgets Jack promoted. He carried over the name "Earl Products, Co." from his brothers' manufacturing firm in Chicago.

Jack Ruby in the Dallas County Jail, with attorney Phil Burleson. Burleson was the only member of the Ruby defense team that took part in the case from the initial defense through the appeals and preparation for a new trial. The photographs were taken by Earl Ruby with a miniature camera.

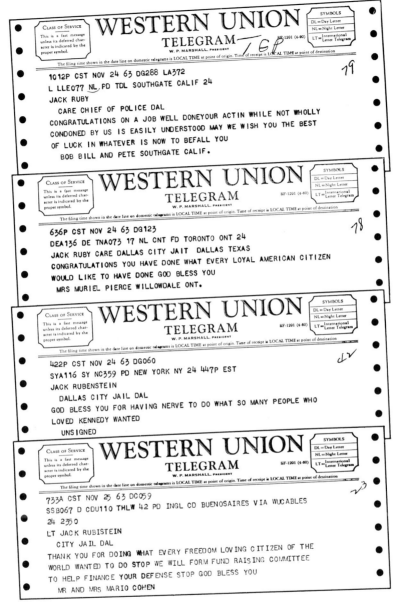

**WESTERN UNION TELEGRAM**
SF-1201 (4-60)
W. P. MARSHALL, PRESIDENT

79

1012P CST NOV 24 63 DG288 LA372
L LLE077 NL PD TDL SOUTHGATE CALIF 24
JACK RUBY
   CARE CHIEF OF POLICE DAL
CONGRATULATIONS ON A JOB WELL DONEYOUR ACTIN WHILE NOT WHOLLY
CONDONED BY US IS EASILY UNDERSTOOD MAY WE WISH YOU THE BEST
OF LUCK IN WHATEVER IS NOW TO BEFALL YOU
   BOB BILL AND PETE SOUTHGATE CALIF.

**WESTERN UNION TELEGRAM**
SF-1201 (4-60)
W. P. MARSHALL, PRESIDENT

78

636P CST NOV 24 63 DG123
DEA136 DE TNA073 17 NL CNT FD TORONTO ONT 24
JACK RUBY CARE DALLAS CITY JAIT DALLAS TEXAS
CONGRATULATIONS YOU HAVE DONE WHAT EVERY LOYAL AMERICAN CITIZEN
WOULD LIKE TO HAVE DONE GOD BLESS YOU
   MRS MURIEL PIERCE WILLOWDALE ONT.

**WESTERN UNION TELEGRAM**
SF-1201 (4-60)
W. P. MARSHALL, PRESIDENT

422P CST NOV 24 63 DG060
SYA116 SY NC359 PD NEW YORK NY 24 447P EST
JACK RUBENSTEIN
   DALLAS CITY JAIL DAL
GOD BLESS YOU FOR HAVING NERVE TO DO WHAT SO MANY PEOPLE WHO
LOVED KENNEDY WANTED
   UNSIGNED

**WESTERN UNION TELEGRAM**
SF-1201 (4-60)
W. P. MARSHALL, PRESIDENT

733A CST NOV 25 63 DC059
SSB067 D CDU110 THLW 42 PD INGL CD BUENOSAIRES VIA WUCABLES
24 2350
LT JACK RUBISTEIN
   CITY JAIL DAL
THANK YOU FOR DOING WHAT EVERY FREEDOM LOVING CITIZEN OF THE
WORLD WANTED TO DO STOP WE WILL FORM FUND RAISING COMMITTEE
TO HELP FINANCE YOUR DEFENSE STOP GOD BLESS YOU
   MR AND MRS MARIO COHEN

After the shooting, Jack received hundreds of letters and telegrams from all over the world. The overwhelming majority supported his action. Some wanted Jack proclaimed a national hero—a point of view Jack himself could not understand. Above and on the following pages are samples from over a hundred telegrams in the Ruby family's possession. Jack Ruby, who had always loved the limelight, was never out of its center from the moment he fired the shot into Oswald's stomach until his own death.

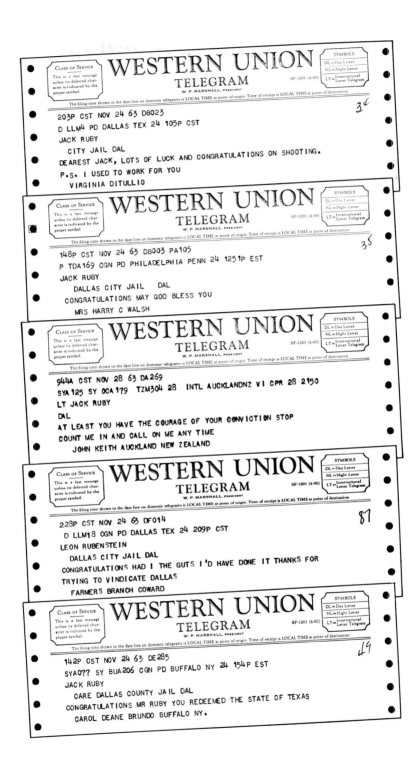

## WESTERN UNION TELEGRAM

W. P. MARSHALL, PRESIDENT SF-1201 (4-60)

The filing time shown in the date line on domestic telegrams is LOCAL TIME at point of origin. Time of receipt is LOCAL TIME at point of destination

34

203P CST NOV 24 63 DB023
D LLM4 PD DALLAS TEX 24 105P CST
JACK RUBY
    CITY JAIL DAL
DEAREST JACK, LOTS OF LUCK AND CONGRATULATIONS ON SHOOTING.
P.S. I USED TO WORK FOR YOU
    VIRGINIA DITULLIO

---

## WESTERN UNION TELEGRAM

35

148P CST NOV 24 63 DB003 PA105
P TDA169 CGN PD PHILADELPHIA PENN 24 1251P EST
JACK RUBY
    DALLAS CITY JAIL    DAL
CONGRATULATIONS MAY GOD BLESS YOU
    MRS HARRY C WALSH

---

## WESTERN UNION TELEGRAM

944A CST NOV 28 63 DA269
SYA125 SY OCA179  TZM304 28   INTL AUCKLANDNZ VI CPR 28 2150
LT JACK RUBY
DAL
AT LEAST YOU HAVE THE COURAGE OF YOUR CONVICTION STOP
COUNT ME IN AND CALL ON ME ANY TIME
    JOHN KEITH AUCKLAND NEW ZEALAND

---

## WESTERN UNION TELEGRAM

87

228P CST NOV 24 63 DF014
D LLM18 CGN PD DALLAS TEX 24 209P CST
LEON RUBENSTEIN
    DALLAS CITY JAIL DAL
CONGRATULATIONS HAD I THE GUTS I'D HAVE DONE IT THANKS FOR
TRYING TO VINDICATE DALLAS
    FARMERS BRANCH COWARD

---

## WESTERN UNION TELEGRAM

49

142P CST NOV 24 63 DE285
SYA077 SY BUA206 CGN PD BUFFALO NY 24 154P EST
JACK RUBY
    CARE DALLAS COUNTY JAIL DAL
CONGRATULATIONS MR RUBY YOU REDEEMED THE STATE OF TEXAS
    CAROL DEANE BRUNDO BUFFALO NY.

## WESTERN UNION
### TELEGRAM
Class of Service
This is a fast message unless its deferred character is indicated by the proper symbol.

SYMBOLS
DL=Day Letter
NL=Night Letter
LT=International Letter Telegram

SF-1201 (4-60)
W. P. MARSHALL, PRESIDENT

The filing time shown in the date line on domestic telegrams is LOCAL TIME at point of origin. Time of receipt is LOCAL TIME at point of destination

3C

243P CST NOV 24 63 DB075
SYA091 SY TOA023 PD COHOES NY 24 332P EST

JACK RUBY
    DALLAS TEXAS COUNTY JAIL DAL
CONGRATULATIONS THANK YOU
    ED KANE CITY MARSHALL CITY OF COHOES NY

---

## WESTERN UNION
### TELEGRAM
Class of Service
This is a fast message unless its deferred character is indicated by the proper symbol.

SYMBOLS
DL=Day Letter
NL=Night Letter
LT=International Letter Telegram

SF-1201 (4-60)
W. P. MARSHALL, PRESIDENT

The filing time shown in the date line on domestic telegrams is LOCAL TIME at point of origin. Time of receipt is LOCAL TIME at point of destination

90

225P CST NOV 24 63 DF008 0A163
0 LBA093 PD LONG BEACH CALIF 24 1145A PST

JACK RUBY
    DALLAS POLICE DEPT DAL
TO A JOB WELL DONE I KNOW THERE MUST BE MANY PEOPLE WHO FEEL
THE SAME AS I DO YOU ARE A GREAT MAN JACK RUBY
    BILL OWENS.

---

## WESTERN UNION
### TELEGRAM
Class of Service
This is a fast message unless its deferred character is indicated by the proper symbol.

SYMBOLS
DL=Day Letter
NL=Night Letter
LT=International Letter Telegram

TGP

SF-1201 (4-60)
W. P. MARSHALL, PRESIDENT

The filing time shown in the date line on domestic telegrams is LOCAL TIME at point of origin. Time of receipt is LOCAL TIME at point of destination

71

504P CST NOV 24 63 DC401 PA173
P TNA307 PD TDTN MARLTON NJER 24 305P EST

JACK RUBENSTEIN, CARE POLICE CHIEF JESSIE CURRY DAL
OUR FAMILY CANNOT FIND IT IN OUR HEARTS TO CENSOR YOU. WE SEND
YOU ALL OUR LOVE AND SUPPORT
    JEAN SCATTERGOOD

---

## WESTERN UNION
### TELEGRAM
Class of Service
This is a fast message unless its deferred character is indicated by the proper symbol.

SYMBOLS
DL=Day Letter
NL=Night Letter
LT=International Letter Telegram

SF-1201 (4-60)
W. P. MARSHALL, PRESIDENT

The filing time shown in the date line on domestic telegrams is LOCAL TIME at point of origin. Time of receipt is LOCAL TIME at point of destination

100

329P CST NOV 24 63 DC355
DEA109 DE RNA035 CRA080 MOA029 7 RX CPT FD EDMONTON ALTA 24
205PMST

MR JACK RUBIN
CITY POLICE JAIL DAL
HEARTIEST CONGRATULATIONS BUT HE DIED TOO FAST
JOE GUIDERE.

---

## WESTERN UNION
### TELEGRAM
Class of Service
This is a fast message unless its deferred character is indicated by the proper symbol.

SYMBOLS
DL=Day Letter
NL=Night Letter
LT=International Letter Telegram

SF-1201 (1-60)
W. P. MARSHALL, PRESIDENT

The filing time shown in the date line on domestic telegrams is LOCAL TIME at point of origin. Time of receipt is LOCAL TIME at point of destination

50

235P CST NOV 24 63 DG003
AA138 A JNA266 PD JACKSONVILLE FLO 24 300P EST

JACK RUBY, CARE DALLAS POLICE HEADQUARTERS
    DAL
THANK YOU. MAY THE LORD AND TEXAS JUSTICE HAVE MERCY ON YOU.
MAY YOU LIVE TO BE A THOUSAND SINCERELY YOURS
    A D PEEPLES

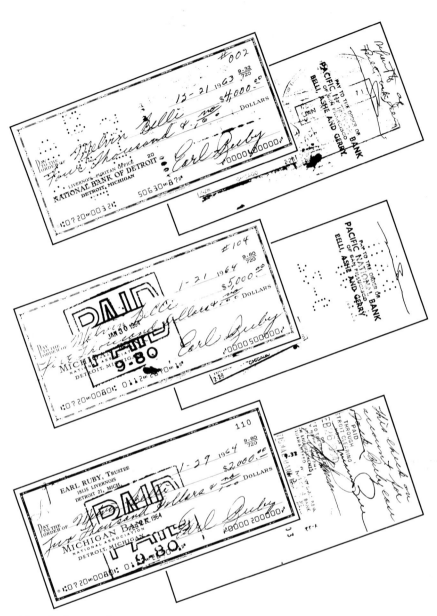

After the jury reached a verdict of guilty and a sentence of death, Melvin Belli was immediately dismissed from the case. For several years afterward, the famous lawyer insisted publicly that he had received no fee for defending Jack Ruby. Not only did he apparently have plans to profit from a book and a movie about Jack's trial, but he did receive substantial cash payments from the Ruby family. The checks above were written by Earl Ruby to Melvin Belli, and bear Belli's endorsement. Belli was not paid for his brief for appeal in Jack's case, which he filed on his own after the family had fired him.

12/26/66

Dear Bro Earl,

I am sitting in a chair at this moment, which makes it possable for me to write to you.

Send my love to Margie, Joyce, Danice and Robbie.

You will never know how much I am forever grateful for what you what you have done for me. I know you have neglected your business, your family, your ~~own~~ own health and mentioning the money you have spent.

Forever my love to you and family.

Your loving bro. Jack.

From the family's private mementos of their brother comes this letter, written by Jack Ruby to his brother a few days before Jack's death. Undergoing treatment for a widespread, metastasized cancer, he wrote the letter from Parkland Hospital, where he was under constant guard. The envelope post-marked Dallas, December 28, 1966, was sent to Earl's business address at Cobo Cleaners in Detroit. Jack died on January 3, 1967. His illness had gone undiagnosed for over a year while he was in police custody awaiting a new trial.

Monday morning, January 9, 1967. Jack Ruby's funeral in Chicago. The small group attending included the author, Alan Adelson, second from the right.

*(above)* The author, Alan Adelson, with Eva Grant, Jack Ruby's older sister. The photo was taken soon after the Detroit attorney began to represent the Ruby family in the matter of their brother's estate. *(below)* Eva Grant on the ramp leading down into the Dallas police headquarters parking garage, where Jack Ruby shot Lee Harvey Oswald. Photo taken almost twenty years after the author's first involvement in the case, on a research trip in preparation for writing *The Ruby-Oswald Affair.*

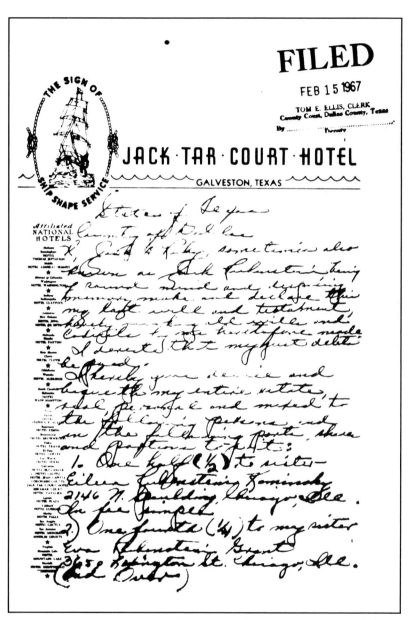

The will written by Jack Ruby in 1950, naming Dallas attorney Jules Mayer as excutor of Jack's estate. Mayer discovered the will in his files after Jack's death, filed it then, and pursued his claims in court, successfully resisting the Ruby family's attempts to regain administration of Jack's meager belongings and donate them to the National Archives.

3. To my sister Eileen Rubenstein Kaminsky, as trustee, in trust for the use and benefit of my nephew Ronald Magid (who) lives with his mother and my family in Chicago, Ill., Said Trustee is to use her own discretion and judgement in advancing, allowing and paying out from the body and principal of this trust estate to and for the maintenance, support, use benefit, education and the furtherance of the best interests and welfare of my said nephew Ronald Magid until he reaches the age of twenty-two (22) years. This trust shall end when Ronald attains his 22nd birthday at which time the trustee shall turn over and pay to Ronald the entire trust estate and all things pertaining thereto.

I hereby nominate and appoint my friend and attorney John F. Meyer, Dallas, Texas to be the sole independent executor of this my last will and estate and I direct that

Page (3)

that no bond be required
of him in such capacity and
that no other action be taken
in the county court then the
filing of this will for
probate and recording and
the listing of all claims due
to and owing by my estate.

Wherefore I Jack L. Ruby
of Dallas Texas as testator
do at Galveston Texas
signed and subscribed my
name below this 24th day
of August, 1950.

Jack L. Ruby
1717 S. Ervay.
Dallas, Texas

# 27

Trying to understand the Oswald side of the assassination became a major undertaking. Although I knew that Jack was not involved in a conspiracy, I had no idea what motivated Oswald. I started with the premise that if the Warren Commission were correct about Jack's role, it probably was correct about Oswald's role, too. My second premise was that every crime has an underlying psychological reason.

Violence rarely occurs without motivation. The perpetrator, whether mentally incompetent or not, always strives for a goal, even though the goal itself may be part of the perpetrator's illness. The goal might be the desire or need for money, thwarted love, revenge, or self defense. Violence is sometimes motivated by political or religious beliefs. The perpetrator always feels justified by his reasoning. It may be more difficult to find the psychotic's logical link between motive and action than it is to define the motive.

The Warren Report was supposed to end all speculation about the facts surrounding the assassination. It did not. Theories continue to multiply, originating from serious historians as well as from amateur sleuths who seem obsessed with finding proof of a conspiracy. Some of these "assassination buffs" are very well organized; one group even issues a regular newsletter. These enthusiasts, while hunting for the needle in the haystack, find irrelevant information, and build it into a conspiracy. In Jim Garrison we have examined one man who seemed compelled to pursue the notion of conspiracy. Some of the others who have not written books were show business personalities Mort Sahl, Dick Gregory, and Les Craine.

I happened to be with Gregory when he made a personal appearance in Detroit. We were driving into town from the airport when he remarked that the freeways had all been built for the eventual revolution. He connected this idea to the Kennedy assassination, saying it had been the first wave of the revolution.

The "buffs" have advanced many theories in books; most of them are contrary to the Warren Report. Generally, the lines of argument are not well thought out, but the books are packed with self-serving footnotes that lend an aura of authority. *Rush to Judgment* does not stand alone; it is one of a growing genre.

I started my investigation of Oswald's history-making act of violence by examining his biography.

Lee Harvey Oswald was born in New Orleans on October 18, 1939, the third son of Marguerite Oswald. His older brothers were his half-brother Edward John Pic, from Marguerite's first marriage, and Robert Oswald, his full brother. Lee's father died two months before he was born, forcing Marguerite to find work. She placed the two older children in an orphanage. It eventually became too difficult for her to maintain even one child at home; Lee, too, was placed in the orphanage. He rejoined the family at age four when Marguerite moved to Dallas.

In Dallas, Marguerite met and married Edwin A. Ekdahl, and the family was again united until the marriage ended in divorce in 1948. This time she convinced her oldest son to quit school and go to work to assist the family financially. Because economic conditions were poor, the boy was unable to find suitable work; consequently, he joined the Marine Corps. John Pic commented: "Lee was brought up in this atmosphere of constant money problems, and I am sure it had quite an effect on him, and also Robert."

Robert followed John into the Marines in 1952, leaving

only Lee and his mother. John was living in New York City with his new wife, and arrangements were made for Marguerite and Lee to move in with them. This plan was short-lived. Lee allegedly pulled a pocketknife on his sister-in-law during an argument. Marguerite and her youngest son moved into their own apartment in the Bronx.

That September Lee enrolled in the public school system. He quickly established a truancy record—serious enough to get him remanded to the Youth House, a public hospital for incorrigibles. He remained there for evaluation from April 16 to May 7, 1953. His examining psychiatrist at the Youth House stated, after the assassination, that he would not have considered Lee a potential assassin. While at the Youth House, Lee scored 118 on an IQ test, placing him in the upper range of bright-normal intelligence.

Lee first became interested in Marxism at the age of fifteen, when an old woman handed him a pamphlet about saving the lives of Julius and Ethel Rosenberg. On October 3, 1956, he wrote to the Young People's Socialist League. "I am a Marxist and have been studying socialistic principles for well over fifteen months."

Lee quit high school at sixteen, after writing a note in his mother's name stating that he was moving to San Diego. The experiences his brothers shared with him about the Marines gave Oswald the impression that, compared to his life of financial hardship and chaos, life in the Marines would be a utopian experience. He decided to follow in his brothers' footsteps and joined the Marine Corps. His mother helped him falsify his age so that he could enlist. It would not be the last time Lee Harvey Oswald would be involved in falsifying documents.

In the service, Oswald received extensive training in aircraft surveillance. He had difficulty relating to people, and showed his dissatisfaction with the world about him. The Marine Corps was not what he expected.

Oswald considered himself a man of great intelligence and felt that many of the officers were not competent to give him orders. To prove his position, he would bait his seniors into discussions of topics in which he was more proficient. When the superior officer showed less knowledge, or was unable to discuss the subject to Oswald's satisfaction, Oswald would judge him unfit and deliberately embarrass him.

After his training in the United States, he was promoted to private first class. On August 21, 1957, he was assigned to an air control squadron at Atsugi, Japan.

Atsugi, built by the Japanese during World War II as a training base for their kamikaze pilots, was then the base for the closely-guarded, secret U-2 reconnaissance planes. In order to work on the base, Oswald was given a low-level security clearance. The hangers in which the planes were stored were heavily guarded.

There was evidence that, while he was stationed in Japan, Oswald did make contact with Russian agents, whose movements were less restricted there than they would be in the United States. Neither the Warren Commission nor the House Select Committee chose to pursue this line of investigation.

Oswald's dissatisfaction with the Marine Corps continued to grow. Secretly he began making plans to defect to the Soviet Union. He felt, however, that he had to get out of the Marines first.

Apparently, he thought he had found a way out when he wounded himself one night with a small-caliber pistol. Paul E. Murphy, who served with Oswald at Atsugi, stated, "One night in the barracks in Japan, I heard a shot in the adjoining cubicle. I rushed to the cubicle to find Oswald sitting on his footlocker looking at a wound in his arm. When I asked what had happened, he very unemotionally replied, 'I believe I shot myself.'"

Possession of a small-caliber pistol is a court-martial offense and Oswald did not want to be court-martialed. He told the physician at the naval hospital at Yokosuka that he injured himself when he dropped a .45 caliber pistol. If Oswald had shot himself with a .45 caliber pistol, he might have taken off his arm.

The injury did not qualify Oswald for a medical discharge. He merely had a short stay in the hospital. Soon afterwards, he went with his unit to the Subic Bay Airfield in the Philippines. Subic Bay was another U-2 base.

In the Philippines, a Pvt. Martin E. Schrand, who had trained with Oswald, was shot to death while on guard duty. Schrand was guarding one of the hangers that housed the U-2 plane. The official cause of death was a gunshot wound caused by a bullet entering under the right arm and exiting through the left side of the neck. While on guard, the Marines there were issued a rifle and three shells, with a positive injunction not to place a shell in the chamber unless they intended to use it. An accidental shooting was virtually impossible.

Rumors circulated on the base that Lee Harvey Oswald had somehow been responsible for the death of Martin Schrand. Those who accepted the rumor as truth have speculated that Oswald wanted a close-up view of the U-2.

When Oswald and his unit returned to Japan, he was court-martialed for the unlawful possession of a pistol and sentenced to twenty days hard labor. Within six months he was again court-martialed, this time for a petty offense: being abusive to a superior officer while off duty. Oswald's reputation for baiting superior officers probably contributed to his being charged for such a minor infraction.

In November 1958, Oswald's squadron returned to the United States. After a brief furlough, he was assigned to El Toro Air Base in California. Here he obtained a Russian-language text book and subscribed to Russian-language newspapers.

He applied to and was accepted by the Albert Schweitzer College in Switzerland for the spring term of 1960. This, according to his brother Robert, was part of his overall plan. Robert believed he had no intention of attending that school, but thought acceptance there would give him a legitimate excuse for going to Europe.

With only four months left in his enlistment, Oswald was removed from radar work and placed on janitorial duties because of his attitude. About that time, his mother injured herself at work, giving him an excuse to leave the service. His application for immediate hardship discharge stated that he was his mother's sole means of support. Believing her son wanted to be at home with her, Marguerite assisted Oswald by sending letters from her doctor and friends. She also submitted an affidavit attesting to the facts in her son's application. On September 3, Oswald began the process of separation from the Marines. He also applied for a passport.

After signing a pledge that he would not divulge any information gained while in the service that would affect national defense, he was released. He returned to Fort Worth where his mother was living, but he stayed only three days. Then Oswald left for Moscow.

# 28

Oswald departed on the freighter *SS Marion Kykes* for Le Havre, a French seaport on the English Channel. He arrived on October 8 and within a few days crossed the channel to England. From England he flew to Helsinki. There he applied for entrance to the Soviet Union. On October 15 he arrived in Moscow on a six-day visa.

  •     While he was in Russia, Oswald kept a diary, and that diary, coupled with statements made later by his wife and Americans whom he encountered in Russia, provide a fairly detailed account of his stay in the Soviet Union.

In Russia, a foreign visitor is supplied with an Intourist guide. Ostensibly the guide helps the visitor to see the sights and find points of interest. Most visitors, however, feel their guides are Russia's way of maintaining a close watch on foreigners within its borders, and for insuring security in restricted areas.

Oswald immediately declared to his guide that he wanted to renounce his U.S. citizenship and become a citizen of the Soviet Union. This was the day before his twentieth birthday. Ironically, the guide gave Oswald a copy of Dostoyevski's *The Idiot* for a birthday present.

On the morning of October 21, the day that his visa was to expire, Oswald had an appointment with a police officer regarding his request for Soviet citizenship. The official, described as balding and stout, wore a black suit and spoke fairly good English.

"What do you want?" the official asked.

"Soviet citizenship," Oswald answered.

"USSR only good in literature. Go back home," was the response.

When Oswald persisted, the official informed him that he would see if his visa could be extended.

At 6 P.M. Oswald received word that he must leave the country by 8 o'clock that evening. Being able to live in Russia had become a utopian dream to Oswald. He wrote [The quotations from Oswald's writing reflect his own spelling and syntax.]:

> I am shocked!! My dreams! I retire to room. I have $100.00 left. I have waited for two years to be accepted. My fondest dreams are shattered because of a petty official; because of bad planning. I planned too much! 7:00 PM I decide to end it. Soak wrist in cold water to numb the pain. Then slash my left wrist. Then plang wrist into bathtub of hot water.

Because Oswald knew his guide would be there almost immediately to take him to the airport, the sincerity of the suicide attempt is questionable. The guide did come, and Oswald was rushed to the hospital. The next day he was well enough to complain about the hospital food.

Oswald was released from the hospital on October 28. He was again interviewed, this time by four officials, including the first one.

"How is your arm?" an official asked.

"Okay," Oswald responded.

"Do you want to go to your homeland?" another asked.

"No, I want to be a Soviet citizen. I want to reside in the Soviet Union," Oswald replied.

"What papers do you have to show who and what you are?" an official asked.

At this point Oswald probably told the officials that he was a former Marine who had information about the U-2 planes. He showed them his discharge papers from the Marine Corps.

"Wait for our answer," an official responded.

"How long?" Oswald asked.

"Not soon," was the reply.

Oswald spent the next three days in his hotel room. He felt the three days were like three years. He remained fully dressed and ate only once during that period. Finally, on October 31, after his guide had left for the day, he hailed a taxi and went to the American Embassy.

He walked up to the receptionist. "I want to see the consul," he demanded.

She pointed to a ledger and replied, "If you are a tourist, please register." Oswald took out his passport as the receptionist directed him to the office of Richard Snyder.

Snyder was typing a letter when Oswald arrived. When he finished his task, he looked at Oswald and invited him to sit down.

"I have decided to take Soviet citizenship and would like to legally dissolve my U.S. citizenship."

Snyder's chief assistant looked up from his work.

Snyder asked Oswald several questions and warned him to be cautious. "Do not take any steps before the Soviets accept you. You are a fool," he continued. "It takes a long time for the paperwork."

"My mind is made up," Oswald retorted. "From this day forward I consider myself no longer a citizen of the U.S.A." Oswald presented Snyder with his passport and left.

Although Oswald does not mention it in his diary, Richard Snyder remembered the conversation quite well. "His attitude was arrogant and aggressive." Snyder recalled. "He stated that he had recently been discharged from the Marine Corps. He also volunteered the information that he had offered the Soviet authorities any information which he had acquired as an enlisted radar operator in the Marines."

Oswald returned to his hotel room certain that this "showdown" would allow him to remain in the Soviet Union. What Oswald did not know was that surrendering his passport to Snyder did not automatically cancel his U.S. citizenship.

Two reporters in Moscow attempted to interview Oswald that day. Neither succeeded. On November 15, having heard nothing yet from the Soviet government, Oswald called one of the reporters. In an interview Oswald announced that he had defected to Russia.

The next day an official visited his hotel room and informed him that he could stay in Russia until the question of his status was resolved. Oswald remained in Moscow until January 4, 1960, when he was given a resident document that would expire in one year. He had not been granted the Russian citizenship he had requested. He was assigned to work in a radio factory in Minsk.

In Minsk Oswald was given an apartment with a view of the river from two balconies. At the radio factory Oswald was befriended by the head of his department, Alexander Zeger, a Polish-born Jew who had emigrated to Argentina in 1938, and back to the USSR in 1955. They were able to converse in English. Until May 1, Oswald neglected his diary. He spent May Day, the national holiday, with the Zeger family at their home.

Dawn, May 1, 1960. Peshawar, Pakistan. Francis Gary Powers, age thirty, was piloting a Utopia Number Two (U-2) reconnaissance jet fourteen miles above the surface of the earth. His mission was to fly high across the Soviet Union, photographing strategic installations, including a Russian ICBM Base. He knew his job and how to achieve his mission. He did not know that a former Marine radar specialist had defected to the Soviet Union, one with specialized knowledge of the U-2. He did not know that former Marine had promised to tell the Soviets all he knew about the systems Powers trusted with his mission and his life.

The Soviets managed to guide a missile to an altitude of 70,000 feet, detonate it on target, and avoid all the radar-jamming devices carried by the U-2. Before the defection of Lee Harvey Oswald, they had been unable to do this. Some coincidences are strong enough to cause serious speculation.

Over the flat farmlands of Sverdlovsk, the U-2 Francis Gary Powers flew was shot down. He became the first U.S. spy pilot to be apprehended within the Soviet Union.

Ironically, if Oswald was instrumental in the Soviets' bringing down the U-2 plane, he was also the major cause of John F. Kennedy's election as president of the United States. The U-2 incident, as it became known, caused the Soviets to break off the summit meeting during which President Eisenhower and Premier Khrushchev were to deal with the Berlin Crisis.

In his memoirs, Khrushchev states his conviction that the U-2 incident helped Kennedy win the White House:

> Not long before the events in Berlin came to a head, I had met Kennedy in Vienna. He impressed me as a better statesman than Eisenhower. Unlike Eisenhower, Kennedy had a precisely formulated opinion on every subject. I joked with him that we had cast the deciding ballot in his election to the presidency over that son of a bitch Richard Nixon. When he asked me what I meant, I explained that by waiting to release the U-2 pilot, Gary Powers, until after the American election, we kept Nixon from being able to claim that he could deal with the Russians; our play made a difference of at least half a million votes, which gave Kennedy the edge he needed.

Eisenhower's initial denial that he knew of the U-2 flight also helped Kennedy in his campaign for the presidency.

Oswald wrote in his diary during the summer and fall of

1960 that he was beginning to understand the society he had chosen to live in. Mass gymnastics, compulsory after-work meetings, required attendance at lectures, and the sending of the entire shop collective to pick potatoes on a Sunday at a state collective farm—Oswald soon became weary of these "patriotic duties." He started to complain about his new "homeland."

He wrote that he dreaded the coming Russian winter. He also revealed several affairs he had. In an entry dated January 1, 1961, he admitted he had fallen in love. His proposal for marriage was refused because he was an American. A second utopia began to crash.

On January 4, 1961, Oswald was finally offered Soviet citizenship but turned it down. Instead, he asked for and received a one-year extension of his residence permit. He wrote that he was reconsidering his desire to stay in Russia. "The work is drab, there is nowhere to spend the money I earn, no night clubs or bowling alleys, no places of recreation except the trade union dances; I have had enough."

On February 1, 1961, twelve days after Kennedy was inaugurated as President, Oswald wrote to the American Embassy in Moscow of his desire to return to the United States, "that is if we could come to some agreement concerning the dropping of any legal proceedings against me."

Technically, he had done nothing wrong. Defecting is not a crime in the strict sense. His citizenship remained American. Why was he concerned with legal proceedings? The only possible concern he might have had was his agreement with the Marine Corps not to divulge secret military information. He probably worried that the American authorities had made the connection between the downing of the U-2 and his gaining specialized knowledge about the plane during his time in the Marine Corps.

Snyder immediately replied to Oswald's letter, requesting him to appear at the consulate for a personal interview and to fill out the necessary papers. In the letter Snyder indicated that Oswald's inquiry about legal proceedings puzzled him. In a dispatch dated the same day, Snyder inquired of the State Department whether Oswald would be subject to any legal proceedings, and if so, whether he should tell him. In the dispatch Snyder stated that if it were clear that Oswald had committed no expatriating act, he would return Oswald's passport to him by mail. The reply from the State Department indicated merely that they had no way of knowing whether Oswald had committed any violation of federal law, so that no guarantees could be given. Snyder was instructed not to return the passport by mail.

Oswald confided his desire to return to the United States to his friend Zeger. The latter admonished him not to reveal this to any Russian.

March 12, 1961, Oswald responded to Snyder's letter. He stated that it would be difficult to appear in Moscow for an interview. "Can't it be done by mail?" he asked.

Snyder's reply insisted that Oswald come to Moscow.

On March 15, Oswald met Marina N. Prosaskoba at a trade union dance. Within a month Oswald proposed to Marina and she accepted. Because he was not as lonely as he had been, Oswald delayed his plans to return to the United States.

Two days later the *Pravda* and *Tass* newspapers revealed that rebel forces launched from the United States had attacked Cuba. Khrushchev—although he had already sent military aid—threatened direct military intervention.

On April 30, 1961, Oswald and Marina appeared at the marriage bureau, signed the registry, and received their marriage stamp. Oswald celebrated his second May Day, a married man.

Although Oswald's marriage had slowed the process, it did not change his desire to return to the United States. While critical of Kennedy's increasingly tough stand against a Marxist Cuba, he had come to feel about Russia as he had felt about the marines—thoroughly disillusioned. In mid-May he wrote his third letter to the Embassy. This time not only did he demand deportation without prosecution, but he also informed the authorities of his marriage and demanded that his wife return with him. He warned that if the embassy did not respond, he would see to it that his relatives in the United States would get "something done in Washington." According to his diary, however, he had not spoken to Marina about the move as yet.

By the end of June, Oswald finally decided to tell his wife of his plans to return to the United States, and requested that she accompany him. He explained that he had seen her country and wanted her to see his. Marina encouraged his efforts.

The first week in July, Oswald learned he was going to be a father. With this news he stepped up his efforts to obtain his passport and get permission for his wife to leave the Soviet Union. With his vacation due, he decided to go to Moscow to visit the American Embassy.

He seemed to be able to make the travel arrangements without difficulty, even though Mr. Snyder, in his testimony before the Warren Commission, indicated that he should have had trouble getting permission to travel. This lends credence to the theory that he received preferential treatment from the Soviets.

Oswald arrived in Moscow on July 8, 1961; because it was Saturday, the Embassy was closed. Marina followed him on Sunday. She, too, was able to travel freely.

On Monday Oswald and his wife appeared at the Embassy, where he was given a form to renew his passport. The passport originally issued to him was still valid until September 10. Oswald again spoke of the possibility that he would be facing criminal prosecution on his return to the States. Snyder assured him again that there were no grounds for such fears. This satisfied Oswald that he was not suspected in the U-2 incident.

On August 20, 1961, Oswald found out which documents were required to obtain an exit visa for Marina. He and Marina filled out twenty forms. When he filed the papers, he was advised that a response would take three and a half months. Marina was called before the Young Communist League, which attempted to dissuade her from going to the United States.

On October 18, 1961, Oswald's twenty-second birthday, Marina took her vacation and visited an aunt in the Ural Mountains. When she returned to Minsk two weeks later, she felt reluctant about going to the United States. Oswald attributed her change of heart to the strain of her pregnancy and the anticipation of another hard Russian winter.

Oswald's desire to return to the United States did not arise from a conclusion that the form of government in the United States is preferable to that in Russia. The United States, however, could provide him greater mobility in his search for a utopia—a state that would remain true to Oswald's interpretation of the principles of Marxism. Such a place would assure Oswald of a living without imposing on him a totalitarian government that robbed him of his right to own property and his freedom to travel.

Neither Russia or the United States was such a place. Oswald had even become disillusioned with the Communist party in the United States. In addition to his diary, Oswald wrote several essays of political commentary on Russia. In "New Era" he wrote the following:

> The communist party of the United States has betrayed itself! It has turned itself into a traditional lever of a foreign power to overthrow the government of the United States, not in the name of freedom or high ideals, but in servile conformity to the wishes of the Soviet Union and in anticipation of Soviet Russia's complete domiciliation of the american continent.

Oswald went on in this essay to denounce the Soviet form of communism. He predicted the final overthrow of the American government, but declared that no good would be accomplished by such a revolution. The United States would merely become a puppet of Soviet Russia. He continued:

> The right of private personal property, religious tolerance, and freedom of travel, which have all been violated under Russian communist rule, must be strictly observed.
>
> No man, having known, having lived, under the Russian communist and American capitalist system, could possibly make a choice between them. There is no choice; one offers oppression, the other poverty. Both offer imperialistic injustice, tinted with two brands of slavery.

If only Russia had held true to the principles of Lenin, Oswald might have found his utopia there. He was now forced to continue his search for a country that could fulfill his utopian ideals.

Oswald probably noted Castro's announcement on December 12, 1961, that he was a Marxist-Leninist and that he would lead Cuba in becoming a communist country.

Thirteen days later, on Christmas Day, Marina was called to the passport and visa office, where she was informed that her application had been granted. She would be allowed to leave the Soviet Union with her husband.

It seems unusual that Marina obtained permission to leave so easily. The policy of the Soviets toward allowing its citizens to immigrate to countries outside the communist block had always been *nyet*. Marina's education as a pharmacist required only a high school diploma, so her loss to the state was of minimum consequence, but such reasoning had had little effect on decisions made in the past. Was Russia granting one last request to someone who had found special favor in some way with the higher powers? Was there something to be gained in the future? Or was this the most convenient way to rid themselves of a person who would always be a potential source of embarrassment?

Marina's getting the official approval of the Soviet government to leave the country did not guarantee her entry into the United States. Oswald had to get permission from the American authorities before Marina could emigrate. True, she was married to an American citizen, but that American citizen had no means of support when he returned to the United States. The American consulate said that Oswald must produce some evidence that Marina would not become a public charge if she were allowed into the United States. They suggested that a relative sign an affidavit to that effect.

On February 15, 1962, June Lee Oswald was born, but her father was not able to see his daughter until Marina brought her home from the hospital eight days later. Russian hospital regulations forbade visitors in maternity wards. In announcing June's birth to his brother, Oswald noted in his letter that, in exchange for a Russian colonel, Francis Gary Powers had been released just five days before the birth of his daughter. Oswald claimed that he was at the Powers trial in Moscow. In the same letter he asked his brother to send all the newspaper clippings about his defection to Russia.

In the meantime the American consulate was in a quandary on how to handle Oswald's request to return to the United States. If the U.S. government refused to grant a visa for Marina and the newborn baby, it would appear to be punishing her for Oswald's attempt to renounce his U.S. citizenship. Failure to issue a visa to Marina would have allowed Russia to proclaim to the international press that they did everything possible to avoid separating the Oswald family, but were foiled by the United States. Such a move could have weakened other U.S. attempts to get permission for Soviet relatives of U.S. citizens to emigrate to the United States.

Oswald could not supply the necessary affidavit of support for Marina and the baby. Following typical government logic, the American consulate solved the problem as described in the following inter-office memo:

It appears that [Oswald] can find no one in the United States who is able and willing to execute an Affidavit of Support for his wife. Furthermore, Oswald has been able to obtain no concrete offer of employment in the United States. On the other hand, he is trained in a trade which should make him readily employable and he and his family will be able to live with his mother in Texas, until he has found work and becomes otherwise settled.

Taking into consideration the latter factors, Oswald's legal obligation to support his wife, and the unusual circumstances of the case, which make it difficult for Oswald to provide the usual financial evidence, the responsible consular officer is willing to accept Oswald's unsubstantiated affidavit as sufficient to overcome the public charge provisions of the law.

On May 16, 1962, Oswald sent a two-sentence note to his employer in Minsk: "I ask to be discharged from work starting May 18, 1962. I will be leaving." On May 23, the Oswalds left Minsk and travelled to Moscow, and on June 1 they left Russia.

# 29

The Oswalds traveled by rail to Rotterdam where they boarded the *Maasdam* bound for New York. Oswald spent most of his time aboard ship writing, still preoccupied with the fear that he would be arrested upon his arrival. Marina was left to tend the baby in her cabin.

In anticipation of his pending arrest, Oswald wrote two sets of questions and answers. One of the questions he posed to himself was whether or not he was a communist. He decided that he would answer yes, he was, although he hated the USSR and the socialist system. He would state that he believed Marxism could work under different circumstances.

On paper, he wondered why American communists, capitalists, and even fascists professed to be patriots, although their beliefs were contradictory. He felt there could be no mediation among them.

He compared the turn-of-the-century American Industrial Revolution to the Russian Revolution because they both answered the needs of the peoples involved. According to Oswald, both had possessed the potential to improve dramatically the lives of the common people, but both had failed. Oswald believed that industrialization brought about a deterioration of society, "a general decay, classes into shapeless societies without real cultural foundations." He speculated that the fight for the marketplace, which led to imperialism, finally resulted in the European Common Market.

He believed that Marx and Engles had made some basic mistakes. The biggest mistake was the concentration of power in Moscow, which made the existence of separate states almost meaningless. Oswald remembered all too well that the final decision on his own exit visa had had to come from Moscow.

Oswald made note in his writing of "fanatical" capitalist supporters in the United States called the "minute men." While Oswald had lived in Russia, the John Birch Society had gained international attention through the actions of some of its supporters. Edwin A. Walker, a U.S. major general stationed in West Germany, had been accused of indoctrinating his troops in John Birch Society dogma, and of proclaiming that former President Truman and former First Lady Eleanor Roosevelt were communist sympathizers. Bernard Weissman, who had placed the black-bordered advertisement in the *Dallas Morning News,* was a soldier in West Germany at that time. Walker was officially reprimanded for his actions and transferred to Hawaii. Oswald also noted that Russia had its counterpart in the existence of politically fanatical groups.

He ended his on-ship writings with comments about the monies he was given in Russia by the Red Cross. He believed they were actually payment from the KGB for his denunciation of the United States. He observed that when he became disgusted with Russian life and began negotiating with the American Embassy for his return, the money was cut off.

The Oswalds landed in New York City on June 13, 1962. They were not met by federal officials and reporters as he had feared, but by a representative of the Travelers' Aid Society. They were escorted to the special service welfare center when he announced he needed aid to travel to Texas. The welfare center called Oswald's brother, Robert, to see if he could assist financially. Robert protested so vehemently that the interviewer had to turn the matter over to the administrator of the center. In the end,

Robert put up the funds. The Oswalds landed at Love Field the next day and were met by Robert and his family.

Probably disappointed that he was not met by the media, Oswald asked Robert if he had been contacted by any reporters. Robert told him that his picture had appeared in the *Star Telegram* with the caption "Ex-Marine Reported on Way Back from Russia."

Oswald did not immediately look for work. He seemed more interested in his writing, perhaps believing that he might be able to make a living by publishing a book about his experiences in Russia. When he did decide he should become gainfully employed, he looked for a position as a Russian interpreter. He soon found out that such employment did not exist in the Dallas-Fort Worth area. He did make contact, however, with Peter Gregory, a teacher of Russian, in order to be certified proficient in Russian.

Oswald held the illusion that he was capable of finding a white-collar position. He was a high-school dropout, dishonorably discharged from the service because of his defection to Russia. His radar training did not qualify him for a management-level job, nor did his experience in the Minsk radio factory.

On June 26, 1962, Oswald finally met with FBI officials. An investigation of Oswald had been initiated by the FBI about the time Oswald started proceedings for his return to the United States. The investigation was prompted by Marguerite's attempt to send money to her son in Russia. Any time money is sent to a Soviet bloc country, the FBI investigates the transaction. Both Robert and Marguerite had been contacted and interviewed by an FBI agent. Marguerite explained that her son was in Russia as a secret agent of the American government, but he would be returning home soon. The agent asked Robert and Marguerite to inform him of Oswald's arrival. In a routine inquiry, the agent learned Oswald was home. He had Oswald come in for an interview on that same day.

Oswald appeared at the Fort Worth FBI office about 1:00 p.m. He appeared tense and agitated. Oswald was insolent and refused to answer some of the interviewer's questions. He stated that he did not care to relive the past. The sole reason for the interview, according to the agent, was to ascertain whether he had promised the Soviets anything for allowing him and his family to return to the U.S. Oswald was asked about his statement to Richard Snyder at the American Embassy in Moscow that he had offered to give the Soviets classified information gained while he was in the marines. He denied that he had ever made such a statement. The agent concluded that Oswald's behavior was affected by his recent return to the states, and decided to interview him again later.

Oswald kept in touch with the Texas State Employment Agency, looking for work. In mid-July he was informed of a position that required a little sheet metal experience. He applied for the job, and falsely claimed he had had sheet metal experience while in the service. He was given the job at the Leslie Welding Company, but it was not the kind of work he wanted.

At the time, Oswald was living in his mother's apartment in Fort Worth. By the time he received his second paycheck, he and his family had moved to a duplex on Mercedes Street, not far from Leslie Welding. Since he could not drive, he walked to work.

The move, however, was not a happy one. Robert Oswald relates that when he came to help his brother move, his mother was screaming and her eyes were red from crying. Marina looked bewildered. It seemed that none of the three boys wanted to live with their mother.

On August 16, 1962, FBI agents interviewed Oswald a second time. The agents claim that the interview took place in front of the Oswalds' duplex, but Marina testified later that the agents entered their duplex to interrogate her husband. This time Oswald appeared somewhat more cooperative and answered most of the agents' questions, except about why he went to Russia in the first place. When asked if he was a Soviet agent, he denied it, stating he knew of no reason why Russian agents would contact him in the United States. The agents felt that even though Oswald was arrogant, he was no threat. They temporarily closed his file after Oswald agreed to contact the FBI if any Russian agent approached him.

During Oswald's first months back in the United States, two events occupied the headlines in newspapers around the world. The Soviets constructed the Berlin Wall, and, when it came to a military showdown, President Kennedy backed off from his plans to demolish the wall with a convoy of bulldozers. The wall remained intact.

Closer to U.S. shores, the Soviets began to install medium-range missiles in Cuba. Kennedy responded by instituting a naval blockade of Cuba, and Khrushchev agreed to remove the missiles if Kennedy would guarantee that the U.S. would stay out of Cuban affairs. Kennedy pledged to a policy of noninterference, Khrushchev removed the missiles, and Cuba remained dedicated to communistic principles. Oswald most likely saw this compromise between Kennedy and Khruschev as a sign of weakness in both leaders, and he almost certainly resented the two superpowers' presumption in determining the destiny of Cuba.

Oswald was not ready, however, to align himself with the Cuban people. In fact, because of his stay in Russia and his marriage to Marina, he was to become a part of the Russian community in Texas.

# 30

George Alexandrovich Bouhe was born in St. Petersburg (now Leningrad) in 1904. Because he spoke English, he worked for the American Relief Commission while he was in high school. As a result of his association with Americans, he emigrated to the United States in 1924, and became involved in banking. In 1939 Bouhe moved to Dallas, where there were no other Russian-speaking persons. He worked as the personal accountant of a prominent Dallas geologist, Lewis W. MacNaughton.

In 1950, approximately fifty people emigrated from Russian-speaking countries to the Dallas-Fort Worth area. Since none of them spoke English, Bouhe took it upon himself to assist these emigrants. He organized a Greek Orthodox church, and helped them find jobs. By 1962, he was the uncontested leader of the Russian community in Dallas-Fort Worth.

Oswald had met one member of this community when he first returned to Fort Worth and explored becoming a Russian interpreter—Peter Gregory. When Oswald met Gregory, his son, Paul, was away at school. When Paul came home for the summer, his father mentioned Oswald's Russian wife. Since Paul was studying Russian, he contacted Marina for "lessons." The lessons consisted of conversations about life in Russia.

Near the end of the summer, Paul invited the Oswalds to dinner at his father's home. Also invited were George Bouhe and Anna Meller, another member of the Russian community. Bouhe brought with him some old maps of St. Petersburg and engaged

Marina in a discussion on what buildings were still standing and about Russia in general. The maps served as an excellent icebreaker for Marina and the other guests, and she thoroughly enjoyed herself. Oswald had mixed emotions about Marina's making new friends.

Until the dinner at Peter Gregory's house, Marina had remained a virtual prisoner in her own home. The English-Russian language barrier had made her afraid of going out at all. Oswald had wanted it that way, but after that evening Marina had people she could talk to.

The following week George Bouhe and Anna Meller visited the Oswalds' Mercedes Street home. They were shocked by the conditions under which the Oswalds were living. There was no food, Marina and the baby were poorly dressed, and the baby slept in a makeshift crib. They noticed that Marina needed dental work, so they arranged for her to meet Elene Hall, another member of their community, who was a dental technician. Elene Hall told them that Marina could get low-cost dental care at Baylor University Dental School.

The Oswalds became acquainted with more members of the Russian community. They met George and Jeanne De-Mohrenschildt and their daughter and son-in-law, Alexandra and Gary Taylor. All of these people began having a significant impact on the lives of the Oswald family. Several of their new acquaintances came once a week to the Oswald home, where they spent the evening conversing in Russian. They usually arrived with food and presents for Marina and the baby. While Oswald appeared irritated at this charity, all believed that he welcomed any handout he could get.

The members of the Russian community came to dislike Oswald—and not just because he failed to adequately provide for his family. Some actually feared him. George Bouhe admitted he thought Oswald might become violent. At their get-togethers, Oswald was often outspoken and crude. He sensed that their guests really came to see Marina and he became jealous. He wanted to be the center of their attention, but his attempts often intensified their lack of respect for him. Most of the Russians were well educated and could see through his attempts to appear important. True, he read many significant books, but he regularly misused the words that he learned from them. They doubted whether he really understood what he read.

They also criticized his attempts to keep Marina from learning English, sensing that he used her inability to communicate as a means of controlling her. They openly encouraged her to learn English. It had become obvious that the only reason they kept coming to Oswald's house and bringing gifts was because of their love for Marina and their concern for both her and the baby.

During their weekly get-together on Sunday, October 7, 1962—an evening when Marguerite showed up uninvited—Oswald announced that he had been laid off by Leslie Welding Company. He explained that the work had been seasonal. None of what he said was true; he was tired of his job and curious about how much help he might get from this new group of "friends."

Immediately they started to discuss how they might help the family with this new problem. It was agreed that Oswald would be able to find work more quickly in Dallas. Marina would go with the Taylors to Dallas that evening, because she had a dental appointment the next day at Baylor. All of the Oswalds' belongings would be stored in Elene Hall's garage, and Oswald would then go to Dallas where he would look for a job.

Oswald headed for Dallas the next day. He requested by letter that his last paycheck from Leslie Welding Company be sent to a post office box in Dallas. Marina stayed at the Taylors' for three days and then returned to Fort Worth, where she stayed with Mrs. Hall for almost a month. During that time, all of Marina's and the baby's expenses were paid by members of the Russian community. Oswald never asked about the expenses, nor did he thank anyone. Oswald was, however, making payments on the loans from the State Department and his brother during this period.

Anna Meller's husband knew a woman at the Texas State Employment Commission who was able to find Oswald a job at Jaggers Chiles-Stovall in the photographic department. Oswald began working there on October 12. While their efforts to find Oswald a job had been successful, the members of the Russian community had reached a point of intolerance for Oswald himself. George Bouhe and Anna Meller refused to help Oswald any further, but because Marina lived with the Taylors, Oswald continued to see them.

Alexandra Taylor had come to her own conclusion about Oswald. He was anti-Russia and anti-capitalism. He wanted a government that gave everything to the people without taxation and allowed individuals to do exactly as they pleased. Oswald wanted to be an important person, but he resented important people. He was not sure about what he wanted, but he wanted it for nothing. His peculiar political views seemed unshakable.

Before long, the Russian emigrés had all but abandoned the Oswalds. Their concern for Marina could not overcome their dislike of her husband indefinitely. Only George and Jeanne DeMohrenschildt continued to see them.

On November 2, 1962, Oswald found a new home for his family in the Oak Cliff section of Dallas. He retrieved his possessions from Elene Hall's garage and brought them to 604 Elsbeth Street in a U-Haul trailer. Marina did not want to move in, calling the place a pigsty. She stayed up until 5 a.m., scrubbing everything.

Life in the Oswald family was not tranquil. Oswald accused Marina of "whoring," not for physical gratification, but to obtain gifts from the Russians. He even said that since she liked them so much, she should go live with them. The fighting got so bad that Marina finally did leave. She called Anna Meller and went to her home with the baby.

The next day members of the Russian community met with Marina. They promised to help her if she left Oswald, but warned her that the help would stop if she stayed with him.

Marina stayed at the Meller's small apartment for the next week. A meeting at which Marina would announce to Oswald her intention to leave him for good was arranged for the following Sunday at the home of George and Jeanne DeMohrenschildt.

As soon as Oswald arrived, George confronted him. "Do you think it's heroic to beat a woman?" he asked.

Oswald did not answer.

Marina accused Oswald of brutality and announced that she wanted a divorce.

Oswald pleaded, "I don't know what I'll do if you leave me. I don't want to go on living."

Marina remained adamant. She just wanted to get her belongings and get away from Oswald.

With the assistance of the DeMohrenschildts, Marina went to Oswald's Elsbeth Street apartment and retrieved her belongings. She moved in with Declan and Katya Ford. Declan, a geologist, was not of Russian descent, but Katya was a member of the Russian community.

Two days later Oswald came to the Ford house and begged Marina to return. Marina stood her ground. Oswald phoned her several times and finally persuaded Marina to see him alone. When they got together, Oswald dropped to his knees and begged her to return. He kissed her feet and promised to change. His persistence wore her down. That same evening she and the baby returned to Elsbeth Street. Members of the Russian community were furious. With the exception of the DeMohrenschildts, they agreed to have nothing more to do with any of the Oswalds.

Thanksgiving morning the Oswalds took the bus to Fort Worth, where they were met by Oswald's brother, John Pic, who was then an Air Force sergeant. He was staying with Robert,

Oswald's other brother, for the weekend. For the first time since childhood, all the brothers were together. Marguerite was not invited to their meeting.

That was the last time Oswald saw his brother John. He would not see his brother Robert again until November 22, 1963.

# 31

Marina was about to experience her first Christmas in the United States. When Oswald refused to buy a tree, she found a small branch and decorated it with nineteen cents' worth of paper.

Jeanne DeMohrenschildt kept in touch with the Russian girl. She felt especially sorry for Marina when she realized how desolate Christmas would be for her. Since Declan and Katya Ford were planning a Christmas party, Jeanne called Katya and obtained a reluctant invitation for the Oswalds. Jeanne later recalled, "I wanted Marina to be at some Christmas party, because it is her first Christmas in the United States; she could have some kind of fun." Jeanne and her husband hoped that the Oswalds might make some new friends.

The party did not go well. Marina ate as if she had not eaten a square meal for several days, and people noticed. Oswald spent most of his time with a Japanese girl who had come to the party and ignored Marina the entire evening. Most of the other guests at the party were not impressed with the Oswalds.

The DeMohrenschildts continued, however, on friendly terms with Marina and her husband. Perhaps this relationship lasted because Oswald and George DeMohrenschildt both strongly supported the civil rights movement. Both were also sympathetic to Cuba, and Cuba remained constantly in the news. Radio Cuba had begun shifting from a Soviet-style communistic ideology to an ideology more similar to that of the Chinese. The USSR under Lenin had held that the world would ultimately be communistic, but believed that each nation would, by revolution from within, turn to communism. Stalin abandoned Lenin's position and advocated that the USSR must overthrow those countries whose political ideology was in conflict with communism. Khrushchev, however, returned the USSR to a Leninist position. He advocated peaceful coexistence with the West, for according to the Communist Manifesto all nations would ultimately embrace communism. The Chinese, on the other hand, embraced communism in the Stalinist tradition and sought to impose communism by military means on any country that seemed ripe for takeover.

George DeMohrenschildt's background made him a unique member of the Russian community in the Dallas-Fort Worth area. He was born in 1911, in a town called Mozyr, in czarist Russia close to the Polish border. His father was an aristocrat and an important official in the czarist regime. The family lived in St. Petersburg, but fled to Polish-occupied Minsk with the coming of the revolution in 1918.

Not long after the Red Army ejected the Poles, George's father was arrested and banished to Siberia. With the aid of his physicians, the elder DeMohrenschildt was able to escape with his family to Poland, where George spent the rest of his childhood. After he graduated from high school, George served his compulsory year and a half in the Polish Army by attending the famous military academy at Grudziadz. George then attended the Institute Superieur de Commerce in Belgium and received his master's degree in finance and maritime transportation. He completed a doctorate in international commerce at the University of Liege.

While attending these institutions, George financed himself by selling ready-to-wear clothing throughout Europe. He became accomplished in a half dozen languages, but still considered Russian his native tongue.

George emigrated to the United States in 1938. After a summer in New York City, he decided to become involved in the oil industry and took a job with Humble Oil Co. Although he eventually became friendly with the chairman of the board, he started on a rig as a roustabout so that he could learn the oil business from the ground up.

When the war started in Europe, he was called up by the Polish Army, but literally missed the boat. He attempted to enlist in the American Army, but was rejected because of high blood pressure. Throughout the conflict, he engaged in various activities promoting the war effort, including working for French intelligence and making propaganda movies.

George was married four times. The first union, begun in April 1943, produced his daughter, Alexandra (Gary Taylor's wife). The marriage was soon dissolved, and George enrolled at the University of Texas to study petroleum geology.

In 1946, he took a position in Colorado, and remained until 1949, overseeing the oil development there. During this period he married and divorced again. There were no children this time.

From Colorado George moved to Texas, where he went into partnership to form a drilling company. He married again, this time to a physician. They had two children, both of whom had cystic fibrosis. One lived only a short time. George was very affected by these events and founded the National Cystic Fibrosis Foundation. This marriage, too, ended in divorce, and George left the country to do consulting for oil developers in Central America and Africa. He eventually took his expertise to countries behind the iron curtain.

His fourth marriage, to Jeanne, lasted until his death.

In many ways George DeMohrenschildt was a Renaissance man who happened to be a Russian immigrant living in Texas. He was widely read, versed in international politics, knowledgeable in several fields of science, and very competent in economic matters. George also possessed a literary and artistic side. He had done some writing and had put on an art show to exhibit some of his work.

Why would a man of his caliber be drawn to Oswald?

They seemed like opposites. George said that he merely wanted information about Russia and Minsk where he had lived as a boy, but his interest in Oswald seemed greater than a desire to learn more about where he grew up.

George and Oswald talked politics for hours. George was the only person to whom Oswald would actually open up. George seemed to be one of the few people that Oswald regarded as a superior human being. George's assessment of Oswald, however, was less than flattering. He described Oswald as a "semi-educated hillbilly," noting that such a person could not be taken seriously. None of Oswald's ideas ever grew beyond a vague, crude form. Because he lacked a good educational background, Oswald never really understood the complicated economic treatises he was reading. He picked up some fairly sophisticated terminology, but when he tried to impress someone with it, he usually demonstrated that he did not comprehend the language he employed.

George said, "I never would believe that any government would be stupid enough to trust Lee with anything important. Even the government of Ghana would not give him a job of any type.

"The guy was always under some kind of pressure . . . some inward pressure.

"The most important answer I think I got from Oswald, and that was one of the reasons we liked him and thought that he was rather intelligent in his estimation of Soviet Russia, is the fact that we asked him, both my wife and I, why did you leave Soviet Russia, and he said very sincerely, 'Because I did not find what I was looking for.' I knew what he was looking for: Utopia."

# 32

The Christmas party at the Fords' certainly did not brighten Marina's spirits, and nothing seemed to improve her situation as Christmas came and went. On New Year's Eve, Oswald went to bed early, leaving Marina up alone and depressed. With remorse Marina reflected on her marriage to Oswald. The New Year was always a happy holiday at home with her friends. Now she had none.

She decided to write a letter to a past boyfriend in Russia; she spoke of her loneliness and her inability to return. She said her husband did not treat her as he should, and wished she were back in Russia. She ended the letter, "I kiss you as we kissed before."

The letter was returned for insufficient postage, and Oswald took it from the mailbox. Instead of responding in a fit of jealousy as he had been known to do, he accused Marina of purposely putting insufficient postage on the envelope so he would discover the letter and become jealous.

January was uneventful. Oswald had nearly finished his training in photography at Jaggers Chiles-Stovall, and his employers expected his performance to improve. He signed up for a typing class at the local high school. Oswald might have thought that, coupled with his photographic experience, typing skills might help him get a job with a newspaper. He wrote to *The Militant*, a left-wing newspaper, offering his services, but he received no response.

On January 26 Oswald made his last payment on the loan

from the State Department, which had financed his family's trip to the United States. He had already repaid his brother for his air fare from New York.

The next day Oswald sent a coupon from a magazine to Seaport Traders in the name of A.J. Hidell for a .38 caliber pistol. The purchase price was $29.95. The pistol was to be returned to his post office box. The post office records indicate that the persons allowed access to the post office box were Oswald, Alex James Hidell, and Marina.

Evidently, while still employed at Jaggers Chiles-Stovall, Oswald forged identification papers for Alex James Hidell. Why the name Alex James Hidell? The forged documents all had Oswald's picture on them. According to Marina, it was a combination of his name and Fidel (Castro). Marina could not pronounce Lee, so she called him Alik.

Oswald had become very interested in a new "celebrity" who had moved to Dallas. Major General Edwin Walker had resigned from the Army because of continued pressure over his right-wing indoctrination of his troops in West Germany. When he resigned, he declared, "My career has been destroyed. I must find another means of serving my country in time of her great need. To do this I must be free from the power of the little men who, in the name of my country, punish loyal service to it."

In Dallas General Walker maintained a high profile as a spokesman for the extreme right. He attacked the civil rights movement and criticized U.S. tolerance of communist Cuba off its shores. He quickly became an enemy of the extreme left. *The Worker*, a radical left-wing national newspaper, ran an article entitled "General Walker Bids for Fuehrer Role." The article declared, "The general thus becomes the first open candidate for leadership of the mass movement which the military-Monopolistic-Fascist plotters are now hoping to organize throughout the nation."

George DeMohrenschildt had similar feelings toward

General Walker. After a party at the DeMohrenschildts, George commented to the Oswalds in Russian that one of their German guests was a fascist "from his brains to his bones."

"Fancy meeting a real, live fascist. Are there really any in America?" Marina asked.

George explained to Marina that the John Birch Society was a fascist organization and General Walker had been seeking to establish himself as the fascist leader in the United States.

Although Priscilla Johnson McMillan records this incident in her book *Marina and Lee*, there is no mention of it in the Warren Commission's report.

On Sunday, February 17, Oswald handed Marina paper and pencil and ordered her to write to the Russian Embassy in Washington. She wrote, as he dictated: "I beg your assistance to help me return to the homeland in the USSR, where I will again feel myself a full-fledged citizen." She also asked for financial assistance.

The fighting between Oswald and Marina intensified to a point where their landlord asked them to leave. They found a place on Neely Street a few blocks away. According to the landlord, they moved their belongings in the baby's carriage.

Marina invited Ruth Paine, a friend she had made through the DeMohrenschildts, to visit her in their new home March 12. Ironically, while Ruth Paine, a Quaker, was visiting Marina, Oswald was there ordering a 6.5 mm Mannlicher-Carcano rifle from a mail-order company in Chicago, for $19.95 plus shipping. He placed the order in the name of A. Hidell.

From Marina, Ruth Paine learned that Oswald wanted to return his wife to Russia. Ruth thought that Oswald should allow Marina to come and live with her. She was separated from her husband, and Marina would make a fine companion. Ruth was trying to learn Russian well enough to teach the language, and Marina would certainly help her in this. Oswald, however, had made no mention of divorce. Perhaps he thought that if Marina were in Russia, she could more easily travel to the country that had become Oswald's new utopia—Cuba.

Oswald was given notice at Jaggers that he was being dismissed, and that his last day of employment would be April 6, 1963. On the prior Sunday, while Marina was hanging diapers in the yard, Oswald approached her with a camera, asking her to photograph him with his rifle in one hand, *The Militant* in the other, and his pistol in his belt. Two of these snapshots, along with photographs of the Walker residence, were later discovered in a notebook in which Oswald recorded his activities. He had also given one of the prints to George DeMohrenschildt.

According to Marina, on April 7, 1963, Oswald left Neely Street with his rifle and notebook hidden in a raincoat. He evidently buried them. He would retrieve them later.

Oswald had not informed Marina that he was fired, so he stayed away from the house during working hours the first three days after his dismissal. On Wednesday, April 10, 1963, he came home as usual and had supper. After supper he left for what Marina thought was his typing class.

At 9:00 P.M., General Walker was in his library preparing his income tax return. All the lights in the house were on and the shades were up. He was sitting at his desk in a corner next to a window. Suddenly, there was a blast and a crack right over his head. The general got up and found a small hole in the wall. When the police examined the hole, they found a bullet, but were unable to determine the caliber.

Oswald returned home later that night to confess to Marina that he had committed the crime. She was horrified, expecting the police to arrive at the door at any moment. They did not.

If Oswald's attempts to get Marina back to Russia were part of a plan to get her eventually to Cuba, how would Oswald himself get to Cuba? Perhaps assassinating one of Cuba's major critics and enemies would have helped Oswald get to his utopia. But he had failed.

# 33

Three days after the attempt on Walker's life, George and Jeanne DeMohrenschildt visited the Oswalds with an Easter gift for the baby. Since they were about to leave for Haiti on business that would keep them there until after the assassination of the president, this would be the last time they would see Oswald.

Marina was showing the home to Jeanne when they came across the rifle in the closet. George heard them talk about it and, whether jokingly or seriously, quizzed Oswald about the shot at Walker. They all saw Oswald's reaction, and it caused an uncomfortable silence.

On April 21, 1963, Oswald read in the morning paper that former Vice President Richard Nixon was in Dallas, and that he was calling for the administration to oust the Communists from Cuba. According to Marina, Oswald put on a good suit and got out his pistol. He said he wanted to get a look at Nixon. Marina somehow forced Oswald into the bathroom, where he remained the rest of the day.

Because of the attack on General Walker, his threatening behavior concerning Nixon, and his being out of work, Marina suggested to Oswald that he go to New Orleans. Oswald had been born in New Orleans, and he could probably find a relative who would put him up until he could find work. Oswald agreed and arrangements were made for Marina to stay with Ruth Paine until he could have her and the baby join him.

Oswald phoned his Aunt Lillian Murret from the New

Orleans bus station on April 25 and asked her if he could stay with her until he found work. He moved in that day. On May 9, he found a job at the Reily Coffee Company and was able to rent an apartment for his family on Magazine Street. According to his application for employment, one of his references was Sgt. Robert Hidell, the assumed name he had been using.

The next day Ruth Paine drove Marina and her child to New Orleans. Marina was pregnant, and Ruth suggested that she return to Texas to have the baby. When they arrived at the apartment, they found the place run-down and bug-infested. Marina and Oswald began arguing, and Ruth Paine left as soon as possible.

In New Orleans Oswald used his street address instead of a post office box number. Apparently he was out of hiding. He also became openly involved in the political debate about Cuba. On May 26 he wrote the Fair Play for Cuba Committee (FPCC) in New York, asking for formal membership in the organization and suggesting that they open a branch in New Orleans.

An answer came quickly from the national director of the FPCC. Oswald was sent a membership card but was informed that it would be difficult to establish a chapter in New Orleans. Anti-Castro sentiment in that part of the country ran high. The FPCC, however, would welcome his efforts in trying to broaden their support.

Obviously elated with his membership, Oswald immediately had printed, at his own expense, a thousand handbills which declared "HANDS OFF CUBA!" and invited people to join the Fair Play for Cuba Committee. He also had five hundred membership application blanks and three hundred membership cards printed.

Oswald again exerted pressure on Marina to repatriate herself to the USSR.

On June 16, at the Dumaine Street Wharf, where the *USS Wasp* was moored, Oswald began passing out his handbills.

Because he was on private property, his activity was stopped. Perhaps he was again attempting to establish a series of pro-Cuba actions that would gain favor for him in Cuba. He recorded all his actions in his notebook. He was planning to visit the Cuban Embassy in Mexico City, where he would show the notebook. Oswald hoped he would be granted a visa to Cuba by the embassy.

Oswald applied for his passport on June 24, and received it the next day. Because he had paid off his loan from the State Department, they evidently saw no reason to deny his request for a passport.

On July 1, Marina again wrote to the Russian Embassy, asking that she be allowed to return to the Soviet Union as soon as possible. She stated that she was homesick. She also requested a visa for Oswald so that he could return with her. Marina later explained that when she wrote the embassy, Oswald was in the kitchen crying. The times of unemployment had been deeply upsetting to him. Perhaps he would be better off back in Russia. Oswald, however, when he mailed the letter to the embassy, enclosed the following note:

> Please rush the entrance visa for the return of Soviet citizen, Marina N. Oswald. She is going to have a baby in October; therefore, you must grant the entrance visa and make the transportation arrangements before then.
>
> As for my return entrance visa, please consider it separately.

Oswald seemed to have no intention of traveling with his family to Russia.

Oswald was fired from his job at the Reily Coffee Company on July 19, 1963. In attempting to purchase another rifle, he had failed to show up for work on time. The reasons for dismissal were inefficiency and inattention to his work

Now Oswald could receive unemployment compensation

and continue his pro-Castro activities in the city that held the second highest concentration of anti-Castro Cubans in the nation.

The FBI raided a cottage in St. Tammany Parish on August 1, seizing more than a ton of dynamite and twenty bomb casings. The newspapers reported that the material was to be used in a military operation against a nation with which the United States was at peace. The next day the news reported that the military operation had been planned against Cuba.

August 5, Oswald went to a store owned by Carlos Bringuier, a delegate to the Cuban Student Directorate. He offered to use his Marine Corps experience to assist in training anti-Castro forces. He declared his own willingness to fight against Castro.

Bringuier suspected that Oswald might actually have been pro-Castro. He was even more concerned that he might have been an FBI agent attempting to learn more about the cache in St. Tammany Parish.

Oswald wrote in his notebook:

> I infiltraled the Cuban Student Directorite and than harassed them with information I gained including having the N.O. city atterny general call them in an put a restraining order pending a hearing on some so-called bonds for invasion they were selling in the New Orleans area . . . .

The next day Oswald returned to Bringuier's store and left his *Marine Guidebook*. Some people have cited this incident as proof that Oswald was anti-Castro.

A few days later, Bringuier was enraged when he and two companions discovered Oswald on Canal Street passing out FPCC handbills. Bringuier explained to the gathering crowd that just a few days earlier Oswald had come to him offering assistance to the anti-Castro cause. Now he had a sign on his chest proclaiming "Hands Off Cuba." Bringuier's accusation caused some of the spectators to begin shouting at Oswald "Go to Cuba" and "Traitor."

A police officer came and told Bringuier to move on. He stated that Oswald had a right to hand out literature. At that moment one of Bringuier's companions grabbed a bundle of Oswald's handbills and threw them into the air. Yellow sheets drifted to the ground as Bringuier closed in on Oswald, taking his glasses off. Oswald crossed his arms, ready to become a martyr for his cause. "Okay, Carlos, if you want to hit me, hit me," he declared.

At that moment a squad car arrived and the four men were taken to the First District Police Station. Oswald appeared cool. He seemed as if he had prepared himself for this ordeal. He spoke of the FPCC as a national organization with a large membership but refused to name members because Bringuier and his companions were in the room. According to the police report, Oswald had four pieces of identification on him, all with his proper name.

In the morning Oswald was interrogated by a commander at the First District Police Station. He informed the commander that the New Orleans chapter of FPCC had thirty-five members who met monthly at different members' homes. The commander later commented on Oswald's calmness. He seemed to have an almost professional demeanor. He expounded on Marxism, Russia, and the United States. When the commander asked him about his opinion of Kennedy and Khrushchev, Oswald observed, "They seem to get along very well together."

At the end of his session with the police commander, Oswald asked to see a representative of the FBI.

The day of the trial, Oswald walked into the segregated courtroom and sat in the area assigned to blacks. This also infuriated Bringuier. When the judge arraigned the four, Oswald pleaded guilty. Bringuier explained how he met Oswald, and showed the *Marine Guidebook* with Oswald's name on top of the first page. The judge dismissed Bringuier and his two companions. Oswald paid a ten-dollar fine.

The confrontation with Bringuier managed to gain Oswald some media attention. A radio talk show moderator of a program entitled "Latin Listening Post" approached Oswald for an interview. Oswald spoke with the moderator for thirty-seven minutes, which was edited to five minutes of radio time. Examination of the tape indicates that Oswald was regurgitating Radio Havana propaganda.

When asked why he thought the United States government had pushed Cuba into the Soviets' arms, Oswald replied, "Castro's Cuba, even after the revolution, was still a one-crop economy, basing its economy on sugar. When we slashed the Cuban sugar quota, of course, we cut their throats. They had to turn to some other country. They had to turn to some other hemisphere to sell this one product. They did so, and they have sold it to Russia."

For over a year, Radio Havana had been trying to convince its U.S. radio audience that this was the case. Actually, the United States cut its sugar import quota from Cuba after Castro reached an agreement with Russia. Radio Havana definitely shaped Oswald's attitude toward Cuba and toward the U.S. government.

As a result of the five-minute tape, the moderator arranged for a half-hour debate involving Oswald, Bringuier, and some other anti-Castro advocates. Considering that Oswald was the only one taking a pro-Castro position, he handled himself quite well. When Bringuier questioned him regarding Castro's characterization of President Kennedy as a ruffian and a thief, Oswald responded, "I do not agree with that particular wording. However, I and the Fair Play for Cuba Committee do think that the United States government, through certain agencies, mainly the State Department and the CIA, has made monumental mistakes in its relations with Cuba, mistakes which are pushing Cuba into the sphere of activity of let's say a very dogmatic communist country, such as China."

Oswald had definitely begun to identify China as a country more true to communistic ideals than Russia. Perhaps he was influenced by Kennedy's press-conference statement that "... we would be far worse off—the world would be—if the Chinese dominated the communist world. Mr. Khrushchev's means are destruction, but he believes that peaceful coexistence and support of these wars of liberation, small wars, will bring about our defeat. The Chinese communists believe that by constantly hitting, and if war comes, a nuclear third world war, they can survive it anyway with 750 million people. So we are better off with the Khrushchev view than we are with the Chinese communist view, quite obviously."

The level of cooperation that existed between Kennedy and Khrushchev convinced Oswald that Russia was losing its role of real leadership in the communist arena. Khrushchev had agreed to permit two or three on-site inspections of a nuclear test ban each year. He had withdrawn several thousand Soviet troops from Cuba. Kennedy and Khrushchev had agreed on a joint weather and communications satellite program and had reached an agreement on the U.S. policy of selling wheat to the Soviet Union and other iron curtain countries. In the meantime, Khrushchev had turned down an invitation to visit China.

In a remark to the moderator, after the television debate, Oswald asserted that the Russians had gone soft on communism, and that Cuba was the only revolutionary country in the world.

According to Marina's testimony to both the Warren Commission and the Select Committee on Assassinations, her husband's only desire while in New Orleans was to go to Cuba. When asked how he planned to get there, Marina explained that her husband wanted to "kidnap" an airplane.

Because it was a matter of weeks before Marina would have their second child, Oswald and Marina agreed that it would be best if she returned to Dallas and stayed with Ruth Paine.

Oswald conceded to Marina that he would attempt to get to Cuba by legitimate means. He would go to the Cuban consulate in Mexico City and apply for a visa. If he were successful, he would send for her and their children.

Oswald abandoned his plan of having Marina return to Russia and then travel to Cuba. On September 17 he applied for and received a tourist card to travel in Mexico.

# 34

Oswald had worked out a list of reasons for the Cuban Embassy to issue him a visa for entry into Cuba. He listed them in his notebook. He cited his military experience, his having been stationed in the Far East, his having been a resident of the USSR and his being fluent in Russian, his commitment to Marxism, his being an organizer and street agitator, and his being a radio speaker, lecturer, and photographer.

Ruth Paine arrived on September 20, unaware of Oswald's plans to go to Mexico. She felt he was friendlier than he had been on her previous visit. A few days later, Oswald packed all of his family's belongings into the Paine station wagon, including his Mannlicher-Carcano rifle.

Oswald boarded a bus for Houston on September 25. The next day he crossed the border at Nuevo Laredo and arrived in Mexico City at 10 A.M., September 27. Not long after his arrival, he registered at the Hotel del Comercio and immediately headed for the two embassies. According to Marina he went first to the Russian, " . . . in the hope that having been there first, this would make it easier for him at the Cuban Embassy."

When he reached the Cuban Embassy, Oswald was met by a secretary. He told her that he had to see the consul personally, for he had documents that would persuade the consul to grant him the visa.

The consul was called in and Oswald showed him his membership cards in the U.S. Communist Party and Fair Play for

Cuba Committee, documentation that he had lived in the Soviet Union, and proof that he was married to a Soviet citizen. The consul told Oswald that he still could not grant him a visa. Permission had to be obtained from the Cuban government. He had Oswald complete an application for a visa. The application required a photograph of Oswald, which he went to have taken. He returned the photograph to the Cuban embassy.

The next day Oswald returned to the embassy, hoping this time at least to obtain an in-transit visa through Cuba to Russia. He again asked to speak directly to the consul. When his request was denied, Oswald became discourteous and was asked to leave. He left, mumbling to himself and slamming the door behind him.

Oswald felt rebuffed. It seemed as if nothing he had to offer the Cubans could persuade them to grant him a visa. He had been more successful in persuading the Russians.

A dejected Oswald returned to the States, arriving in Dallas about 2 P.M., October 3. He went straight to the Texas Employment Commission and filed for unemployment. That same afternoon he registered at the YMCA. It was one full day before Oswald telephoned his wife and went to visit her.

Two days later (October 5) the White House announced that the president would make a political trip to Texas around November 21.

Since there was no room at the Paine residence for Oswald to stay, he found himself a room in the Oak Cliff section of Dallas, across the Trinity River from downtown. His landlady, Mary Bledsoe, disliked him almost from the beginning. She testified that he would leave early in the morning and return mid-afternoon, only to retire to his room. She was upset when she heard him speaking on the phone in a foreign language. At the end of the first week she asked him to leave.

Oswald spent the next weekend at the Paine residence. Thinking it might make him more employable, Ruth Paine gave him a driving lesson.

Oswald continued to look for work, but was unable to land a job. One of Ruth Paine's neighbors, who had heard about Oswald's hunting for employment, knew through her younger brother that there was a job opening at the Texas School Book Depository.

The same day Oswald picked up his belongings from Mrs. Bledsoe and moved to 1026 North Beckley, where he registered as O.H. Lee.

On Oswald's behalf, Ruth Paine called the Texas School Book Depository and spoke to Roy Truly, the depository superintendent. Oswald interviewed the next morning and was hired.

According to Roy Truly, Oswald indicated he had just gotten out of the Marine Corps with an honorable discharge. Truly did not check Oswald's background. He put Oswald with another employee who showed him how to fill book orders. They worked together a few hours and then he left Oswald on his own. Given the thousands of titles that the School Book Depository handled, Oswald seemed to catch on quickly.

Still expecting the birth of their second child, Oswald gave Ruth Paine the telephone number at his rooming house so that she could call him with the news. He forgot he had registered under a fictitious name. The baby was born Sunday, October 20, two days after Oswald's own birthday.

The following week Oswald attended a speech given by General Walker. Walker had rented the Dallas Memorial Auditorium to counter the effect of an appearance there the following night by Adlai Stevenson, ambassador to the United Nations, who was speaking in celebration of United Nations Week. Walker declared that the main battleground in the world was the United States. Walker attacked Stevenson, calling him a symbol of the Communist conspiracy and the United Nations. Oswald observed the man he had already tried to assassinate. Was he planning another attack? We will never know.

The following night became history. Stevenson was

struck in the head with a picket sign, spat upon, and booed. Many of the pickets admitted they had attended Walker's rally the night before.

Oswald was at his rooming house that night, perhaps listening to this announcement on Radio Havana: "The CIA acts under the direct orders of the president, in this case Mr. Kennedy, and is responsible solely to him for their activities and adventures. When they launch a pirate attack against the Cuban coastline, and murder a militiaman or a teacher, when they commit acts of sabotage against a Cuban vessel or industry, they are acting under direct orders of the United States president." It explained that the recent Cuban attack on an American freighter was to prevent its landing arms and saboteurs.

Papers the next morning carried the news that a United States force in Guatemala was on a secret mission, possibly to train Cuban exiles for another strike against Cuba.

Oswald spent the following weekend at the Paine residence with his wife and children. Earlier, Ruth Paine had developed an active dislike for Oswald because it seemed to her that he wanted to get rid of Marina. During these weekend visits, however, she began to see him as a person who cared for his family, who tried to make himself helpful around the house, and who tried to fit in socially. She knew that he really preferred to stay to himself. She also noted that he watched television avidly.

On October 28, Oswald went to work at the depository, returning to his rooming house for the evening. Radio Havana announced that the United States was exporting explosives and other materials of death and destruction through the mail, claiming that these were the activities of the CIA. The station declared that "Any new Yankee offensive will be met with the firmness of our national motto."

Two days later Radio Havana announced that the Castro government had captured several U.S. Central Intelligence Agency operatives. Castro accused the United States of systematically raiding Cuba.

For the next several days Oswald spent most of his spare time at the rooming house. The house had seventeen bedrooms. Oswald's room was eight by ten feet with four windows. According to the landlord, Oswald was well behaved, although he never talked to the other renters. He came home every night right after work and would often stay in his room listening to the radio. The housekeeper reported that if someone else were watching television, Oswald would watch only for a few minutes and then leave. "He would go to his room, shut the door, and never say a word."

When his room was searched after the assassination, a portable shortwave radio was found. Radio Havana was a shortwave broadcast system. During this time Oswald checked out from the public library *The Shark and the Sardines*, a book very critical of U.S. involvement in Latin America. The author of the book was Juan Jose Arevalo, former president of Guatemala.

This was the situation for Lee Harvey Oswald at the beginning of November, 1963.

As the month began, the FBI was looking for Oswald, investigating further his time in Russia and his activities since his return. On November 1, FBI Agent Hosty stopped at the Paine residence, trying to locate Oswald. Ruth Paine informed him that Oswald was living somewhere in the Oak Cliff area, but she did not have the address. Hosty also learned that Oswald was employed at the Book Depository. As he was about to leave, Marina came into the room. Hosty could tell that Marina was disturbed when she learned who he was. She jotted down Hosty's license number incorrectly. The paper with the license number was later found among Oswald's papers. That same day Oswald rented a post office box in the name of the Fair Play for Cuba Committee.

On November 2, the news of President Kennedy's trip to Texas was confirmed. The only city mentioned was Houston. The next day it was announced that the president would visit Dallas, but no details about time or place were given.

November 5, Agent Hosty visited Ruth Paine again to see if she knew where Oswald was living.

On Friday, November 8, Governor Connally announced that President and Mrs. Kennedy would tour Houston on November 21, and attend a breakfast the next morning in Fort Worth. From the breakfast the president would go to Dallas for a noon luncheon. The site of the luncheon was still uncertain. This was the first confirmation of the date and time of Kennedy's visit to Dallas.

After work that day, Oswald rode out to the Paines' residence to spend the weekend. He planned to apply for a driver's permit the next day, but because it was Election Day, the license bureau was closed.

Critics assert that Oswald was identified at two places that day: a car dealership in downtown Dallas and a rifle range. Based on the testimony of both Ruth Paine and Marina, Oswald did not leave the residence.

Oswald asked to use Ruth Paine's typewriter that weekend. He began a letter to the Russian Embassy in Washington. In addition to telling about his trip to Mexico, he stated that he had been contacted by the FBI. He wrote, " . . . on November 1, Agent James F. Hosty warned me that if I engaged in FPCC activities in Texas the FBI would take an interest in me." He also made another request for a visa.

Because he had Veteran's Day off, Oswald spent the day at home with his family. As a result, Marina did not feel he should come the following weekend, and told him so when he called on November 14.

The newspapers reported on Friday, November 15, that because of his very tight schedule, the president would probably be unable to motorcade through downtown Dallas. The next day, however, it was announced that there would be a motorcade. Oswald could not have known before this time, one week before

Kennedy's fatal trip to Dallas, that he would be able to see the President's car from the building where he worked.

During the next week, President Kennedy again criticized Cuba's communistic government. "We in this hemisphere must also use every resource at our command to prevent the establishment of another Cuba. Cuba is a victim of foreign imperialism, an instrument of the policy of others, a weapon in an effort dictated by external powers to subvert the other American republics." Kennedy urged the people in Cuba to rid themselves of their communistic bondage. Radio Havana responded by calling Kennedy an imperialist and hypocrite.

The next day, Marina asked Ruth Paine to phone her husband at the rooming house. Ruth was told that no one named Oswald lived there. Marina became furious. When Oswald called the next day, he explained that he did not want his landlord to know his real name, because of his earlier defection to Russia. He also did not want the FBI to know where he lived. Oswald did not call his wife again.

The route of the motorcade was published the morning of November 21. It showed that the motorcade would pass by the School Book Depository Building. It is hard to imagine that Oswald could have planned to shoot President Kennedy from his place of work before he even knew the route of the motorcade.

In order to get his rifle, Oswald had to go to Ruth Paine's house. On the weekends he had been catching a ride to her house with Wesley Frazier, the brother of the woman who suggested Oswald apply for the job at the School Book Depository. According to Frazier, Oswald asked him for a ride shortly before noon on November 21. Because it was not a weekend, Frazier asked why. Oswald explained he had to get some curtain rods for his room. Oswald had decided to shoot the president.

Sometime that day, Oswald took some brown wrapping paper from the shipping department; he later fashioned it into a carrying case for his rifle.

Frazier dropped Oswald off at the Paine residence about 5:30. Both women were surprised to see him. He had never come unannounced before. They felt it was probably his way of making up for using an alias at the rooming house.

The only mention of the presidential visit the next day was by Ruth Paine. His only response was, "Ah, yes."

Nothing unusual happened that evening. Oswald watched a movie on television and went to bed at nine o'clock. Ruth noticed later that the light was on in the garage, but did not think it unusual. Oswald had several items stored in her garage, and it was not unusual for him to go to the garage to get something. At this time he probably fashioned the brown paper into a case and wrapped his bolt-action, clip-fed 6.5-mm Mannlicher-Carcano for use the next morning.

The weather report for the morning called for rain. Apparently Oswald was unconcerned that the president might be covered by a plastic bubble. Perhaps Oswald did not care whether he killed Kennedy. He only wanted to make the attempt.

Oswald awoke before 7 A.M. He took approximately fifteen dollars of the money he had on him and left the rest. He slipped his wedding ring into an antique tea cup. He dressed, and after making a cup of instant coffee, went to the garage to get his disassembled rifle.

He walked across the street to Frazier's car and deposited the package in the back seat. When Frazier got into his car, he noticed the package but had no reason to question it. He thought it was a curtain rod.

Frazier later testified that when they arrived at the Depository parking lot, Oswald walked in front of him carrying the bag. He entered the building before Frazier and that was the last Frazier saw of Oswald and his package.

The president's schedule that morning in Fort Worth called for him to appear at a street rally in front of his hotel at 8:15 A.M. It was raining, but the president stuck to his commitment.

At 9:30 the president gave his last public speech at a breakfast. From there he went to the airport and boarded Air Force I, arriving in Dallas at 11:40.

The presidential party disembarked by the rear ramp of the aircraft. A small reception was held on the airfield. Mrs. Kennedy was given some red roses. After greeting well-wishers near a fence, President and Mrs. Kennedy took their seats in the back of the car, with Governor and Mrs. Connally on the jump seats.

The motorcade began. In the lead were Police Chief Curry and Sheriff Decker. Fifty feet behind was the presidential car, then the presidential follow-up car manned by secret service agents. Behind these came the vice president with his follow-up security cars. At the rear of the motorcade were the press buses.

The motorcade and accompanying motorcycles kept in contact with each other via police radio. Instead of using the normal police channel, they used channel 2. Channel 1 continued to be the normal working channel for the Dallas Police. All transmissions on both channels were recorded on dictabelts and their transcripts appear in the exhibits in the Warren Commission volumes.

The motorcade passed through the Dallas streets, adjusting speed according to the crowds along the streets. Its speed never exceeded thirty miles per hour. It made one stop where a large group of people held a banner which read, "Please, Mr. President, stop and shake our hands." The president complied.

By the time the motorcade reached Main Street, the crowds were surging into the roadway. They thinned down, however, as the parade reached the end of Main Street and turned right onto Houston Street, approaching the Depository Building.

The Texas School Book Depository was resurfacing the floors on the upper level. The sixth floor on that day was disheveled, with boxes piled on boxes. At the window on the southeast end of the sixth floor, from which he planned to fire the shots, Oswald pushed and piled boxes to hide himself from anyone inside the building.

While Oswald was assembling his rifle—a matter of inserting and tightening five screws—the elevator stopped at the sixth floor. A coworker exited. Normally it should have taken about six minutes to reassemble the rifle. That day it took longer.

The coworker sat down within forty-five feet of Oswald to eat his lunch. He later testified, "Well, at the time I couldn't see too much of the sixth floor, because the boxes at the time were stacked so high."

The coworker left when he finished his lunch. Oswald was alone again. It was now 12:20.

As the motorcade made the turn from Houston onto Elm, it slowed even further and began its descent toward the triple underpass. People were scattered about Dealey Plaza, mostly along the curb. All were trying to get a glimpse of the president and first lady.

The presidential car made the turn with its follow-up car just five feet behind. As the follow-up car straightened out of the turn, a shot rang out. Pigeons roosting on the Hertz Rent-A-Car sign and on the roof of the depository took flight. At the same moment the president lurched forward to the left, grabbing his throat with his right hand.

Within seconds two more shots exploded, one catching the president in the back of his head, tearing away part of his skull and brain.

The dispatcher on Channel 2 announced the time as 12:30; the next transmission was from Chief Curry: "Go to the hospital—Parkland Hospital. Have them stand by."

"Get a man on top of the triple underpass and see what happened up there."

"Have Parkland stand by."

Sheriff Decker then took over the transmission. "I'm sure

it's going to take some time to get your man in there. Pull every one of my men in there."

"Dallas," the dispatcher responded, "I repeat, I didn't get all of it. I didn't quite understand all of it."

"Have my office move all available men out of my office into the railroad yard to try to determine what happened in there, and hold everything secure until homicide and other investigators should get there," Decker repeated.

The motorcade raced to Parkland Hospital. The president was pronounced dead within half an hour.

# 35

As the shots that killed Kennedy were fired, three employees were watching the parade from the fifth floor of the Texas School Book Depository. They heard the shells ejected from the murder weapon drop to the floor.

The employees had a commanding view of Dealey Plaza. They saw people falling to the ground as the motorcade suddenly speeded up. The three ran to the west side of the building to see what had happened to the motorcade. Panic-stricken people ran from the scene, many of them headed for the railway tracks.

After the third shot, Oswald ejected the shell and chambered a fourth round, but he was finished. He quickly left his perch, moving along the eastern side of the building to the staircase on the northeast side. Evidently not caring (or perhaps hoping) that it would be identified as his, Oswald discarded his rifle close to his clipboard and ran down the stairs.

Marion Baker, a patrolman from the motorcade who was in front of the depository when the shots rang out, rushed into the building. There he encountered Roy Truly. With Baker in the lead, the two ascended the staircase. As Baker reached the landing on the second floor, he saw a figure in the lunchroom. Drawing his service revolver, Baker approached Oswald, who stood calmly holding the full bottle of Coke he had obtained from the nearby vending machine. Truly was right behind Baker and identified Oswald as an employee. The two left. Later Truly said, "He didn't seem to be excited or overly afraid or anything."

Oswald walked down the southeast corner stairway and out the main entrance of the building. He walked seven short blocks east on Elm, then boarded a bus that would have taken him to Oak Cliff. On the bus was Oswald's former landlady, Mary Bledsoe. She saw Oswald.

As the bus headed back into the congestion around the Texas Book Depository Building, its direction left much to be desired for one who had just shot the president of the United States. He asked for a transfer and got off the bus. Oswald walked three blocks to the Greyhound station and hailed a cab. He had the cab driver drop him off four blocks south of his North Beckley rooming house. The time was 12:54.

According to the housekeeper, Oswald entered the rooming house just before 1 P.M. He went directly to his room. There he put on his light zippered jacket and placed his Smith & Wesson in his pocket.

The housekeeper claimed that while he was in his room, a patrol car pulled in front of the house "and just slightly ticked its horn three times." Conspiracy advocates claim this proves that Oswald had at least one accomplice who was involved in trying to help him escape from Dallas. The license number of the car given by the housekeeper turned out to be out of service, and police records cannot place such a car in the area. Moreover, the housekeeper's employers indicated that she was prone to fibbing about such things.

Oswald left the house and headed south.

At 12:45 the police radio dispatcher made the following Channel 1 announcement:

> Attention all squads. At Elm and Houston reported to be an unknown white male, approximately thirty, slender build, height five feet ten inches, 165 pounds. Reported to be armed with what is believed to be a .30 caliber rifle. Attention all squads, the suspect is believed

to be a white male, thirty, five feet ten inches, slender build, 165 pounds, armed with what is thought to be a 30-30 rifle. No further description or information at this time.

A similar announcement was made at 12:48, which was followed by requests for a more thorough description such as clothing. One of the officers making a request did not identify himself.

Oswald's route took him south on Beckley, then southeast on Crawford. At the corner of Tenth and Crawford he turned almost due east, putting himself directly ahead of a cruising patrol car approaching him on Tenth.

The driver of the car, Patrolman J. D. Tippit, a veteran of over ten years, patrolled the Oak Cliff area, District 78, during daylight hours. Since this was a residential area, he rode alone.

After the shooting, the radio dispatcher ordered nearby patrol cars to the downtown area, and specifically ordered Tippit into the central Oak Cliff area.

At approximately 1:15, cruising east near the intersection of Tenth and Patton, Tippit overtook Oswald. Oswald's general description was similar to the one given by the police radio dispatcher. According to eyewitnesses, Tippit pulled over to the curb. Oswald stepped over to the passenger side of the car and spoke to Tippit through the window. Tippit then got out of his patrol car, and as he walked toward the front of the vehicle, Oswald pulled out his revolver and fired several shots at the officer. Four of them found their mark. Patrolman Tippit died where he fell. Oswald turned and headed south and continued toward Jefferson Avenue.

Oswald walked on to Zangs Boulevard, where he found patrol cars everywhere. He needed a refuge for a while, so he ducked into the Texas Theater. If it had not been for an alert salesman in a store nearby, Oswald might have eluded his pursuers. The salesman saw Oswald duck as a patrol car passed and then watched him enter the theater. The salesman told the cashier at the theater what he had seen, and the cashier called the police.

When the police arrived, the house lights were lit and the officers proceeded to check each of the few patrons seated in the auditorium. When the officers reached Oswald, he attempted to go for his pistol but was quickly subdued. He cursed as he was led from the theater, claiming police brutality. The police found on Oswald all of his credentials, official and forged.

If Oswald had continued south on Zangs Boulevard, he would have come to the Red Bird Airport. Perhaps he was going to do what he had threatened to do in New Orleans—hijack a plane to Cuba. It is hard to know what Oswald's intentions were on that day. It does not seem unreasonable that this man, who probably gave military secrets to the Soviets so that he could remain in their country, would take a shot at the President of the United States in order to curry favor with another communist power. What about his actions after the assassination? Were they an attempt to gain even more notoriety? Whatever personal needs those actions satisfied for Lee Harvey Oswald, the world will never know what they were. Jack Ruby's act of vengeance inadvertantly silenced the only sure source of information on the president's assassin.

# 36

After Judge Robertson rejected the Hooten will and ac-cepted Jules Mayer's will for probate, I was forced to take a wait-and-see attitude on any further legal action to return Jack Ruby's estate to his family. The Estate of Jack Ruby was totally in the hands of Jules Mayer; the family and I heard nothing. Occasion-ally Earl would ask if there were new developments, but I had no answer for him.

The assassination buffs and I had one thing in common. We knew that in time the Warren Commission investigation would be reopened. It was hard to predict, however, what it would take to get Congress to reopen the investigation of the Kennedy assassination. I was surprised when it finally happened thirteen years after the assassination. Cuba was involved.

A Senate Committee on Governmental Operations uncov-ered evidence that indicated that the CIA might have worked with the Mafia in an attempt to assassinate Fidel Castro. John Roselli, who had been identified as a member of organized crime, had unsuccessfully made such an attempt. The Senate committee's findings prompted the House of Representatives to form the Select Committee on Assassinations. It was 1976.

The press criticized the committee for getting off to a slow start. First the original chief counsel resigned; within a month, the chairman followed him. Louis Stokes of Ohio took over the committee chairmanship, and G. Robert Blakey became chief counsel. Many serious students of the Kennedy assassination considered Blakey's appointment unfortunate. He had been a former special prosecutor with Robert Kennedy's Strike Force, and had been chief counsel to the McClellan committee. He would later claim that prior to his appointment with the committee on assassinations, he had an open mind on the conspiracy issue and had accepted the conclusions of the Warren Commission. If that was the case, Blakey's role on the committee must have had a profound affect on his point of view. He ended up writing *The Plot to Kill the President: Organized Crime Assassinated J.F.K.*, which was published in 1981.

As chief counsel, Blakey played a major role in determining which evidence the committee would evaluate. The committee started its work by interviewing a series of Warren Commission critics and sifting through the theories that had been propounded over the years about the assassination of Kennedy and subsequent murder of Oswald. The highlight of these interviews was the discovery of the dictabelt recordings of the two police channels. The original dictabelts were found, but it was soon discovered that their fidelity was so poor it rendered them useless. A second-generation tape was located at one of the radio stations in Dallas. This one was declared fit for use.

By applying modern computer technology, experts selected by Blakey determined that not three, but four shots were fired in Dealey Plaza that day. Incredibly enough, they even "determined" from this sound recording the direction of the fourth shot: it had been fired from the grassy knoll in Dealey Plaza. This mysterious fourth shot was fired just before Oswald's last shot.

When I read about this "new evidence," I felt compelled to review the reports that had previously addressed the number of shots fired at Kennedy. Fifty-six people in the Plaza at the time recalled three shots; five recalled four shots—four of these people were on the overpass where the echo would come into play—and three persons recalled only two. Of course, who was I to argue with computer science?

Then I learned that one of the recordings had been made from a motorcycle officer's radio; the button had been left depressed on Channel 1. I wondered how a recording of Dealey Plaza could be made on that channel. All communication in the motorcade was supposed to be conducted on Channel 2.

At 12:24, after the shots were fired, the dispatcher on Channel 2 announced, "Unknown motorcycle—up on Stemmons with his mike stuck open on Channel 1. Could you send someone up there to tell him to shut it off." A mike on Stemmons Freeway could not pick up sounds from Dealey Plaza. In addition, a carillon could be heard in the recording. There are no carillons in Dealey Plaza.

Six years later, in 1982, the National Research Council would reexamine the tape evidence of a fourth shot. A young jazz musician from Mansfield, Ohio, had obtained a copy of the tape and noticed that, at the moment on the tape when the fourth shot was supposed to have been fired, there seemed to be cross talk between the two police channels. He brought this to the attention of the National Research Council. With the use of sound spectrograms, they found the "crossed" transmission to be the words, "Hold everything secure until the homicide and other investigators get there." Sheriff Decker had spoken those words on Channel 2, about one minute *after* the assassination had taken place.

In spite of the conflicting evidence that the committee did have at the time they conducted their investigation, they continued their investigation as if a fourth shot had been fired. If a fourth shot had been fired, there must have been a conspiracy with at least two people involved. And if there was a conspiracy, was Jack Ruby part of it? Earl received a subpoena to appear before the committee on September 26, 1978. He asked me to go with him.

As Earl's legal counsel before a house committee, my role would be limited. Even so, I was eager to go. Perhaps I would have a chance to present my theory on the assassination.

Before we could enter the committee hearing room, we had to pass through metal detectors. As we did, one of the guards remarked to Earl that we were lucky we came today. Earl asked why and was informed that Jack Ruby's brother was going to testify this morning. We looked at each other and almost burst into laughter.

The design of the hearing room was unusual. First, we entered from the center of the room. Most courtrooms are entered from the back. The room was huge, larger than the largest federal courtroom I had ever been in. The spectators' section behind a bar to our left stretched across the entire room. In front of the bar was a counsel or witness table. In front of the table were the House members' seats, facing the table, elevated about the height of a judge's bench in most courtrooms. To the left of the table was a platform with television and audio equipment. The entire left side of the room was windowed, allowing natural light into the room.

As we entered the hearing room, we were each given a set of mimeographed papers and directed to the spectator section. Blakey was just finishing a speech summarizing some of the committee's "findings."

The committee found that Barney Baker had placed a telephone call to another one-time associate of Jack Ruby on the evening of November 21, 1963. The person Baker called was David Yaras of Miami. Yaras was a close friend and associate of Lenny Patrick. He had also been acquainted with Ruby during their early years in Chicago. Like Lenny Patrick, Dave Yaras had served, it is alleged, as a key lieutenant of the Chicago Mafia leader, Sam Giancana, reportedly as an executioner. In an FBI interview in 1964, Yaras stated that he had last seen Ruby over ten years prior to the assassination.

I leaned toward Earl and jokingly asked, "Was your

brother in the Mafia?" His strained half-smile indicated his shock and disgust with Blakey's accusation.

"Once again," Blakey concluded, "the ultimate meaning of these facts and circumstances remains yet indeterminate. It would be appropriate now to call Mr. Ruby."

Earl and I rose and walked to the witness table.

Although no Treasury agent would ever admit it publicly, the federal government uses its powerful Treasury Department for criminal investigations. Almost immediately after the assassination, Earl was subjected to an intensive audit of all his open tax returns. Earl with his co-stockholder from Chicago owned the largest dry cleaners in the Detroit area. They had a contract to do the cleaning for the customers of the J. L. Hudson Company, the biggest department store in Detroit. They operated a large plant in the city and had several dry cleaning stores in the greater Detroit area. Each store filed its own tax return. An intensive audit means verification of each and every deduction taken on all the returns. For example, every long distance telephone call was examined and verified. When such an audit is conducted for information, as opposed to checking for correctness, a special intelligence agent is assigned to the case. A special agent is usually brought in when a revenue agent suspects fraud. Earl's case was different. He was not informed of the presence of the special agent. Because I had worked for the Treasury Department, I realized what was happening and gave the special agent a joking bad time about it.

In principle, I do not disagree with this system. If, for instance, Jack had been involved in a conspiracy and it was his job to eliminate Oswald, there would have been some sort of payoff. To whom would the payoff go? Jack was in jail. Earl's brothers and sisters were not affluent enough to be able to hide such sums of money, but Earl might have been able to. An intensive audit would turn it up. Even though there were some questions raised concerning a reallocation of income between corporations, no extra sums of money were discovered.

The only item in question that might have related to Jack Ruby at all was a telegram to Havana, Cuba. When questioned, Earl could give no answer other than that he did not send it. Many of his employees had access to the phones; it could have been sent by any one of them. The IRS allowed the telegram as a business deduction. Ironically, after the audit was finally completed, Earl received a personal refund.

As counsel before a house committee, I could only advise Earl of his legal rights; I could not object, nor could I argue a point. A witness appearing before a congressional committee is required to answer all questions or face a possible charge of contempt of Congress. If a witness refuses to answer a question on the grounds that his answer might incriminate himself, the committee has the option of granting the witness immunity. Failure to then answer the question can result in the witness being charged with contempt of Congress.

James E. McDonald, a rather young, handsome gentleman, interrogated Earl on behalf of the committee. He began by asking about Earl's associates when he was a youngster in Chicago. He quickly found that because of the age difference between the brothers, Earl knew Jack's friends only by sight or reputation, but not personally.

McDonald focused next on the telegram to Havana. Again Earl could offer no explanation except that he had not sent it. The line of questioning that followed became so intense that in a regular court of law I would have objected that McDonald was browbeating the witness. I had no authority, however, to do so in this hearing. When McDonald suggested that the telegram was really sent by Jack but charged from Dallas to Earl's number, Earl became visibly upset. I decided it was time I intervened.

"Mr. McDonald," I interrupted, "the telegram bill indicates the telegram originated at a Cobo Cleaners telephone number.

It was not charged from another number; it would indicate that on the bill."

Why so much emphasis on a telegram to Cuba dated April 1, 1962? In his opening remarks right before Earl began to testify, Blakey connected Jack Ruby with the Mafia. I felt I knew the direction in which Blakey and McDonald were leading the committee. I was certain they would also bring up Lewis McWillie. I knew about McWillie, but I was convinced that his story about Jack Ruby had nothing to do with the assassination of Kennedy or the murder of Oswald. Blakey and McDonald probably thought otherwise.

This is McWillie's story:

I had been working in gambling joints around Dallas-Fort Worth since the early 1940s. When I worked my way up to ownership of a club in the early 1950s, some of the dealers and I would stop in an all-night restaurant early in the morning hours where there was this fellow at the counter with a hat on. A hat in Dallas was unusual. Finally, I asked who he was.

"That's a fellow named Jack Ruby that runs a club called the Vegas Club out on Oak Lawn," I was told.

Finally, one morning the fellow walks up to me and says, "Is your name McWillie?" I said yes. He explained who he was and that he was having a problem at his club because the city officials were enforcing the curfew law against him and not the other clubs. He thought it was because he was Jewish. I suggested he speak to a Mr. Schepps, an important leader in the Jewish Community. Well, I guess it worked. He didn't have no more trouble after that. From then on I could never get rid of Jack Ruby. He was around me all the time.

In 1958, I went to Cuba to manage the Tropicana. I

was promised a percentage of the place when it got to doing good, which it never did much good on account of the revolution coming up and all that. They were looking for business, so I suggested that I call Jack Ruby and have him get a hold of Tony Zoppi. Tony Zoppi is a well-known columnist like (Jim) Bishop, Earl Wilson, people like that. That's the kind of man he was in Dallas and all society people read his column. He wrote me back that they'd come over on a certain date. So I sent him two tickets, which the place paid for. Then I explained to him we would pay off their room. We figured we would get a lot of publicity from it, and people from Dallas would come to Cuba.

Later, Jack came and said that Tony couldn't make it. Jack stayed about six days. He was there (at the Tropicana) every night he was in Havana, and after that he went back to Dallas. Every morning when I got up he was there. When I left the place, he went with me to eat and went to bed. He bugged me all week.

The casino didn't pay Jack's way when he got there because he didn't bring Zoppi. He stayed in a little hotel just around the corner from my apartment. Had we known that Zoppi wasn't coming, we would have told Jack to stay home.

I had no knowledge of John Roselli's or Sam Giancana's efforts to assassinate Castro. The first time I heard about it was in the newspapers.

I expected to hear this story again, but I was wrong. My interruption caused McDonald to change his line of questioning. I was glad I had intervened.

McDonald asked questions about Jack's relationship with Earl after Jack had become an adult. It seemed that even after Jack grew up, he still could not keep a secret. Sooner or later Jack always had seemed to confess all to Earl—no matter how stupid or questionable his actions.

McDonald asked hypothetically, "In your opinion, if Jack had been involved with anyone in shooting Oswald, do you think it would be likely that it would come out in conversation when you were alone with him, or when he was with members of the family?"

This question gave Earl the opportunity to talk about Jack's deathbed denial of any conspiracy. One of the exceptions to the hearsay rule of evidence is the so-called deathbed confession. The courts have assumed that when a person is on his deathbed and about to meet his maker, he will not lie.

Earl and Elmer Gertz visited Jack in Parkland Hospital a few days before he passed away. Because the media had followed closely the story that Jack was terminally ill with cancer and that his condition was deteriorating, Jack was painfully aware he was going to die. Once again he denied any involvement in a conspiracy. He stated that he had acted alone and unaided in his shooting of Oswald. Earl and Elmer Gertz tape-recorded this conversation, and for the committee record, Earl repeated Jack's statement to McDonald.

Again McDonald suddenly dropped his line of questioning and changed the focus of the hearing. He introduced a film clip that had been shot by the British Broadcasting Company. It was taken after the trial and in it Jack rambled incoherently. After the film clip was shown, McDonald asked Earl what Jack was trying to say. Earl did not know, and it was obvious that he was grieved by seeing on screen this pitiful image of his brother. I decided to interrupt again.

I tried to offer some insight into the paranoia that Jack was experiencing at the time the film was made. I explained that at the contesting of the will, psychiatric testimony made it clear that Jack's mental processes had deteriorated since the trial, and that these rambling sessions had become common for him. When I finished, I felt that no one had understood what I was trying to say. I was wrong. After a short recess, the congressmen on the committee had a chance to ask questions. About half the questions were directed to me.

When Earl and I were excused, we headed for the door, with at least a dozen newsmen right behind us. In the hall their questions all dealt with alleged Mafia characters. Nothing we said seemed to move them from their preoccupation with the theory that organized crime was behind the assassination of John F. Kennedy. The congressional committee had definitely given the media encouragement to go conspiracy hunting. I nudged Earl away from the reporters and out the front door.

Following Earl's testimony, Captain Jack Revill, who had been a lieutenant on the Dallas Police Force in the so-called Special Services Bureau (vice squad) at the time of the assassination, was called to testify. When asked about Jack's involvement in drugs, gambling, or organized crime, Captain Revill denied any knowledge of such involvement. Asked his personal impression of Jack, Captain Revill said: "Jack Ruby was a buffoon. He liked the limelight. He was highly volatile. He liked to be recognized with people, and I would say to this committee: If Jack Ruby was a member of organized crime, then the personnel director of organized crime should be replaced."

Reville's testimony reminded me of what John Roselli said about his interrogation by federal agents about a possible Mafia connection to the assassination. Ovid Demaris recorded Roselli's remarks in his book, *The Last Mafioso: The Treacherous World of Jimmy Fratiano* (New York: Times Books, 1981).

They had me up at the Carrol Arms Hotel, Bobby Baker's old stomping grounds, for a secret session, and I really fixed their fucking wagon. All hot, you know, about who killed Kennedy. Sometimes I'd like to tell them the mob did it, just to see

the expression on their stupid faces. You know,
we're supposed to be idiots. Right? We hire a
psycho like Oswald to kill the President and then
we get a blabbermouth, two-bit punk like Ruby to
shut him up. We wouldn't trust those jerks to hit
a fucking dog.

The final report of the Select Committee on Assassinations became available in July 1979. Within two weeks I had the
eleven volumes and final report in my possession. The reading
began again. The report clearly stated that, "The committee's
awareness that it might have evidence that Oswald was not the
lone assassin affected the manner in which it conducted the
subsequent phase of the examination." Because the committee
believed that there was at least a possibility that two gunmen were
in Dealey Plaza when Kennedy was shot, they had hunted for a
conspiracy. Even the presence of two gunmen in the plaza,
however, would not in and of itself prove that there was a
conspiracy.

To its credit, the committee was not as interested in
testimony as it was in scientific evaluation. In every area possible,
a panel of the most eminent scientists was assembled to study the
evidence.

After the shooting, President Kennedy was rushed to
Parkland Hospital, where he was taken immediately to the emergency room. Dr. Malcolm Perry was one of the first to attend the
president. Kennedy was lying on his back when Perry and the
other physicians first saw him. They observed a small, circular
wound in the neck region below the Adam's apple. Dr. Perry
performed a tracheotomy to assist the patient's breathing. There
was also a massive head wound which was later described as a
blast to the right posterior section of the skull. Within twenty
minutes they realized that there was no way to save the president

and they pronounced him dead. During this whole time the President's back was never examined.

An impromptu press conference followed the official announcement of Kennedy's death. United Press International quoted Dr. Perry as saying that the entrance wound was below the Adam's apple. Critics of the Warren Commission have used Perry's statement as one of the reasons for their skepticism of the validity of the later official report of the autopsy performed at Bethesda Naval Hospital.

While the press conference was being held, Kennedy advisors wheeled the casket containing his body to the waiting limousine where it was removed to Love Field and placed aboard Air Force One. Mrs. Kennedy wanted the autopsy to be performed at the naval hospital.

The Dallas County medical examiner objected strongly to the body being removed from the county. The jurisdiction for the autopsy was technically Dallas County, but the hectic and unique circumstances surrounding this death overruled following the letter of Texas law. The body arrived at the hospital in Washington D.C. at approximately 7:35 p.m. E.S.T.

Agents of the FBI attended the proceedings in which Commander James J. Humes, director of laboratories of the National Medical School, headed the pathologic team that was to determine the cause of death. During the autopsy there were twenty-nine people in the room, including the two FBI agents. There was some debate over whether Dr. Humes should perform a complete autopsy or only partial. The general consensus was that a "quick post" should be done.

Initially, the pathologists examined the exterior of the body, taking photographs and X-rays and in doing so took note of the tracheotomy. Dr. Ebersole, acting chief of the radiology department, took several X-rays of the skull, chest, and trunk. The film was immediately developed and returned to the autopsy room. No complete bullet of any size could be located either in the back or the brain area, although two fragments were removed. These fragments were to become a source of controversy. The receipts for the fragments classified each as a "missile."

Dr. Humes probed the wound in the president's back with his finger and concluded that the missile had traveled a short distance because he could feel the end of the track with his finger. The pathologists speculated as to whether the bullet had fragmented. When Dr. Humes learned that a bullet was found on the stretcher at Parkland Hospital, he concluded that the bullet had fallen out of the wound, thus causing the bulletless missile track.

The pathologists under Dr. Humes' direction formulated two general conclusions: (1) One missile entered the rear of the President's skull and exited in the front of the skull; (2) One missile entered the back of the president and was apparently dislodged during cardiac massage at Parkland Hospital.

The next day Dr. Humes met with two of the autopsy pathologists to discuss the preparation of the report. Dr. Humes called Dr. Perry in Dallas and was informed of the tracheotomy at the level of what Dr. Perry still thought was the entrance wound. As a result of these conversations, Dr. Humes changed his opinion and stated that the missile penetrated the body in the back, traversed the body and exited in the neck. This conclusion was written into the final report. After the final report had been prepared, Dr. Humes destroyed his notes. Although this is a common practice among medical examiners, critics have cited this as one more reason for questioning the validity of the autopsy.

The congressional committee selected a panel of nine eminent forensic pathologists to reevaluate the autopsy material. The panel went to great lengths to authenticate the material they had. There was even discussion among the panel members of disinterring the remains of the dead president. They soon determined this to be unnecessary because of the extensive reports, photographs, and X-rays that they did have access to. Because of the delicacy of the matter, the Warren Commission had not examined any of the autopsy documentation, but had relied on the testimony of the physicians in attendance. Dr. Perry declined to express an opinion to the commission about the origin of the missiles. He stated:

> I didn't clearly identify either an entrance or an exit wound. In the press conference I indicated that the neck wound appeared to be an entrance wound, and I based this mainly on its size and the fact that exit wounds in general tend to be somewhat ragged and somewhat different from entrance wounds.

The panel examined the X-rays, photographs, and clothing and determined that the neck wound was higher than the uppermost extension of Kennedy's right lung. If the missile had struck the lung, it would have collapsed and blood would have been present within the cavity. Pieces of the president's clothing had entered his back with the missile, so it was obvious that the back wound was an entry rather than exit site. The panel confirmed that the same bullet that struck Governor Connally had struck the president. This was the bullet found on the stretcher at Parkland Hospital.

Computer-assisted image enhancement of Kennedy's massive head wound displayed inward beveling at the back of the skull, which provided definite evidence of an entrance wound. Based on this new evidence, the panel of experts concluded that both wounds to the president were from the rear.

The panel then addressed the question of why, if the President had been struck from the rear, he appeared to fall backward in the home movie taken of the assassination. At the time of the assassination there were 510 photographs taken by seventy-five photographers, but the movie taken by Abraham Zapruder was the most useful visual record. The movie established the timetable used by the Warren Commission, their critics, and the House Select Committee to fix the exact timing of each event during the shooting.

The Warren Commission numbered each frame on the film as a means of labeling the precise moment when the shots hit the president and Governor Connally. It was at Frame 312 that the first effect of the massive head wound is indicated by the president's reaction. At that frame his head moved forward slightly, and then from Frame 313 to Frame 323 the president's head moved backward. Even those not critical of the Warren Commission found this difficult to understand, and quite frankly, so did I. Any elementary student of physics is familiar with the corollary to Newton's law that when a stationary object is struck by a moving object, the stationary object will move in same direction as the moving object. One billiard ball striking another is the classic example used to illustrate this law.

The members of the panel, however, concluded that there was a scientific explanation for the backward movement of Kennedy's head. They agreed that the time a bullet actually moves through tissue is usually less than a thousandth of a second. "A bullet of 150 grains weight, passing through eight inches of tissue, entering at 2,000 feet per second (approximately the velocity of the 6.5 mm Mannlicher-Carcano bullet) and exiting at 1,000 feet per second will pass through the body in .00045 seconds, and impart to the tissue 998 foot pounds of energy, the equivalent of more than 4,100 horse power." The transfer of this energy, the panel continued, produces a temporary cavity which develops after the bullet has passed through. Thus the bullet would be 100 feet away from its target at the time the photograph shows the destruction. As a result of this push through the head, the larger exit wound in front of the skull would permit a greater exodus of tissue under pressure, and a resulting backward movement of the head. It was what the panel termed a reverse jet effect. The short interval between the two motions, the panel explained, supports this explanation.

Most of the Warren Commission's critics had used the firearms evidence to discredit the commission's findings. The Select Committee on Assassinations chose a panel from the Association of Firearm and Tool Mark Examiners, the Forensic Science Foundation, and the American Academy of Forensic Sciences. This panel reached the following conclusions:

(1) The windshield of the presidential limousine was fractured from the inside during the assassination.

(2) The three expended cartridge cases found on the sixth floor of the School Book Depository Building were fired from Oswald's rifle.

(3) Oswald's rifle did not have a hair trigger that would affect accurate aiming and firing.

(4) Oswald's 6.5 mm Mannlicher-Carcano rifle could easily be mistaken for a German Mauser, as it was when found on the sixth floor by a sheriff's deputy.

(5) An individual could attain better accuracy using the iron sights rather than the scope on Oswald's rifle.

(6) In the case of Officer Tippit, the bullet cases found at the scene were fired from Oswald's revolver. The panel could not unequivocally prove that the bullets recovered from Officer Tippit's body were fired from Oswald's revolver.

A panel of experts examined the photographic evidence to determine if anyone was visible on the grassy knoll who could be considered a second assassin. The experts agreed that there was no one. Since critics had claimed that a picture of Oswald's head had been superimposed on the photograph purported to be him holding his rifle in his backyard, the experts examined the photograph. They determined that the photo was genuine.

A panel of handwriting experts selected by the congressional committee disproved the two-Oswald theory. According to that theory, the Oswald that went to Russia was not the same Oswald that returned. If this theory were true, Oswald's mother would have detected the false Oswald. By examining handwriting samples of Oswald before and after Russia, the panel determined that the same person had written all the samples.

The report of the Select Committee on Assassinations satisfied most of the major critics of the Warren report. By maintaining that there was at least a possibility that four shots were fired in Dealey Plaza, they had not totally denied the possibility of conspiracy. Many American theorists thrived on the possibility, as if they wanted to believe that there had been a conspiracy and that the Warren Commission had covered it up.

# 37

Before the National Research Council released its report on its investigation of the possibility of a fourth shot having been fired at Kennedy, the chief counsel of the Select Committee on Assassinations had published his definitive statement on the assassination. G. Robert Blakey, in conjunction with Richard N. Billings, had written *The Plot To Kill The President: Organized Crime Assassinated J.F.K.* (New York: Times Books, 1981).

Blakey postulates that the leaders of organized crime developed a bitter hatred of the Kennedy Administration because of the war it waged against racketeering. They were also upset over the Kennedys' failure to overthrow Castro, who had curtailed their lucrative gambling operations in Havana. The Mafia decided that Kennedy no longer deserved to live.

Blakey implies that the Mafia might have tolerated the pressure they were feeling from the Kennedy administration, except for one thing: Kennedy violated the mob's own code of ethics:

> It is well understood by prosecutors and police that there is a line that must not be crossed. You are all right just as long as you do not sleep with them! You do not take favors, either money or sex. If you do, and then take action against them, retaliation awaits. (p. 375)

According to Blakey, Kennedy crossed that line when he

had an affair with Judith Campbell.

Blakey weaves a story of intrigue, citing Jack Ruby's supposed longstanding association with the criminal element, men such as J. Lewis McWillie. Jack had visited McWillie, who allegedly had ties with organized crime, in 1959 at a casino he managed in Havana (p. 52). According to Blakey, Ruby had been involved with people in Cuba who probably had had contact with Oswald.

In a chapter entitled "Dallas in Light of Modern Science," Blakey develops the story of the tape evidence that a fourth shot had been fired, ignoring later evidence that discredited the tapes. The plot thickens with the revelation that Oswald's uncle Stutz Murret was a bookmaker and exerted Mafia control over Oswald. As for Jack, anyone coming from Maxwell Street in Chicago had to be involved in some way with the Mafia.

Blakey, who had declared that Jim Garrison's theories were a hoax, nevertheless intermingles many of Garrison's theories with his own throughout *The Plot to Kill the President.*

When I finished reading the book, I immediately contacted Professor Blakey. It was the summer of 1982. On the telephone I identified myself and he immediately remarked that it appeared that he had egg on his face. I asked if I could meet with him, and we arranged a meeting in his office in the Law School at Notre Dame. I wanted to know why a man of his stature and credentials would add such trash to the many volumes of serious study on the subject of the assassination.

My wife accompanied me on this trip. Perhaps it was the contrast between the scholarship and discipline that one associates with the Law School of Notre Dame and the sensationalized and commercialized book that Blakey had written, but as we entered his office, I suddenly felt so angry that I could not talk for a few minutes. My wife's summary of the meeting describes my confrontation with the author of *The Plot to Kill the President.*

## Interview with Robert Blakey
### Saturday, July 31, 1982
### by Charlene Adelson

Tuesday, earlier this week, Alan called Mr. Blakey at home to make an appointment to visit with him. A meeting was planned for the following Saturday morning.

At approximately 9:30, Alan called from our hotel room to set the specific time and to obtain directions to Mr. Blakey's office. Since the law school building was locked, we were directed to a specific window under which Alan would call to the professor, and he in turn would come down and open the door.

Standing under the window felt foolish, but it got us in.

When we entered the small, cluttered office, I looked around and saw bookshelves full of books on organized crime. On the wall hung a chart depicting the various alleged Mafia leaders and their spheres of influence. Tucked among the crime-related books were a few of the books on the assassination of President Kennedy I had seen in Alan's library.

For the first time in my recollection, Alan was nervous. He later explained that with what he had to say to Blakey, he was afraid he might be thrown out the open window. Upon reflection, it was amazing that Blakey allowed such a confrontation, knowing full well Alan's credentials.

Alan began by thanking the professor for allowing the interview. Then he asked him, in light of the report of the National Research Council, whether he still felt that his theories were correct.

"The NRC is still working on that project," Blakey replied. "They will submit an amended report in about six months. You should wait until that report is complete. It will vindicate us."

"Professor Blakey," Alan said, "may I call you Bob?"

"By all means," the professor responded.

"Bob," Alan continued, "because of a crossover between the channels, the NRC's report places the tape the committee had, the one where you claim the third and fourth shots were fired, at least one minute after the shooting."

"Wait the six months, and you will see," was the only reply.

"I have my own theory," Alan explained. "No one does anything for nothing. Every person does everything with a goal in mind. Oswald was clearly an opportunist. He quit high school to join the Marine Corps, but then dropped out. Then he went to Russia where, in all likelihood, he assisted in blowing Gary Powers and his U-2 out of the sky. Disillusioned, he dropped out of Russia, bringing home with him a Russian citizen (his wife) and their child. Upon returning to this country he still was not satisfied. So he chose Cuba. When he went to the Cuban Embassy in Mexico City, he was told in no uncertain terms that he did not have the credentials. In his mind, what better credentials would there be than if he took a shot at Castro's political enemy, Kennedy. He'd been planning to go to Cuba even before he went to New Orleans. He wrote the Russian Embassy requesting the return of his wife and child to Russia, because it would be easier to get them to Cuba from Russia than from the United States. Finally, after executing his plan, he had to let it be known that it was he who shot Kennedy. He left his rifle and his clipboard in a conspicuous place where they would be quickly traced to him. He left his makeshift carrying case near his perch. He left the School Book Depository Building and was the only employee absent after the assassination. Then he returned to his rooming house to get his pistol, and headed toward Jefferson and Zangs, briefly going out of his way to murder a police officer, thus identifying himself even further. Had it not been for the vast number of patrol cars in the area, he would have continued down Zangs about five miles to the Red Bird Airport. Then he could have forced a pilot at gunpoint to fly him to Havana. You know yourself that Marina testified to both the Warren Commission and your committee that he threatened to do just that. He probably thought he would receive a hero's welcome. We both know however, that Castro would probably have sent him back for fear of retaliation."

"An interesting theory," Blakey reflected.

"But why would a man of your credentials put forward the theory that the mob did it? Your book will be cited as an authority by others for years."

"Don't worry about that," Blakey laughed, "it only sold about 20,000 copies."

"But," Alan objected, "it's on the shelves of all the libraries dealing with the subject of the Kennedy Assassination. A copy was even in the Kennedy Library in Boston when we visited there."

"Three things are fact," Blakey answered. "First, John F. Kennedy was shot by a sniper on Elm Street in Dallas on November 22, 1963. Second, the rifle that shot the President was owned and operated by Lee Harvey Oswald. And, third, Jack Ruby shot and killed Lee Harvey Oswald two days later in the basement of the Dallas Police Headquarters. From there, moving out in any direction, like a ripple effect, the facts become blurred. Who is to say what is fact and what is fiction?"

"Let's examine your client," he continued, referring to Jack, although Alan really represented the whole family. "The actual shooting of Oswald didn't cast any light on the assassination itself. If, however, it could be shown that Jack associated with people who wanted the President dead, and especially if those same people were associated with Oswald, we would have a strong indication of a conspiracy in the assassination. Isn't that true?"

"If you can make such associations, you may have something," Alan responded slowly.

Blakey continued, "Jack grew up in what Earl called the 'ghetto' of Chicago, Maxwell Street. Jack hung out with street gangs who on occasion ran errands for Al Capone."

"So what!" Alan interjected. "Jack did all kinds of things to make a buck during the mid-twenties. At fifteen, how was he to know what was right or wrong?"

"Well, whether you know it or not, Mickey Cohen considered Capone to have had an influence on his life. We believed, moreover, that Jack was a member of the notorious Dave Miller Gang. However, I have no evidence beyond association," Blakey frankly admitted.

"That's the trouble with your whole theory," Alan said, looking directly into Blakey's eyes. "It's all guilt by association. How do you account for a person like Arthur Goldberg, who was Secretary of Labor under John F. Kennedy and later a Supreme Court Justice? He certainly knew and associated with the same people, not to mention other Maxwell Street graduates such as Meyer Levin, Hyman G. Rickover, Barney Ross, and William Paley."

"Well, we do know that Jack was involved with the Miller-led street gangs that broke up the German-American Bund in the 1930s," asserted Blakey, as if this in itself was evidence of membership in the mob.

"Mr. Blakey," Alan answered, intentionally addressing him by his last name, "you are not Jewish and more than likely don't remember the Bund activities before the Second World War. I hardly remember them myself, or, more likely, my only memory is what I heard later. Those were meetings of grown men, dressed in brown shirts, conspiring to end Judaism. I cannot find fault with Jack's activities in that regard." Thus ended that subject.

"You know that Jack was connected with the Scrap Iron and Junk Handlers Union until 1940," Blakey said with a note of triumph.

"Get off it, Bob," Alan responded, knowing what Blakey was hinting at. "While Jack was with the union, it was a law-abiding organization. It wasn't until after Jack left that it became a 'shakedown organization,' with Dorfman as president. If you're trying to say that all union officials are crooked, I need only cite the case of Walter Reuther."

The subject was again quickly dropped.

"I suppose now you want to bring up the Guthrie Affair?" Alan suggested.

"Well, where there's smoke there's fire," Blakey responded.

"I think this is one you dreamed up," Alan retorted. "This is a perfect example of the kind of distortion that runs throughout your book. You state that in 1946, Jack played a role in an effort by the syndicate to take over Dallas, which was wide open to gambling and prostitution. The newly-elected sheriff, Steve Guthrie, was approached by a syndicate man from Chicago, Paul Roland Jones, who attempted to bribe him. According to your book, Ruby's name came up several times in the negotiations as the operator of a 'fabulous' club which was to be a front for syndicate gambling operations. You correctly point out that all of the meetings between Jones and Guthrie were recorded. In the twenty to twenty-two tapes still in existence, Jack's name never appears. You fail to mention that the man who made the recordings, Dallas Police Lt. George Butler, who was present at all of the meetings, also could not place Jack's name in any of the conversations. While on the one hand you admit that Jack was not involved, your next paragraph states that Jack had close ties with those who were involved. You state that in 1947 (a year later), when Jack went to Dallas to assist his sister in her Singapore Club, he knew Jones and his codefendants as patrons of the club. Once again, guilty by association. No hard evidence.

"To compound the effect you stated, and I quote, '...while there is no concrete evidence, anymore than there had been from the earlier investigation of the FBI and Warren Commission, that Ruby was actually involved in the attempt by the Chicago syndicate to take control of gambling and prostitution in Dallas, our investigation did determine what probably happened.'

"From that statement you then explain, based on hearsay, that the notorious Lenny Patrick ordered Jack out of Chicago. Although you indicated that Patrick denied the story, you follow that with an admission by Earl's brothers and sisters that Patrick had been a neighborhood acquaintance. What one has to do with the other, I cannot understand."

Blakey said nothing.

There was conversation about Jack's role as a strip club operator, thus making him a target of organized crime. Alan reminded Blakey that Jack only became involved in that line of business at the insistence of his financial backer and partner, Ralph Paul. Jack wanted a place with class and if he could have, he would have operated a much different sort of club.

The last area of discussion between Blakey and Alan dealt with what they called the Cuban Connection. Alan had explained before we met with Blakey that this was the area where Blakey made the connection between Jack and the mob. According to the Warren Commission, Jack had gone to Cuba in August 1959, to visit his good friend, Lewis J. McWillie, a professional gambler who was then working as a pit boss at the Tropicana in Havana. Blakey paints McWillie as an important member of the mob and almost at the right hand of Santo Trafficante. According to Blakey, Jack was highly involved in Trafficante's release from prison.

When Castro took control in Cuba on January 1, 1959, he became the champion of the people. Among other things, he suppressed the gambling interests. As a result of this suppression, McWillie, Jack's friend, invited Jack to spend time in Cuba along with Tony Zoppi, hoping the latter would publicize the casinos and bring business back. Through a number of unrelated circumstances, Blakey made Jack the most important figure in the release from detention of many of the casino owners, particularly Santos

Trafficante.  Blakey cited the testimony of Robert McKeown.

[AUTHOR'S NOTE:   Blakey cited the testimony of Robert McKeown.  McKeown came into the picture as a result of Jack's statement to the FBI in December 1963.  Ruby told the FBI that "at a time when Castro was popular in the United States," he read about a person in the Houston area who had run guns to Castro.  Ruby said he tried to contact this person in hopes of selling Jeeps, but that nothing further developed.  The FBI contacted McKeown in January 1964, when he said a man by the name of Rubenstein from Dallas called requesting him to obtain the release of three prisoners being held in Cuba.  At the time, McKeown was serving probation for gunrunning to Cuba.

When McKeown appeared before the Select Committee in executive session, his attorney of record was Mark Lane.  After being sworn and asked his name and address, he was asked when he first met Jack Ruby.  Because McKeown took the Fifth Amendment, he was given an order of immunity.  McKeown proceeded to testify, making many inconsistent statements.  Many important points were left in question:  (1) How and when did McKeown determine he was dealing with Jack Ruby?  (2) How many people did Ruby want released from Cuba?  (3) When did his first contact with Ruby occur?  (4) How many times did Ruby visit with him in person?  (5) What was the amount of time between the initial phone call from Ruby and his personal visit or visits? (6) When did he first speak to the FBI about Ruby?

McKeown did say that he had been contacted by Oswald in August or September of 1963 about purchasing some high-powered rifles.

Floyd J. Fithian, Congressman from Indiana, challenged this statement of McKeown:

"I find it totally unbelievable that someone like yourself, who took the president's death as tragically as any of us, would subsequently sit down with a member of the Federal Bureau of

Investigation and talk and answer the questions—now you were not on trial. They were not pressuring you; you were not pressuring them.

"I find it almost unbelievable, in retrospect, that during the course of that discussion with an agent of the highest law enforcement group in the United States, that you would overlook the fact that you had seen Lee Harvey Oswald."

McKeown's only reply was that the Warren Commission did not ask him.

At the end of Representative Fithian's questioning, McKeown admitted that he was writing a book with Mark Lane. Fithian turned to the chairman of the committee and gave his summation of McKeown's testimony:

"Mr. Chairman, I am not sure that further questioning would be at all productive. I think the record has shown that we have three, if not four or five, inconsistencies in the witness's testimony and the record will show that the witness is in the process of, if not fictionalizing this, at least commercializing it, in a book arrangement, and I think that that is really what we have learned here today, and I have no further questions."]

Based on testimony by McKeown, Blakey continued that McWillie was not detained and, therefore, couldn't have been one of the persons Ruby was trying to free. One thing for sure, Blakey affirmed, was that Trafficante was in prison during that time. He then pursued a circuitous route, tracing Jack's steps, all in an effort to prove that Jack assisted in Trafficante's release.

Blakey next turned to the many long distance calls Jack made in the months preceding the assassination, his battle with the American Guild of Variety Artists (AGVA), and his financial plight.

Finally Alan said, "Bob, the very nature of your position is inconsistent. First, if Jack had connections as high as Santos Trafficante, he would have been able to have his dispute with the

AGVA settled with one phone call, and he wouldn't have had to make all those calls. Second, if he had those kind of connections, he certainly wouldn't have been in the financial plight he was in. He owed excise taxes in excess of $40,000."

Blakey did not answer.

Alan took this opportunity to end the conversation. It seemed to me that the time was well chosen, for Professor Blakey had run out of answers.

We excused ourselves, thanking the professor for his time. His parting remark was that it was enlightening to speak on a subject to one who was so well-versed on it.

Once in the car, I asked Alan why it is that someone can't see the forest for the trees.

"Well, honey," Alan explained, "when I was with the Treasury Department, somehow I believed everyone cheated the government on his income taxes. I was indoctrinated, I guess. Professor Blakey has been concentrating on organized crime so long he sees it behind every rock.

"As he said, three things are facts: the president was shot, Oswald did it, and Jack shot Oswald. From there, you can expand to anything."

# Epilogue

While in Dallas in 1982 doing research for this book, I decided to call on Jules Mayer. Over the years, nobody in the Ruby family had heard from him. He greeted me on the phone like a long-lost brother and immediately invited my wife and me over to visit him.

The years had taken their toll on the man. He was balding and the hair that remained was gray. He certainly was not the testy individual I once knew.

We chatted for awhile and the subject of Jack's gun came up. He just happened to have it in his office safe.

The gun he handed to me looked almost new. Eva had described the gun as old and broken. She had said that the hammer was broken, so that each time Jack wanted to fire it he had to cock it. As I pulled the trigger it went click, click, click. No defect.

I handed the pistol back to Mayer who, while standing over me, placed it in his belt. "That," he said, "was how Jack carried the gun."

Mayer told me that the only reason he had the gun in his office at that time was to show it to a prospective buyer, who he then found out hoped to rent it and use it in a carnival. He said that he had refused the offer; he was waiting for a better one.

When I returned to Detroit, I told Earl about the gun. He was furious. We all had thought that the gun was in Henry Wade's safe. Now it was out on the street, available to the public at a price for any commercial venture that might come up. This was exactly what the Ruby family had tried to avoid, and was one reason they had wanted the gun presented to the National Archives. Earl wrote the Texas Bar Association, but they replied only that they "saw no indication of any unethical conduct on the part of Mr. Mayer. We are therefore closing our file on this matter."

Jack Ruby's estate will probably never be closed, and the family may never be granted their wishes concerning the possessions of their brother. They will continue to be confronted by speculation on the part of others as to the "real role" Jack Ruby had in the murder of Lee Harvey Oswald. Many more books will be written, claiming to be the definitive statement on those three days in November 1963. New evidence will be countered by more new evidence.

In a way I had played the "evidence game" myself in confronting Professor Blakey. But real insight into the assassination of President Kennedy and the murder of Lee Harvey Oswald is not based on any accumulation of evidence and documentation, it is based on coming to know the persons who were involved. Through my research and reading I have come to know the Utopia-seeking Oswald. Through my involvement with the Ruby family, especially Earl and Eva, I have come to know Jack Ruby. And in coming to know Oswald and Ruby, I have come to a new understanding of those tragic events in Dallas that have affected so many lives and changed the course of history.

# Appendixes

Appendix A

# Timetable of Events Surrounding the Assassination of John F. Kennedy and the Murder of Lee Harvey Oswald

| | |
|---|---|
| October 16, 1963 | Oswald starts work at the Texas School Book Depository. |
| November 1, 1963 | FBI Agent Hosty visits Ruth Paine's residence where Oswald's wife is staying in an attempt to locate Oswald. He is told that Oswald is working at the Texas School Book Depository. |
| November 2, 1963 | President Kennedy's trip to Texas is publicly confirmed. Houston is the only city mentioned in the announcement. |
| November 5, 1963 | Accompanied by another FBI agent, Agent Hosty visits Ruth Paine's residence again trying to locate Oswald. |
| November 8, 1963 | Governor Connally announces that the president and Mrs. Kennedy will be present at a noon luncheon in Dallas on the 22nd of November. The Secret Service is informed that 45 minutes have been allotted for a motorcade procession from Love Field in Dallas to the site of the luncheon. |
| November 16, 1963 | It is publicly confirmed that there will be a presidential motorcade in Dallas. |
| November 21, 1963 | The *Dallas Morning News* publishes route of the presidential motorcade. Oswald asks fellow employee Buell Wesley Frazier for ride to Ruth Paine's house to pick up curtain rods. Oswald stays overnight with wife at Paine residence. |
| November 22, 1963 | |
| 7:15 A.M. | Oswald, with package he claims to be curtain rods, catches ride with Frazier to work. |

| | |
|---|---|
| 11:30 A.M. | Jack Ruby goes to the offices of the *Dallas Morning News* to proofread ads for his nightclub. Ruby is critical of a black-bordered ad entitled "Welcome, Mr. Kennedy" that is in the morning paper. The ad, which is sponsored by The American Fact-Finding Committee and identifies Bernard Weissman as its president, attacks President Kennedy for being soft on Communism. No street address is given for the committee—just a post office box. |
| 11:40 A.M. | President John F. Kennedy arrives at Love Field, Dallas, Texas. |
| 11:50 A.M. | The president's motorcade leaves Love Field. |
| 12:24 P.M. | The police dispatcher on Channel 2, the channel used to coordinate operations for the motorcade, complains that a mike on an unknown motorcycle on Stemmons Freeway is stuck open on Channel 1. |
| 12:30 P.M. | The president's motorcade enters Dealey Plaza and as the presidential limousine passes the Texas School Book Depository Building, John F. Kennedy is mortally wounded by gunfire. The presidential car and three other cars in the procession speed to Parkland Hospital four miles away. |
| 12:31 P.M. | One minute after the president has been shot, Sheriff Decker tells police dispatcher on Channel 2 to order everything secured until investigators get to the scene of the assassination. |
| 12:32 P.M. | Dallas Patrolman Baker, acting on his own, enters Depository Building and with building superintendent Truly begins search of building. They find Oswald on the second floor but Truly identifies him as an employee, and they continue the search. |
| 12:34 P.M. | Dallas police radio mentions Depository Building as possible source of shots that struck the president. |
| 12:35 P.M. | The presidential limousine arrives at Parkland Hospital. Team of doctors note irregular breathing and possible heartbeat and attempt to keep President Kennedy alive. |

| | |
|---|---|
| 12:40 P.M. | Oswald boards bus on Elm Street, six blocks from Depository Building. Bus gets caught in traffic jam due to motorcade and assassination. Oswald leaves bus. |
| | Jack Ruby, still at the offices of the *Dallas Morning News*, hears that the president has been shot. |
| 12:45 P.M. | Police radio broadcasts a description of suspected assassin based on a report given to the police by a person who saw the shots fired from the sixth floor of the Depository Building. |
| 12:46 P.M. | Oswald takes taxi to point on North Beckley Avenue, several blocks away from his rooming house. |
| 1:00 P.M. | After all heart activity ceases and the Last Rites are administered to the president, he is pronounced dead. |
| | According to his housekeeper, Oswald arrives at rooming house, goes to his room, and leaves again. |
| 1:15 P.M. | Patrolman J. D. Tippit, acting on the broadcasted description of the suspected assassin, stops Oswald for questioning. Oswald shoots and kills Tippit. Domingo Benavides observes Oswald empty cartridges from his gun as he walks away. |
| 1:16 P.M. | Benavides reports the shooting of patrolman to police headquarters on Tippit's radio. Description of gunman matches description of suspected assassin. |
| 1:36 P.M. | Jack Ruby, watching television at the offices of the *Dallas Morning News*, hears the announcement that the president is dead. He leaves immediately. |
| 1:40 P.M. | Johnny Brewer sees a man attempting to hide as patrol car passes. He observes the man enter the Texas Theatre without buying a ticket and informs cashier at theatre. She calls the police. |
| 1:45 P.M. | Jack Ruby arrives at Carousel Club. |
| 1:48 P.M. | Police enter theatre, forcefully disarm Oswald, and place him under arrest. |

| | |
|---|---|
| 2:00 P.M. | A casket containing the president's body is transported by ambulance to the presidential airplane at Love Field. |
| 2:15 P.M. | The casket is loaded on the presidential airplane. Departure is delayed until Vice President Johnson is sworn in as president. |
| 2:30 P.M. | Captain Fritz of the Dallas police homicide division, along with representatives of other law enforcement agencies, begins questioning of Oswald. Oswald is questioned intermittently for approximately 12 hours over the next 45 hours. |
| 2:47 P.M. | The presidential airplane departs for Washington, D.C. |
| 3:15 P.M. | Jack Ruby leaves the Carousel and visits his sister Eva who is recovering from surgery. After a short stay, he returns to the Carousel. |
| 4:48 P.M. | The presidential airplane lands at Andrews Air Force Base (5:48 E.S.T.). |
| 5:30 P.M. | Jack visits his sister Eva a second time and stays for about two hours. |
| 6:30 P.M. | A three-and-a-half-hour autopsy of the president's body begins at Walter Reed Hospital in Bethesda, Maryland. |
| 9:00 P.M. | Ruby returns to his apartment about this time and calls his brother Hyman Rubenstein in Chicago. |
| 9:30 P.M. | About this time Ruby leaves his apartment for the Temple Shearith Israel, arriving near the end of two-hour memorial service. |
| 10:30 P.M. | At a delicatessen near his Vegas Club, Jack Ruby buys eight sandwiches and ten soft drinks for officers at the police station. He calls the station and finds out that they have already eaten. |
| | Ruby arrives at the police station to find a way of contacting Dallas radio station KLIF to see if their staff would like the sandwiches and soft drinks he has purchased. |

| 12 midnight | Ruby accompanies reporters to basement for press conference in which Oswald is briefly shown to reporters and District Attorney Wade answers questions. After the press conference, Ruby introduces himself to Wade and several others who are there. He obtains KLIF's private phone number and arranges phone interview between KLIF and Wade. |

**November 23, 1963**

| 1:45 A.M. | Ruby arrives at KLIF with sandwiches and soft drinks and stays for the two-o'clock news broadcast. |

| 2:30 A.M. | Ruby leaves KLIF and eventually finds his way to the Dallas Times-Herald Building where he visits with employees. |

| 4:30 A.M. | Ruby arrives back at his apartment and awakens his roommate George Senator. He phones Larry Crafard, an employee at the Carousel, and asks him to get the club's Polaroid camera and join them. The three drive to one of the "Impeach Earl Warren" billboards in Dallas, and Ruby instructs Crafard to take three photographs of the sign. Ruby is certain there is a connection between the signs and the black-bordered ad that appeared in the *Dallas Morning News*. The three drive to the post office and Jack asks a postal employee for the name of the person who rented the P. O. Box listed in the ad. The employee states that he cannot give out such information. The three men then stop at a coffee shop for about thirty minutes. |

| 6:00 A.M. | After dropping Crafard at the Carousel, Jack returns with Senator to his apartment and retires. |

| 8:30 A.M. | Crafard calls Ruby and asks him for instructions about feeding Ruby's dogs. Ruby cannot go back to sleep. He watches a rabbi deliver on television a eulogy of President Kennedy. |

| 1:30 P.M. | Ruby leaves his apartment at approximately this time and goes to Dealey Plaza. He talks to a policeman and reporter. |

| | |
|---|---|
| 3:00 P.M. | Ruby stops at Sol's Turf Bar and runs into Frank Bellochio. Bellochio shows Ruby a copy of the black-bordered ad, and Ruby states that he believes that the ad is an attempt to stir up anti-Semitic feelings. Ruby shows Bellochio a photograph of the "Impeach Earl Warren" sign and links the sign to the same anti-Semitic conspiracy. |
| 4:00 P.M. | Ruby calls Stanley Kaufman, a close friend and attorney, and talks to him about the black-bordered ad. Ruby believes the black border indicates that the sponsors of the ad knew that the president was going to be assassinated. |
| 4:00 P.M. -midnight | Ruby spends several hours with his sister Eva. He makes several calls and leaves Eva's apartment and returns again. After visiting the Pago Club, Ruby finally returns to his own apartment to stay sometime after midnight. |
| November 24, 1963 | |
| 1:30 A.M. | About this time, Ruby goes to bed and sleeps until after nine o'clock that morning. |
| 10:19 A.M. | Ruby receives a call from Karin Carlin, an employee, requesting money be sent to her in Fort Collin. Ruby agrees to wire her the money that day. |
| 11:00 A.M. | At about this time Ruby leaves his apartment for the Western Union office, which is a block away from the police station. He takes his dog Sheba with him. |
| 11:17 A.M. | Ruby completes the transaction of sending $25.00 to Karin Carlin and receives a time-stamped receipt. As he leaves the Western Union office, Ruby sees a crowd gathered at one of the ramps that leads to the basement of the police station. He proceeds on foot toward the police station. |
| 11:20 A.M. | Lieutenant Pierce drives his car up the ramp at the police station. As a policeman guarding the ramp moves the crowd to one side to let Pierce's car pass by, Ruby starts down the ramp on the opposite side of the car. |

11:21 A.M.    As Oswald is being led out of the basement office of the police station, Ruby steps forward holding a .38 caliber revolver and fires a single shot into Oswald's abdomen. Unconscious, Oswald is rushed to Parkland Hospital.

11:28 A.M.    Oswald is brought into the emergency entrance of Parkland Hospital.

1:07 P.M.    Oswald, without having regained consciousness, is pronounced dead.

## Appendix B
# Important Dates:
# The State of Texas vs. Jack Rubenstein

| | |
|---|---|
| November 26, 1963 | Jack Ruby indicted for murder of Lee Harvey Oswald. Charge: "murder with malice." |
| December 23, 1963 | First bail hearing before Judge Brown. Bail denied. |
| January 10, 1964 | Date set for second bail hearing. Postponed. |
| January 20, 1964 | Second bail hearing. Judge Brown orders that neurological tests be conducted on Jack Ruby. Melvin Belli withdraws motion for bail. |
| February 10-14, 1964 | Change of Venue Hearing. Judge Brown postpones decision until after an attempt has been made to select a jury. |
| February 3-March 3, 1964 | Jury selection. 168 prospective jurors examined. 121 dismissed for cause: 68 by the prosecution, 58 by the defense, 1 for illness. 18 peremptory challenges made by the defense. 11 peremptory challenges made by the prosecution. Change of venue not granted. |
| March 4-14, 1964 | The trial of Jack Ruby. The decision of the jury after less than an hour of deliberation: 1) Jack Ruby was sane. 2) Jack Ruby was guilty of murder with malice. 3) Jack Ruby should die for his crime. Judge Brown confirms the death sentence. Belli fired. |
| March 20, 1964 | Defense counsel files a motion for a new trial. |
| April 9, 1964 | Defense counsel files first amended motion for a new trial. Defense also files a motion for an extension of time to file a second amended motion for a new trial. Judge Brown overrules motion for extension of time. |

| | |
|---|---|
| April 13, 1964 | Defense counsel files a supplemental motion for an extension of time to file second amended motion for a new trial. Judge Brown again overrules the motion. |
| April 22, 1964 | Defense counsel files motion for the hospitalization of Jack Ruby. Judge Brown overrules motion. |
| April 27, 1964 | Defense counsel files a request for a sanity hearing. |
| April 29, 1964 | Judge Brown refuses to allow the defense's second amended motion for a new trial to stand and refuses to hear witnesses on the motion for a new trial. Defense's motion for a new trial is overruled and notice of appeal is filed with the Court of Criminal Appeals. |
| June 16, 1964 | Defense counsel files motion for continuance in sanity hearing. |
| July 27, 1964 | Defense counsel files a motion for an extension of time to file statement of facts (a court-approved transcript of the trial required by Texas law in order to file an appeal) and bills of exception (a list of challenges that are made considering specific rulings of a judge during a trial). Motion for extension of statement of facts is granted with sixty-day limit. Motion for extension of bills of exception is denied. |
| July 28, 1964 | Defense counsel files fifteen formal bills of exception. |
| August 6, 1964 | Judge Brown refuses to approve the fifteen bills of exception. |
| August 21, 1964 | Defense counsel files bystander bills of exception—a "bystander" filing being necessary when the presiding judge has denied approval of the initial filing of the bills of exception. |
| September 25, 1964 | Defense counsel files second motion for extension of time to file statement of facts. Judge Brown grants thirty-day extension. |
| October 22, 1964 | Defense counsel files third motion for extension of time to file statement of facts. |

November 20, 1964      Defense counsel files fourth motion for exten-
                       sion of time to file statement of facts. Judge
                       Brown grants ten-day extension. Judge Brown
                       also signs statement of facts.

March 8, 1965          Hearing before Judge Brown on defense mo-
                       tion for sanity hearing. Defense counsel files
                       motions to disqualify Judge Brown, for change
                       of venue, for Ruby's right to choose his own
                       attorneys, and for an extension to prepare for a
                       pretrial conference and sanity hearing. Judge
                       Brown overrules each motion.

March 18-19, 1965      Hearing before United States District Court in
                       Dallas on defense counsel's petition to place
                       jurisdiction of Jack Ruby under the district.
                       Judge Davidson denies petition but returns
                       case to the Administrative Judge of the Dallas
                       Court instead of Judge Brown.

April 20 & 23, 1965    Hearing before United States District Court in
                       Jacksonville, Florida, on defense counsel's
                       petition for a stay of Judge Davidson's order to
                       return Jack Ruby's case to the Administrative
                       Judge of the Dallas Court. Motion denied.

May 24, 1965           Hearing before Judge Holland on Jack Ruby's
                       choice of counsel. Joe Tonahill, hired by Belli,
                       is removed as Ruby's counsel.

June 1, 1965           Defense counsel files amended motion to dis-
                       qualify Judge Brown.

June 21, 1965          Judge Brown requests that he be removed
                       from any further duty in the case of *The State
                       of Texas* vs. *Jack Ruby*.

July 23, 1965          Hearing before Judge Holland on defense
                       counsel's petition formally to disqualify Judge
                       Brown. No decision.

September 9, 1965      Second hearing before Judge Holland on de-
                       fense counsel's petition to disqualify Judge
                       Brown. Judge Holland passes the defense
                       counsel's petition up to the Court of Criminal
                       Appeals.

| | |
|---|---|
| May 18, 1965 | Texas Court of Criminal Appeals directs Judge Holland to proceed with sanity hearing, allowing Joe Tonahill to be one of defense counsel, and remands Jack Ruby to the custody of the sheriff of Dallas County. |
| June 13, 1966 | Jury sanity hearing. Jack Ruby is held to be sane. |
| June 24, 1966 | Briefs on the appeal of Jack Ruby's death sentence are filed by the defense counsel and the State of Texas. |
| August 12, 1966 | Defense counsel files petition with the United States Supreme Court to review the case of Jack Ruby. |
| October 5, 1966 | Texas Court of Criminal Appeals orders a retrial of Jack Ruby with the venue of the new trial to be changed to some county other than Dallas. |
| November 15, 1966 | Texas Court of Criminal Appeals turns down the State of Texas' motion for a rehearing on court's October 5 decision. |
| December 5, 1966 | Judge Holland selects Wichita Falls, Kansas, as the site for the retrial of Jack Ruby. |
| January 3, 1967 | Jack Ruby dies. The charge of murder with malice will be officially dismissed. |

## Appendix C
# U. S. Department of Justice Report

**U.S. Department of Justice**

Office of Public Affairs

Office of the Director                          *Washington, D.C. 20530*

August 25, 1988

Attached is a copy of the Department of Justice report that
was sent to the House Judiciary Committee in response to a
request by the House Select Committee on Assassinations to review
its 1979 study on the assassinations of President John F. Kennedy
and Dr. Martin Luther King, Jr.

The House of Representatives Select committee on Assassinations completed its review of the assassinations of President John F.
Kennedy and Dr. Martin Luther King, Jr. in late 1979. The results of
that review and a series of recommendations for further action were
included in a final report which was made available to the public. The
recommendations of the Committee included several proposed actions to
be taken by the Department of Justice.

Virtually all of the actions sought by the Committee were
completed by the end of 1983. Those actions and the results were
reported to the former Chairman of the Committee, Congressman Louis
Stokes, and other former Committee members in the form of correspondence and copies of scientific reports. The Department has delayed
issuance of a formal notice of the completion of its response to the
Select Committee report, pending a complete review of all public
comment responsive to Department of Justice-initiated studies of
acoustical evidence by the Federal Bureau of Investigation and the
National Academy of Sciences. We have concluded that the Department
has now completed its response to the Committee recommendations and,

consistent with the request of the Select Committee, hereby report the results to the House of Representatives Judiciary Committee.

Quoted below are the three "recommendations for further investigation" listed on page 7 of the final report of the Select Committee. Listed after each is a summary of the results of the Department of Justice action responsive to the recommendation. It is noted that the results to recommendations "A" and "B" were previously reported in their entirety to former members of the Committee. Similarly, most of the information listed in item "C" was previously reported to the former members. There are no "new developments" included in this report; rather, we are taking the formal action of advising the Judiciary Committee that following a lengthy period of review of unsolicited correspondence and other information available to the Department that we have accepted the conclusions of the National Academy of Sciences panel of experts regarding President Kennedy's assassination and have determined that it appears unlikely that new information will emerge which would provide a productive basis for further investigative activity regarding either the President Kennedy or Dr. King assassinations.

A.     Committee Recommendation: "The Department of Justice should contract for the examination of a film taken by Charles L. Bronson to determine its significance, if any, to the assassination of President Kennedy."

Result of Department of Justice Activity: As reported to Congressman Stokes on April 9, 1981, the Department of Justice was unable, due to the provisions of the Privacy Act and the Freedom of Information Act to offer the owners of the above film ("Daniel film") privacy assurances of the type tentatively offered by the Committee (which was not subject to the legislation cited above). Those individuals insisted upon such privacy assurances in addition to other assurances as a condition of making the films available for government analysis. Consistent with our notice to Congressman Stokes in April 1981 that we would not further pursue the acquisition of those films from their owners absent a Congressional request and Congressional assistance, the Department has taken no further action in this regard. It should be noted that the value of these films in evaluating the acoustical evidence was significantly diminished in view of the conclusions of the National Academy of Science.

B.     Committee Recommendation: "The National Institute of Law Enforcement and Criminal Justice of the Department of Justice and the National Science Foundation should make a study of the theory and application of the principles of acoustics to forensic questions, using the materials available in the assassination of President John F. Kennedy as a case study."

Result of Department of Justice Activity: As reported to former Committee members in October 1980, the National Institute of Law Enforcement and Criminal Justice of the Department of Justice contracted with the National Bureau of Standards, Law Enforcement Standards Laboratory, of the Department of Commerce for a review of the acoustics reports. The Law Enforcement Standards Laboratory concluded that a scientific study of the acoustics evidence would be very expensive to conduct and would be unlikely to yield information of significant value to the field of forensic science.

The Department subsequently requested a study by the Federal Bureau of Investigation Technical Services Division of the acoustics work performed for the Committee. The Department also contracted through the National Science Foundation for a National Academy of Sciences study of the acoustics issues related to the John F. Kennedy assassination. The National Academy of Sciences study, conducted by the Commission on Physical Sciences, Mathematics, and Resources of the National Research Council, was a more thorough effort (at our request) and was the only effort which involved significant review of the actual acoustical evidence--a Dallas Police dictabelt recording. The Department was able to avoid direct involvement in decisions regarding the scope of that study and the composition of the panel conducting the study by arranging for the National Science foundation to oversee the study. The results of both studies were provided to former members of the Committee immediately upon their conclusion.

The Federal Bureau of Investigation Technical Services Division concluded that there was no conclusive proof provided by the Select Committee's experts to support their determination that the sound patterns on the Dallas Police Department dictabelt recording represented gunshot blasts rather than some other sounds or electrical impulses produced internally by the police radio system. The Bureau experts further questioned the basis for the Committee expert's conclusions that the impulsive sounds originated near Dealey Plaza (the site of the Kennedy assassination.) The Federal Bureau of Investigation report raised numerous other concerns regarding perceived inadequacies in the Committee's experts' methodology, which methodology led to the conclusion of a conspiracy.

The National Academy of Sciences made some startling findings, which it announced to the public at the time of the completion of its study. According to that panel of experts, "the acoustic impulses attributed [by the experts who performed the acoustical analyses for the Select Committee] to gunshots were recorded about one minute after the President had been shot and the motorcade had been instructed to go to the hospital." The panel concluded that "reliable acoustical data do not support a conclusion that there was a second gunman."

The Select Committee's goal of advancement of the application of the principles of acoustics to forensic questions was advanced by both acoustical analyses. Both of the studies were reported to the law enforcement community in a two-part article entitled "Acoustical Gunshot Analysis: The Kennedy Assassination and Beyond" published in the FBI Law Enforcement Bulletin (November and December 1983, Volume 52, Numbers 11 and 12 respectively).

C.        Committee Recommendation: "The Department of Justice should review the committee's findings and report in the assassinations of President John F. Kennedy and Dr. Martin Luther King, Jr., and after completion of the recommended investigation enumerated in sections A and B, analyze whether further official investigation is warranted in either case. The Department of Justice should report its analyses to the Judiciary Committee."

Result of Department of Justice Activity: As the Department advised the former members of the Select Committee on October 7, 1980, Departmental attorney and investigative personnel reviewed the entire Select Committee report as well as all relevant Federal Bureau of Investigation reports. The Federal Bureau of Investigation was asked to further investigate any aspect of the assassinations which Departmental attorneys felt had even an arguable potential of leading to additional productive information. The Federal Bureau of Investigation completed those tasks and, as reported previously, developed no information of value.

The Department has continued to carefully review incoming unsolicited correspondence related to the assassinations, without regard to whether such correspondence was generated in response to the Department's acoustical review. While, as a result of the limited resources available for this activity, the Department has advised frequent writers that individual responses were not possible for most submissions, each letter had been reviewed by at least two attorneys and those letters raising either scientific or investigative issues have been referred to the appropriate Department components for further consideration. The flow of such unsolicited correspondence has been the primary cause of our reluctance to formally advise the Judiciary committee of our "completion" of the Department's response to the Select Committee's final report, since, despite the resolution of those specific tasks sought by the Select Committee, we have considered the review of all correspondence to be potentially productive.

The Department has carefully reviewed the National Academy of Sciences report on the acoustical evidence related to the John F. Kennedy assassination. Based upon the panel's methodology and factual conclusions as well as lack of any persuasive criticism of that report following its public release, the Department accepts its conclusions.

The Department has also reached the conclusion that all investigative leads which are known to the Department have been exhaustively pursued either during the Department's response to the Select Committee's report or in one of the previous investigations of the assassinations of President Kennedy and Dr. King.

Finally, the Department agrees with the conclusion of the National Academy of Sciences that "because of the strength of the demonstration that the [Kennedy assassination] acoustical evidence for a grassy knoll shot is invalid, the Committee believes that the results to be expected from such [further acoustical] studies would not justify their cost."

Accordingly, the Department of Justice has concluded that no persuasive evidence can be identified to support the theory of a conspiracy in either the assassination of President Kennedy or the assassination of Dr. King. No further investigation appears to be warranted in either matter unless new information which is sufficient to support additional investigative activity becomes available. While this report is intended to "close" the Department's formal response to the Select Committee final report, it is the Department's intention to continue to review all correspondence and to investigate, as appropriate, any potentially productive information.

Appendix D

# The Jack Ruby Will That Was Never Signed

[The following is an official copy of the last Jack Ruby will. Shortly before he died, Jack instructed his brother Earl to have this will drawn up for him. While Earl was waiting outside of Jack's hospital room for his doctor to arrive to witness the signing of the will, Jack died from a blood clot that lodged in his lungs. This copy of the will was filed by Alan Adelson in the Dallas County Court March 1, 1967.]

*No. 67-467-P2*

LAST WILL AND TESTAMENT OF

JACK RUBY

I, Jack Ruby, presently residing in the City of Dallas, State of Texas, against my will, being incarcerated at the present time, and being of sound mind and disposing memory do hereby make, publish and declare this to be my Last Will and Testament, hereby expressly revoking any and all former Wills and Codicils by me made.

It is my intention that should I be released that I

FIRST would become a resident of the State of Michigan and for that purpose I hereby declare my residence in that State and that this, my Last Will and Testament, shall be probated according to the laws of the State of Michigan.

This being my Last Will and Testament, I do hereby

SECOND reiterate that I have had no association with any persons in connection with the assassination of the late John F. Kennedy and for the world to know that on my death bed I so make this statement.

The property that I might have or any transient assets,

THIRD copyrights or other things of value, I do hereby give, devise and bequeath to my brothers and sisters who survive me, share and share alike, children of deceased brothers and sisters to take by right of representation.

I hereby nominate and appoint Earl Ruby Executor of this

FOURTH my Last Will and Testament, and direct him to pay all my just debts together with all my funeral and administration expenses I further direct that all estate and inheritance and succession taxes of every description occasioned by my death and properly assessed be paid out of the residue of my estate and that my Executor shall not seek contribution from anyone for any portion of the taxes so paid. My Executor shall have the power to do all acts and things that I may do in my own right including, but not limited to, selling, transferring and exchanging property, investing

and reinvesting the funds in my Estate, to compromise and adjust
claims for or against my Estate, to collect all income and to employ
all agents and counsel necessary to the proper administration of my
Estate. To do, in general, any and all things, for the preservation
of and the management of my Estate, and my Executor shall not incur
and liability for any loss or damage incurred by reason of the
exercise of any of the powers so long as the same was done in good
faith and with reasonable care and diligence.

I request that my Executor be required to file only
nominal bond.

IN WITNESS WHEREOF, I, Jack Ruby, on this  -------- day of
December, 1966, have declared this to be my Last Will and Testament,
consisting of this and one (1) other typewritten sheet of paper, and
have hereunto set my hand and seal in the presence of the witnesses
below subscribed who have so subscribed in my presence.


                    _____ L.S.
                            JACK RUBY

SIGNED, PUBLISHED and DECLARED to be the Last Will and
Testament of Jack Ruby, Testator above named, consisting of this and
one (1) other sheet of typewritten paper, in the presence of us, and
at his request, in the presence of each other, have hereunto set
our names as witnesses, the day and the year written above.


_____Residing at_____


_____Residing at_____


FILED                    -2-

MAR 1 1967

TUM E. ELLIS, CLERK
County Court, Dallas County, Texas
By _____
        Deputy

Appendix E

# (Anti-Semitic) "People" of State of Texas -v- Ruby

[The following document was found among papers kept by Eva Grant. Neither the source of the document nor the author of the note at the top of page one is known.   The language of the prosecutor, however, is verified by the court-approved transcript of the trial of Jack Ruby.]

*Dr. mr. Rubenstein — when Jim Conbet was asked what makes a champ?, He replied — "A guy who can get up off the floor and fight another Round. So keep fighting"*

(Anti-Semitic) "PEOPLE" OF STATE OF TEXAS -v- RUBY.

Nor will any attempt be made here to recite or discuss the numerous (over 100) prejudicial errors of the Court that fall into the categories of (1) refusing to grant change of venue, (2) seating hostile jurors, (3) improper rulings on admission of evidence, (4) improper charge to the jury , (5) general misconduct of Court and Prosecutor during trial.

PROSECUTOR INFERENTIALLY REFERRED TO SHYLOCK AND CHRIST.

A prosecutor represents <u>all</u> the people including Jews. It was his duty to be fair and impartial and place before the jury all the facts bearing on guilt or <u>innocence</u>. <u>People -v- DeFrance, 104 Mich. 563.</u>

> "Reference to one's race, creed or color or appeals to hate or prejudice are grounds for a new trial. Where defendant, who was Jewish, produced 4 witnesses in his behalf, the prosecutor stated 'he did not care how many Jewish witnesses the defendant brought there to testify.'"

The Court said:

> "The arguments of a lawyer representing this nation *** are not without great weight and influence *** there was prejudicial error in this trial which prevented it from being fair and impartial ***." <u>People of the U.S. -v- Skuy. 261 F. 316.</u>

The prosecutor was "guilty of malice" by frequently referring to Ruby as "Jewish boy from Chicago", (gangster), "Jewish Messiah", (Christ) "money grabber"("money changers"), and by

many vile and vicious epithets and innuendoes. Such references
are grounds for a new trial, because they influence and inflame
a juror and appeal to hate and prejudice.

> In the case of People -v- Hurwich, 259 Mich. 361,

> "In a prosecution for arson *** where one
> defendant was a Jew *** question on cross-
> examination *** that two bankruptcies and
> a fire is Jewish fortune"

the Supreme Court of Michigan divided 5 to 3 on whether the
prosecutor acted in good faith in asking the question.

The affirmative opinion indicated that "the
question was not asked in bad faith nor that it affected the
verdict."

Although this case turned on the question of the
good faith of the prosecutor, the dissenting opinion said that
the mere asking of such a question showed bad faith and was
improper.

> "The question served as a means to convey to
> the minds of the jurors a senile cackle of
> slapstick days with prejudicial effect if
> not of purpose. There was no excuse for
> asking the question and it should have been
> stricken from the record, counsel admonished
> and its poisonous effect purged by instant
> instruction accomplishing such end." Quoting
> from page 365 of foregoing case.

> "Prosecuting attorney's appeal to racial prejudice,
> in trial of colored man for murder, by stating to
> jury that, if they wanted to live with him to bring
> in verdict of not guilty, held prejudicial error."
> People -v- Hill, 258 Mich. 79.

2C

In People -v- Newman, 113 Cal. App. 679, in a prosecution of defendant for arson who was Jewish

"the prosecuting attorney, in his argument
to the jury, made statements appealing to
racial prejudice when he said: 'I don't
know whether it was Mrs. Leary's cow or
Max Newman's (defendant's) grandmother who
started the fire in Chicago.' *** I once
saw the torso of a little boy friend of
mine blackened and dead in the Morgue, set
by one of the kind of men *** that we are
prosecuting here ***. I want you to think
a little bit about conditions here and what
may come if this is not stopped.'"

"Such statements were so prejudicial that
their injurious effect could not have been
cured by any method that might have been
devised, and the judgment of conviction was
reversed notwithstanding the Court's instruction to the jury to disregard them."

In People -v- Golden, 23 Okla. Crim. 243, 214 P.946,

"We all know the way of Jews' dealings in business
and having their business dealings *** these are
God's chosen people, who the Bible says shall
gather into their arms all the wealth of the
world."

The case was reversed and remanded for a new trial because of these inflammatory remarks.

It was the duty of the Court to prevent and take appropriate measures to reprimand the prosecutor and correct the effect of such highly improper and unethical conduct but both the Court and jury seemed to welcome and enjoy these references.

The Court's personal prejudices or those of any member of his family who had connections with organized Anti-Semitic groups should be investigated. If it is determined such associations existed, this disqualified the Court from sitting in this case and brought to attention of Supreme Court of Texas.

It is a paradox that Ruby, who concerned himself with preventing Anti-Semitism, became a further victim of it and may be executed because of the Anti-Semitism of the Court, prosecutor and jury before whom he was tried.

2D

Appendix F

# Notes and Letters by Jack Ruby

- Fragment of Notes Written in Prison

- Letter to Joe from Prison
  [The exact idenity of the person to whom Jack is addressing
  this letter is not known.]

- Letter to Earl Ruby from Parkland Hospital
  [Jack's sister Eileen typed this letter while he dictated it to
  her by phone from the hospital.]

Fragment of Notes Written in Prison

(7) he really made
them some good
sandwiches and
he said ~~he said~~ he
really took care
of me, and I asked
him how many
sandwiches he
had made and he
said eight and
I said I thought
I told you ten, and
he said he could
make the other two,
and I said never
mind because I
wanted to get
going but I kept
ordering other

(8) items such as
soda drinks and
the kind I wanted
were warm, and
he gave me a
plastic bag of ice.
I also ordered
other kinds of
bakery goods so
if they didn't like
the rye bread
they could change
to another kind
of bread.
He helped me to
the car with
all the packages
and I thanked
him, told him if he
ever wanted a favor
over

(13.)
larger room and one
of the officials
mentioned the room
down in the base-
ment and now I
wasn't too anxious
to leave, because
this was making
history and I was
part of it.
I walked down the
steps or rode an
elevator I don't
remember and be-
fore I knew it I
was in the large
room and they
brought this fellow

(14)
out and made no
attempt to ask him
some questions
but it was useless
and they had taken
him back. Then
Mr. Wade was asked
quite a bit of questions.
Then they all left
I was in the hallway
and two fellows
walked by and I
recognized one be-
cause he used
to work in a
service station
across from the
Vegas Club

Letter to Joe from Prison

Dear Joe —

you have known me a long time, and certainly have judged me as to my character and my behavior when I operated my nite-clubs for 18 years in Dallas, and have never been involved in anything illegal in all the years I've spent in Dallas.

Of course you know how regretful I am for the embarrassement I've caused

the Dallas Police
when I lost my
head that Sunday
morning. Especially
since I've had not
many Dallas police
as my friends.
Well, what I'm going
to write now is
going to shock you.
That I'm being
framed for being
in on the assas-
sination, that I had
been used to silence
Oswald.
The reason why
I know all of these
things, is because

of the many tricks
and ruses that
were played on me
during my incar-
ceration here at
the county jail,
you will find out at
a future date that
what I am stating
here will be true.
you must believe me
Joe, that the only
reason I committed
that horrible crime,
because of my love
for the president,
and his wife.

Please remember
me to Joe body,
Mike Eberhardt,
Blankenship, Carlson
Buddy Nurmiter,
Walter Jarvin, Bill
Everett, Sammy Tilson,
Perry, Capt. Dyson,
Cornwall, Ganaway,
and all the rest
that are too many
to mention here.
Someday Joe, You
will find out what
President Johnson is!
What he had to do
with the assination.
One thing for certain

Joe, he couldn't stand
a polygraph test.

Remember Joe, he was
the only one who
gained by the
assination, and the
Jews are being used
as a scapegoat
for his crime.
How did Oswald, who
never worked a day
in his life suddenly
decide to take a
job at the most
vulnerable spot to
commit the crime,
He went to work

a week or two days
at the book building
before even Kennedy
knew he himself was
coming to Dallas,
Kennedy didn't know
he was coming to
Dallas until a week
before he made the
trip. Who up in
Washington was so
close to the president
to know this information
and to pass it on to
Oswald. Figure that
one out.
Also that shot he
took at Gen. Walker
was a fake pretence

IV to make it look as
though he was crazy.
He would it hit
Walker at 15 ft, and
yet he hit a bull's
eye at 200 yds.???
Some later date
you will find
out who was be-
hind all of this,
by the actions of
the president,
and then you
will find out
we had he fooled
the world! Ir
make some phone
calls to some

Jewish people through the phone books etc. you will find that many have disappeared. Be careful Joe as to how you check on anything and also what I'm telling you here, and also of who you can trust. Stay away from P.T. DEAN, he is in the conspiracy. (think my family has been dealt with. For your own curiosity, try and call these members

1, Call from a phone
booth, so they can't
trace these calls;
- If no one answers
at these numbers,
you will know some
thing is wrong,

Eileen Kaminsky
HO-5-3280
              Chicago
Marrion Carroll
SHELLDRAKE 3-0984
              Chicago
Earl Ruby
   353-3070
the cleaning plant
UN. 3-0400
              Detroit

## Letter to Earl Ruby from Parkland Hospital

Dear Brother Earl,

I don't know how to begin to thank you for all you've done for me these last three years. What would I have done if you hadn't been out there doing your very best for me? I don't think just thanking you will ever compensate you for your XXXX devotion, your time and money, but I feel I must tell you in some way how I feel.

Earl, XXXXXXXXXXX I want you to know I never knew Oswald, I was never involved in any conspiracy and I did not plan to shoot him. After it happened I didn't know XXXXXXXXXXXX XXXXXXXXXXXXXX what I had done, XXX Oh, Earl, how I wish this had never happened. I never realized this could cause so much grief to everyone. How I wish I had these last 3 years to live over again - my life would have been so different. I would have been with all my family whom I love so much. You've all been so wonderful being so loyal to me. I'll never forget it as long as I live.

Earl, I knew you've been coming down here to confer with the lawyers all the time, XXXXXXXXXXXXXXXXXXXXXXXXXXXXXXXXXXXXXXXXXXXXXXXXXXXXX and I was able to see you for short periods, but XX now that I am in Parkland, I XXXXXX XXX talk to you face to face without that glass between us and I want to see you. This is the same hospital where our Beloved President Kennedy died. He was a wonderful man. Earl, thanks again from the bottom of my heart.

Jack Ruby

XXXXXXX

Appendix E:
# A Conversation with Earl Ruby

[On September 9 and 10, 1988, editors of Romar Books met with Mr. Earl Ruby and had the opportunity to discuss with him some key issues about his brother's life. Here is that conversation.]

**Romar Books:** Mr. Ruby, where were you when you first found out that your brother had shot Lee Harvey Oswald?

**Earl Ruby:** Well, I happened to be at Cobo Cleaners that Sunday morning, the dry cleaners that I owned in Detroit. I was there on Sunday because there was some electrical work to be done that couldn't be done while the people were working. They finished about 11 o'clock or so, and one of my employees that had come down to visit asked me to take him home. So we both got in my car, and I was driving west on McNichols, because he lived off of McNichols and the Evergreen Street area. Anyway, while we were driving, I think I was just about to Wyoming, when we heard it on the news—that Jack had killed Oswald.

I had known that someone had shot Oswald. I was talking to one of my very good friends in Chicago who was in the hospital. I wanted to see how he was feeling, and I called him, and in the midst of our conversation, he said, "I have to hang up. Somebody just shot Oswald." That was the first indication. And they didn't give a name then—I didn't think it was my brother. Even the report I heard, I think they said "Rubenstein" and nobody took it to be Jack. But he had legally changed his name, you know, from "Rubenstein" to "Ruby" in '47; so did I and so did my other brother, the three of us.

**Romar:** Did your family become involved in the investigation?

**Earl Ruby:** When it first took place, that *same night*, the FBI came to my family's home. I was living here, Michigan, but they came to my family's home. I immediately flew to Chicago to be with the rest of the family. Agents came to our house; we wouldn't let them in.

**Romar:** Did you know who they were? There must have been swarms of reporters at your door.

**Earl Ruby:** We didn't know. They said they were the FBI, and I said, "How are you going to prove it?" So they said, "Okay, we're going to give you a number, and you call this number, and they'll verify who we are." So they gave me a number, and I called, and they said, "Yes, please let them in and talk to them." So we let them into our house. Now we had two of my sisters there, and my older brother and I (he has passed away, too), and they had four agents. Each of them took one of us into a different room, and questioned us.

**Romar:** To see if your stories matched?

**Earl Ruby:** Right. But nothing came of that, because we knew nothing. Then the IRS—I got to tell you about the IRS. A few days after the assassination and everything—the shooting of Oswald—an IRS agent came into my office at Cobo Cleaners, and he went over my books, and he couldn't find anything wrong—except there was a telephone call that was something—

**Romar:** Was that the one telephone call to Cuba?

**Earl Ruby:** Yes. I didn't even remember what it was, to be honest with you. The phones were open to everybody. They didn't know where the call went, really. It just said to Havana, and not who was called. When the IRS man was about finished, he asked me, "Did you ever get all your money from the business that you sold in Chicago?"—that was before I came to Detroit. And I said no. He said, "I see that on the records." He said, "You know, you have a credit coming, of $5200!" I almost fainted at that. I'll never forget that. By the way, my phones were tapped. You could hear it; you could hear the buzzing of the recordings, of the tap on the line. I can't believe how they could be so obvious.

**Romar:** The FBI was tapping your phone?

**Earl Ruby:** For weeks, for weeks they did. We made a joke out of it, the family did. The person on the other end would say, "Hey, what's that noise?" We said, "It's the FBI, they're tapping our phone!"

You know, of course, that they didn't find anything. There was nothing to find. We have to emphasize that Jack was definitely not part of the Mafia. At one time he was really destitute, really bad. That's when he wrote the will. *[Ed. note: the 1950 Mayer will]* He was even thinking of committing suicide. But then I brought him up to Chicago. I was going to open up a nightclub for him. He and I went looking around; I don't know what year that was. He went down there in '47, so it must have been in the '50s.

**Romar:** Was that the time he sold the nightclubs in Dallas?

**Earl Ruby:** That's right. Anyhow, he came back looking terrible; you'd think he was a hobo. So I gave him money to get clothes with and to live on, and we looked around to buy a nightclub. We looked at one down on Well Street just across from the Merchandise Mart. A very nice place. The deal didn't go through, and then the fellow down there wasn't able to keep up with the payments for the clubs, and he went back to Dallas again.

**Romar:** He seemed to like Dallas very much.

**Earl Ruby:** He did, he did. And he knew a lot of people, from the clubs. And you know, all the policemen knew Jack. I think you have one article about the time he went to the aid of some policemen who were in trouble. Also—and it's recorded in the Warren Commission—he went to the aid of a black pianist that was having a problem, that was being harrassed at some night-club. And he always had something going. Like the dogs. I gave you the picture of Jack with his favorite dogs, there at one of his clubs.

**Romar:** Hadn't he left one of the dogs in the car when he went to the Western Union office? When the shooting took place? Here's the picture.

**Earl Ruby:** Yes, this one on the left. He had taken the older one. Now you know, these pictures have never been out of the family. No publisher or anybody has ever seen any of them before.

**Romar:** In the book, Alan talks about another one of Jack's enterprises—the Twist board, the product in this ad.

**Earl Ruby:** Yeah, I have one of those at home. We have a planter on it!

**Romar:** This says it was made by Earl Products. Wasn't that the name of your company?

**Earl Ruby:** Yes, it was. Earl Products. Not in Dallas, though—Chicago. Look at that! He must have used the same name in Dallas. I didn't even notice that. That's my own business!

**Romar:** Well, it worked in Chicago! Jack must have thought it would work in Dallas.

**Earl Ruby:** I guess. Something else he did, that I gave you a picture of, was with that entertainer they called Little Daddy. I've got a copy of that contract. He took Little Daddy to New York, you know. But he just couldn't do it. He just couldn't get him in.

**Romar:** Earl, why do so many people try to say that Jack Ruby was involved with the Mafia, or that he was following their instructions when he shot Oswald?

**Earl Ruby:** I don't know. You must understand, he did know some Mafia people. The Mafia used to come into his place, because he had a very plush strip-tease place, and where else would they go? And another thing—when I was being interrogated, by these three lawyers, *[Ed. note: in his testimony for the House Select Committee on Assassinations]* they asked me, "Why did he let the Mafia in his nightclub?"

**Romar:** What?

**Earl Ruby:** That's what *I* said. I said, "If you owned it, would you tell them to leave?"

**Romar:** He might not be in business very long.

**Earl Ruby:** Not only that, they're big spenders. I couldn't believe they asked that. Why did he let them in the nightclubs. Unbelievable. He couldn't stand at the door and ask for ID. But again, they're the biggest spenders. They got money like water. And there's no proof of any kind that he worked for those people. Of course, he knew some people from home, like I did. Some of these writers make a big deal of that, like that *Contract on America. [Ed. note: Contract on America by David Scheim (New York: Shapolsky Publishers, Inc., 1988) is a recent proposal of the Mafia conspiracy theory.]* When I went to high school, I knew Irwin Weiner.

**Romar:** Isn't he a person who's been suggested as one of Jack's underworld bosses?

**Earl Ruby:** He was the one Jack called in Chicago, Irwin Weiner. That was *my* friend. We went to school together. He had nothing to do with Jack. I gave Jack his number to call to see if he could help him. Jack was having trouble. And then they put something in that book about another friend of mine, Mike Shore. The three of us went to high school together. Mike Shore was *my* buddy. In fact, I see him every time I go to California. I still see Irwin Weiner. He's a big bondsman for everybody, but he handles the Mafia. Well, what else? His father was a bondsman before him. He got out of high school in '34, with me; we graduated together. And I gave Jack his number. Jack didn't even know him. I was down there at the time—you know, I used to visit him several times a year—and it was my money invested in the nightclub.

**Romar:** The conspiracy theorists use that phone call to argue that Jack was a mobster?

**Earl Ruby:** We just knew people like that. Also, believe it or not, some fellows I used to play ball with, they became holdup men. They were killed eventually. They were holding up the Mafia gambling joints, which were illegal at that time.

**Romar:** They were robbing the mob?

**Earl Ruby:** Oh, yeah, and they found out who they were and they killed four of them. I used to play ball with those guys on Sundays.

**Romar:** But that doesn't make you a holdup man, right?

**Earl Ruby:** That's right. What am I gonna do? "Hey, you can't play ball!" They'd have massacred me. But that's all the proof they have about Jack. Guilt by association.

**Romar:** And very loose association at that.

**Earl Ruby:** That's right. And in the Dallas police files, there's no record of him having been associated with the Mafia. If he were associating with them, why wouldn't the police records have indicated? No record at all. That's what we've got to get across.

**Romar:** He had a clean record?

**Earl Ruby:** Yes! Well, he had some minor things, like fistfights and such. By the way, in Texas, even a lot of women carry guns. There's nothing illegal about carrying a gun. And people would walk down the street with rifles. 'Cause that's the way it was there. I don't know if it is that way now.

**Romar:** It wouldn't have been unusual, in 1963, to find someone like Jack carrying a gun in Dallas?

**Earl Ruby:** That just is not proof that he planned to kill Oswald. There is no proof anywhere. In fact, again these writers about conspiracy say that the Warren Commission didn't know what they were doing, and things of that sort. But they never got any other information, and what's-'is-name, that Robert Blakey? *[Ed. note: author of* The Plot to Kill the President] The other books he wrote, they were all about the Mafia. He would naturally be ready to see anything that way. Whatever. Of course, he made money from this.

**Romar:** Some of the documents you've shown us indicate that you invested a lot of your own money in Jack's businesses. This letter, for instance, is dated August 1953. You were sending him a check for $1,250.

**Earl Ruby:** From that you can realize I wasn't lying, that Jack wasn't getting his money from the Mafia. And the Warren Commission report shows, in my testimony, that I brought the checks. That is right in there. It was my money. And it was my money that paid for the trial and all the expenses, like $60,000. Some of it I got back.

I also brought cancelled checks, when they subpoenaed me to be interrogated in Washington, before this Assassinations Committee—

**Romar:** The House Select Committee on Assassinations?

**Earl Ruby:** Yes, before them. Alan was there, too. He went with me. I brought the checks with me, and I gave them the checks. By the way, they never sent anything back. They kept everything. I'm sure it's there, somewhere in their exhibits and things. But they asked me about it because at that time, at the time of the shooting, I had sent Jack a total of—well, it was a lot of money.

I had given him $15,000 to go to Dallas, by the way. I don't know if you've got the story straight on Dallas. My sister was down there. When I came out of the service, I started this business. Again, Jack had started this business before, and took me in, and that's how I made a living until I went into the service. One of the foremen that I was working for talked me into enlisting in the Navy and I was sent to the Aleutian Islands.

Anyhow, then when I came out of the service, I went right back into the business we were in, but much more than candies and things. And that's what Jack taught me before. So, when I was being interrogated there, I told them that I gave Jack about $15,000 to go down to Dallas. Eva wanted him to help her out in the nightclub. But the stories in the books, they say the Mafia sent him there. It's not true. I gave him the money.

**Romar:** You're the Mafia and you didn't even know it!

**Earl Ruby:** Anyhow, they wanted to know how much money I sent him. I showed them one check for $6,000, several checks totalling I think $16,000 altogether.

**Romar:** Which was a lot of money in the 1950s.

**Earl Ruby:** Yeah, it was. And they said, "Why did you keep sending your brother money? If he didn't pay you back?" And I told them why: if it wasn't for him, I wouldn't have had this money. He's the one that put me in business. Otherwise I would be working in a factory. Or driving a truck.

For eight hours, three lawyers asked me questions. Nothing came of it, of course. There was nothing to hide.

Some of these stories that came out tried to show that he was the head of the Mafia. All the money he got for the clubs was either mine or Ralph Paul's. One of those books even—you won't believe it—in the first part of the book, he writes Jack is a big shot in the Mafia; later on, he writes he is destitute. Now you know that anybody that's a big shot in the Mafia, he's not going to be destitute.

**Romar:** That sounds right.

**Earl Ruby:** But, that's how smart this writer was. And they just keep on. Just lately, in the *Globe,* there was this terrible, terrible story, that this woman who used to be a waitress at one of the clubs saw Jack with Oswald, and with five men that *looked* like the Mafia.

**Romar:** They just looked like mobsters?

**Earl Ruby:** That's what she said. Of course, she made one mistake. She says they went back and had a meeting in the apartment behind the Carousel. There is no apartment behind the Carousel. She says she has been hiding all these years because no one would believe her. Of course no one believes her; she's not telling the truth.

**Romar:** It is a strange story.

**Earl Ruby:** Did you hear of that Mafia guy that turned government witness, Fratianno? In the book that he wrote—I mean, he didn't write, he had a ghostwriter—In that book it states, "Why would we hire a punk like Jack Ruby to do a major killing of any kind?" He mentioned that because they were trying to say the Mafia hired Jack. And this Mafia guy is in that—what do you call that—witness protection program. And I wrote him—they told me where to send the letter—but he never answered me. So I called the writer of the book, to see if I could talk to him, but he won't do anything else, won't try to get another statement. He said it should be enough that he made that statement in the book. But I wanted it public. I want it published in the newspapers, the UPI or AP.

**Romar:**  A long time you've been fighting this.

**Earl Ruby:**  Yes, but it doesn't seem to help. With the conspiracy angle, and the Mafia, they get all the publicity. They don't care if it's the biggest lie they've ever seen. Why do people want to read *Contract on America?* It's terrible that they say those things. That's why I'd really like to get some more details from the Justice Department. They just released their final conclusions, you know, the final report saying that they didn't find any evidence of conspiracy.

**Romar:**  We have a copy of that report, and I believe we're going to publish it in the book.

**Earl Ruby:**  Did you ever watch the Ruby-Oswald, what did they call it? Just "Ruby-Oswald," on CBS. Have you ever seen it? The main point of this thing is, Michael McGreevy and his dad wrote this script, for this dramatization. He kept in touch with me all the time. I helped him; he came to my house. The show was very good and turned out very well. And then after it was produced, Michael got a call from a publisher—I don't even remember the name. Remember he had just been paid probably a couple hundred thousand dollars from CBS to devote all his time for a whole year, and he had interviewed a thousand or more people, and that dramatization doesn't show any conspiracy. So he went to New York to see about doing this book. The publisher said, "We are very much interested in your writing a book for us; however, you've got to put some conspiracy in the book or it won't sell."

**Romar:**  They wanted him to add fiction to the story?

**Earl Ruby:**  Or it wouldn't sell. And Michael said, "How can I do that? I just was paid two hundred thousand dollars to do all this investigating for CBS. This would be a conflict of interest. They could probably sue me."

**Romar:**  For contradicting what he said in the dramatization.

**Earl Ruby:**  So—that's a true story.

**Romar:**  There are several new books out now, about the assassination, about Oswald, and of course they talk about Jack. Most of them say that Jack was in some way involved with the assassination.

**Earl Ruby:**  Most of it I know, and if it refers to Jack it has to be hearsay or association. Oh, I don't know what we can do. I had a plumber over yesterday, and he was telling me that he watched an HBO comedy skit where they involved Jack, and it was terrible. He wanted to know if I could sue, but you can't sue, unless they mention my name. They don't, of course. And all these things, if Jack were alive, they wouldn't be able to print all of this. But there's nothing you can do. I still can't believe that you can't do something, because it's hurting *us.* The family. My sister Eva's out of her mind over all this. These things they say—it's unbelievable—what my sister's suffering. Me it doesn't bother too much; I don't believe it. But she lived there and she knows there was no Mafia. She knows the money came from me or Ralph

Paul, his buddy, and some from my brother Sam, too. Sam loaned him some money.

**Romar:** And he died a poor man. You don't die a poor man when you have the kind of connections they claim Jack had.

**Earl Ruby:** Yes, right. He was the head of the Mafia. How ridiculous. These books, the media, they can say what they want. Unless you are involved like this, you never really know what happened.

**Romar:** After the shooting, Jack got a lot of response from the public as well as the media, didn't he?

**Earl Ruby:** People sent checks, small amounts, just so they could have his signature on the back. From all over people wrote, sent telegrams. I don't know if you're aware—there were thousands of letters that Jack got from all over the world. We didn't even get them all. The sheriff wanted to know what to do with them all. He said, "This is a whole truckful. What am I going to do with it?" He gave us some that had some money in them, but not a whole lot.

**Romar:** If the telegrams were any indication—

**Earl Ruby:** And most of the letters came from Catholics, of course. They were really beautiful. And Jack—I don't know if you got that story—but he used to supply gifts for the Catholic orphanage in Dallas.

**Romar:** No, we didn't know that.

**Earl Ruby:** By the way, even when I went to see him in the jail, many times they would let me talk to him alone in a little room. You know, the sheriff liked him. And even during the trial, you know where they bring the defendant out of, they have a side room for him. I was in there all the time, talking to him with the guards and everything. They let me go in there. They all liked him. And I had the—unbelievable—Sheriff Decker told me one day, "Any time you come here, twenty-four hours a day, any day, you can come and see Jack." So I used to go there right from the airport, once at two o'clock in the morning.

**Romar:** That must have made it a lot easier for you.

**Earl Ruby:** They really liked him. For instance, those pictures of Jack in the jail. I took those myself. No one has ever seen those outside the family.

**Romar:** This was right after the shooting?

**Earl Ruby:** Oh, sure. Oh, sure. And there were, I told you, God knows how many thousands of letters. The deputy told me there was a whole truckful of them, wondered what to do. I told him, "You'd better dump it." I kept some. I just took a few. And I think I may have finally thrown them out. Real nice. Like one letter was from a young child—I'll never forget; this was a very nice one, maybe from a ten-year-old—It said, "I remember you, Jack Ruby. When I was hungry, you bought me something to eat."

**Romar:** So some of the people who wrote knew him personally.

**Earl Ruby:** We heard from all kinds of people.

**Romar:** Did you hear from any famous people? For instance, one of the pictures you gave us shows Jack with Tennessee Ernie Ford at his club sometime in the fifties.

**Earl Ruby:** Yes, that is him. In fact, he called me, after it was all over. He never contacted Jack, or made any effort to contact Jack when all this was going on. Afterward, when it was all over, he called me up and said he'd like to have a letter from somebody, or one of Jack's letters to me; he'd like to have one.

**Romar:** He wanted it for a souvenir?

**Earl Ruby:** Yes. I said forget it. Another one that called me was Hank Snow. He's a western singer. He was a star in the Grand Old Opry.

**Romar:** An entire industry seems to have grown out of the events surrounding the assassination, and of course Jack became an important focus of that attention.

**Earl Ruby:** You know, Tony Zoppi was Jack's best friend. He wrote a column about the theatrical industry, the nightclubs. He had made arrangements for us, the two of us, we were going to go to Paramount Studios—he had an appointment all arranged—to produce a movie about Jack. The appointment was for January the sixth, 1967. Jack died the third. It was called off, of course.

Somebody else who got in on the act—You want to hear something about that Melvin Belli?

**Romar:** He defended Jack at his trial.

**Earl Ruby:** That's right. For years, you know, he tried to tell the media that he never got a dime for the case—he never got a dime. I had—and I *kept* telling the media—I had three cancelled checks to him for $11,000, with his signature on the back, made out to him, endorsed by him. And he denied getting them. Finally, after about ten years, he admitted he got the money.

**Romar:** He admitted he had it.

**Earl Ruby:** Right. I think somebody from the media went to him and told him they had seen the checks.

**Romar:** After the jury came back with the guilty verdict, didn't Belli leave the defense team? At what point was he taken off the case?

**Earl Ruby:** The same day, I'm almost positive. That afternoon. They came to me and said, "We think we should fire him now." And he deserved to be fired. He mishandled the whole case. He tried to disgrace Dallas. He was writing a book and making a movie, at the same time that he was supposed to be taking care of the case. And the special investigator that we hired to help prepare the defense—he was a police detective and became a special investigator. He came to me—and this is the absolute truth—he was in tears about the manner in which Belli was handling the case. Belli was asking *him* what to do.

**Romar:** Who, then, started filing the appeals?

**Earl Ruby:** Well, then we got Burleson, who had worked on the defense, and we got Sol Dann, William Kunstler—he was the head of it—Elmer Gertz, and Sam Houston Clinton, Jr., who is a judge now. I talked to him the other day.

**Romar:** Although Belli had headed the defense, he took no part in the appeal process?

**Earl Ruby:** No! No! Belli was not involved at all, but he filed a brief. We wouldn't have any part of him, we didn't ask him to, but he filed the brief anyhow.

**Romar:** On the appeal.

**Earl Ruby:** Yes.

**Romar:** After you *fired* him, he filed the brief.

**Earl Ruby:** Well, yes. You know, he was disgraced. He'd gotten a guilty verdict and a death sentence. Kunstler was the chief counsel on the appeal.

Now another thing about Belli, how terrible he was really. He had an associate, Sam Brody, a criminal defense lawyer from Los Angeles, who was excellent. And Sam came to me one night while we were getting ready for the trial. He said to me, "I'm going back to LA tonight. I don't like the way Belli is handling this case."

**Romar:** His own associate?

**Earl Ruby:** Really. The truth. At the same time Belli was supposedly or allegedly taking care of the trial, he was writing a book by Joe Moscow. And Joe Moscow came to me, he said, "I can't put up with it anymore, I'm leaving." And he left. He was down in Dallas, writing the book at the same time. I knew he was planning to write a book, but that's too much, while he was supposed to be defending Jack. And making a movie too.

**Romar:** I believe he's written several books about cases he's handled.

**Earl Ruby:** Something else that came up the other day—Percy Foreman passed away.

**Romar:** The famous Texas attorney?

**Earl Ruby:** Yes. The article about him said that he was involved in the defense of Jack Ruby, but he was never involved. We didn't hire him. We interviewed him; he went to see Jack; we didn't hire him. We should have had him; that was the worst mistake we made. You know, that Belli team, they denied they were making a movie. And somehow, Aynesworth—he got all the dope on it.

**Romar:** Hugh Aynesworth?

**Earl Ruby:** Yes, Hugh. We were very close. Anyhow, somehow he got hold of a letter that was correspondence from Joe Tonahill to a movie producer, telling him how well they were working on the movie in Dallas, during the trial. Because we were trying to get rid of Tonahill, we had to go to court.

So Tonahill denied everything, and I'm up there with the letter in my pocket, and they gave me the signal, to show the letter, to read the letter. So I read the letter. Tonahill must have died. There was a jury there. Some very strange things happened.

I want to tell you something that came up early on. It was when the trial first started that Tom Howard was more or less pushed out by Belli. Tom came to me and said, "I think we can work out a deal with Henry Wade where Jack will get ten years." And Jack had served a couple of years by that time.

**Romar:** By the time the trial came up.

**Earl Ruby:** Yes, so by the time the trial was over, he could possibly be coming out in a few months or so, on parole. So I told Zoppi, because Zoppi and Belli were running around together every night, entertaining, whatever. Now the next day, Belli cornered me, and he said to me, "What the hell do you think you're doing, trying to make a deal? I'm running this trial, and I'm gonna walk Jack right out of there." That's what he said.

Going back to Sam Brody—who had more experience in criminal work than Belli—he told me that we should work on getting this deal, and work for a small sentence, you know, so Jack could get out. That's one of the reasons Brody left. It was Belli's ego.

**Romar:** Wasn't it after the verdict that Jack started having real problems with nightmares?

**Earl Ruby:** Yes, yes. You can't blame him. Belli got him sentenced to the electric chair. Well, he bawled the hell out of me for even mentioning a deal. It wouldn't have made any difference, though. Jack wouldn't have lived.

**Romar:** Still, he might not have been facing the electric chair.

**Earl Ruby:** Right.

**Romar:** Wasn't there some other publicity-hunting connected with the trial?

**Earl Ruby:** Well, it's all money behind it. And Judge Brown, he was writing a book about it, actually writing a book while he was judging the trial. That is not something judges are supposed to do. And you know what? Judge Brown and all those lawyers, the state's attorney, what's his name—Henry Wade?

**Romar:** Yes.

**Earl Ruby:** They used to come to Jack's club! They used to come to the club. It was a joke, really.

**Romar:** How soon was the appeal actually filed after Jack's conviction?

**Earl Ruby:** Very shortly after the verdict. In fact, they were asking for a change of venue on the appeal, so they sent me up to Wichita Falls. I drove up there to Wichita Falls. I checked around, I talked to people, all the business people and the rabbi, and asked them their opinion about having the trial in that town. And they all said, "Yes, that could be. He could get a fair trial." But it never got to that, of course.

**Romar:** I understand. Before they could transfer Jack to Wichita Falls for the new trial, they discovered that he was ill. Did Jack's attorneys plan to bring up the sanity issue in the new trial?

**Earl Ruby:** I don't think so, because it would not have made any real difference. The way it worked, if they did plead insanity, he would go to— well, it's like a jail, an institution. When the person is judged sane, he goes on trial again. It starts all over again, so there's nothing gained. That's what I think; that's how I understand it. But it's been twenty-five years ago.

Of course, Jack died in jail, from a blood clot. You knew he didn't die from cancer.

**Romar:** When did you realize that Jack was ill?

**Earl Ruby:** He had complained to me—I was seeing him every few months while he was in jail, and would stay there a week or two or whatever—he was complaining to me all the time about pains in his chest for at least a year.

**Romar:** Even during the trial?

**Earl Ruby:** Before the trial, but after the shooting. In between that time, when he was in jail. The trial didn't come up till later. He was complaining about pains in his chest, and they were giving him Pepto Bismol.

**Romar:** Of course, it was much later that they realized how ill he was.

**Earl Ruby:** Yes, well, they took him to the hospital finally. You know, don't you, what happened when Jack died. We didn't get the will signed.

**Romar:** How did that happen? Alan had already prepared the will.

**Earl Ruby:** And I took it down there, and Eva and I took it to the hospital, to have Jack sign it. Jack was under guard, of course, there in Parkland Hospital, and we couldn't just take anyone into the room. He was waiting for his new trial, but he was still in custody there. And we had to find someone to witness the will.

**Romar:** And you couldn't get anybody in?

**Earl Ruby:** Well, no. They had a twenty-four-hour nurse, so we asked the nurse. She said, "I'll go and ask the chief nurse." The chief nurse said no. So she's out. They had twenty-four-hour policemen outside the door. I went out to this fellow, and asked him if he'd be a witness. He said, "I have to ask the sheriff." The sheriff said no, he didn't want him to get involved. So— we didn't have a witness.

So I called Phil Burleson, and I asked him. He said, "I'll tell you what. Call Dr. Jaffe"—he was taking care of Jack—"he's going to be there tomorrow morning at nine o'clock, and ask him if he'll be a witness." So he gave me the number. I called Dr. Jaffe; he said, "Sure, I'll be glad to do it." So we got there—Eva and Eileen, those are my two sisters, and myself—we got there about a quarter to nine, and I was the one who went in to see him. About five minutes to nine, the nurse said to me, "You're going to have to leave. I'm going to give him his sponge bath."

So I walked out, and we were all sitting there on a bench outside the door, when all of a sudden there was all kinds of commotion going on. And I had talked to Jack, you know, we were having a conversation, just a minute before. Anyhow I had left the room, was sitting on the bench next to Eileen and Eva, when all of a sudden I heard them call something, like "blue" or something.

**Romar:** Was it "code blue"?

**Earl Ruby:** Yeah, that's it, and here they come down the hall. The doctors were running; the interns and the nurses were running, into his room. And four of them came pushing a big machine, the thing that hits you on the chest, I think—and I never saw him again. He had a blood clot, in his leg and it went to his lung. And I never saw him again.

So, now we've got the will.

**Romar:** Still unsigned. Just a few more minutes, and you would have avoided all those years of legal battles with the probate for Jack's estate.

**Earl Ruby:** So he *[Ed. note: Jules Mayer]* came up with the old will. And he, well he got the gun. But he didn't get the other stuff. I'm still working on it. I called Bill Kunstler, who is a brilliant lawyer, I don't know if you know about him, an ACLU lawyer, brilliant. Anyhow, he was the chief counsel in charge of the appeal, when they reversed the verdict. We had about five great lawyers.

**Romar:** Was there no further action you could take after the court accepted the 1950 will?

**Earl Ruby:** No, no. When they made the ruling, it was all over. We had tried everything. Not only that, but in Dallas we didn't have a chance. Not only was the will permitted to be used, but since we were from Michigan, they treated us like outcasts. So then it came out that Mayer wants to sell the gun. We can't stop it really; we wanted to donate it to the archives, but it's too late for that. He'll sell it, and he'll take his fee and then give the rest of the money to the family. But I have to get a lawyer to be sure we get our share. That's all we can do now.

**Romar:** It's been over twenty years now—twenty years to settle an estate that consisted of a watch, a ring, a suit, and a handgun.

**Earl Ruby:** You know—Jack Ruby, it looked like he didn't plan to kill Oswald because he shot him in the stomach. I know he was sorry, later on he was sorry that it happened. That's why he wrote those notes, all the handwritten notes, so it could be told. In his handwritten notes, he put it all down, of where he was and what he did from the time Kennedy was shot until he shot Oswald.

**Romar:** It's like a diary, then.

**Earl Ruby:** Sort of. That notepaper, that's maybe the only paper they would give him. He had beautiful handwriting.

**Romar:** Was he writing the notes right after he was arrested? Or was this later?

**Earl Ruby:**  Well, it was when he was in jail sometime. I told you. Eva had the notes of the timetable, what took place every fifteen minutes, but we can't find that now—I talked to her the other day. You have the part after the assassination of Kennedy, where he was writing about where he went on Friday night. He went to the synagogue, and then you know, of course, even Rabbi Silverman there said Jack broke down and just cried like a baby.

**Romar:**  That's how strongly the president's death affected him.

**Earl Ruby:**  And it's all true. You know what I told one guy, one of those at the Assassinations Committee—he was asking me questions, and he was saying words to the effect that I wasn't telling the truth. Well, I said, "I'm here, and I was sworn in, and I'm telling the truth, and this is the truth, whether you believe it or not." And Jack was telling the truth. That's all that he wanted, was for people to know what really happened.

# Index